Schizophrenia

Full national clinical guideline on core interventions in primary and secondary care

developed by the

National Collaborating Centre for Mental Health

commissioned by the

National Institute for Clinical Excellence

published by

Gaskell and the British Psychological Society

British Library Cataloguing-in-Publication Data

A catalogue record for this book is available from the British Library.

ISBN 1-901242-97-8

Distributed in North America by Balogh International Inc.

Printed in Great Britain by Cromwell Press Limited, Trowbridge, Wiltshire.

Additional material: data CD–ROM created by PATH (www.pathmedia.co.uk); training resource CD–ROM created by Windrush Technology Limited (www.windrush.net).

developed by   National Collaborating Centre for Mental Health
Royal College of Psychiatrists' Research Unit
6th Floor
83 Victoria Street
London
SW1H 0HW

commissioned by   National Insitute for Clinical Excellence
11 Strand
London
WC2N 5HR
www.nice.org.uk

published by   Royal College of Psychiatrists
17 Belgrave Square
London
SW1X 8PG
www.rcpsych.ac.uk

and

British Psychological Society
St Andrews House
48 Princess Road East
Leicester
LE1 7DR
www.bps.org.uk

Contents

Guideline Development Group membership

Dr Tim Kendall (Chair)

Co-Director, National Collaborating Centre for Mental Health; Deputy Director, Royal College of Psychiatrists Research Unit; and Medical Director and Consultant Psychiatrist, Community Health Sheffield NHS Trust

Mr Stephen Pilling (Facilitator)

Co-Director, National Collaborating Centre for Mental Health; Director, Centre for Outcomes Research and Effectiveness; and Consultant Clinical Psychologist, Camden and Islington Mental Health and Social Care Trust

Professor Tom Barnes (Lead, Topic Group on Pharmacology)

Professor of Psychiatry, Imperial College Faculty of Medicine, London; Lead, Topic Group on Pharmacology

Professor Philippa Garety (Lead, Topic Group on Psychological Interventions)

Professor of Clinical Psychology, Guy's, King's and St Thomas' School of Medicine and the Institute of Psychiatry, King's College London and Trust Head of Psychology, the South London and Maudsley NHS Trust

Professor Max Marshall (Lead, Topic Group on Service-level Interventions)

Professor of Psychiatry, University of Manchester

Ms Emma Harding

Service User, and Senior Project Worker, User Employment Programme, SW London St George's Mental Health NHS Trust

Mr Bill Hare

Rethink Severe Mental Illness

Mr Graham Estop

Mental Health Charities in NICE

Mr Peter Pratt

Chief Pharmacist, Doncaster and South Humber NHS Trust and Community Health Sheffield NHS Trust

Dr Paul Rowlands

Consultant Psychiatrist, Derbyshire Mental Health Services NHS Trust

Professor Irwin Nazareth

Professor of Primary Care and Population Studies, Royal Free and University College London Medical School

Ms Liz Newstead

Lecturer/Clinical Nurse Specialist, Dorset Healthcare NHS Trust/Bournemouth University

Ms Christine Sealey (Observer)

Guidelines Commissioning Manager, NICE

National Collaborating Centre for Mental Health staff

Dr Catherine Pettinari   Senior Project Manager

Dr Craig Whittington   Senior Systematic Reviewer

Ms Ellen Boddington   Research Assistant

Ms Rachel Burbeck   Systematic Reviewer

Mr Lawrence Howells   Research Assistant

Mr Daniel Michelson   Research Assistant

Ms Celia Morgan   Research Assistant

Ms Laura Russell   Project Secretary

Dr Judit Simon   Health Economist

Acknowledgements

Special advisers to the Guideline Development Group

Dr Sarah Davenport (Ashworth Hospital Mersey Care NHS Trust)
Dr Richard Gray (Institute of Psychiatry)
Professor Rob Kerwin (Institute of Psychiatry)
Dr Frank Margison (Manchester Mental Health and Social Care Trust)
Dr Robert Poole (Mersey Care NHS Trust)

Stakeholder organisations registered for this guideline

Acute Care Collaborating Centre
Age Concern England
All Wales Senior Nurses Advisory Group (Mental Health)
Association for Quality in Health and Social Care
Association of the British Pharmaceuticals Industry (ABPI)
AstraZeneca UK Ltd
Bristol-Myers Squibb Pharmaceuticals Ltd
British Association of Behavioural and Cognitive Psychotherapy (BABCP)
British Dietetic Association
British Medical Association
British National Formulary (BNF)
British Psychological Society, The
BUPA
Chartered Society of Physiotherapy
Chronic Conditions Collaborating Centre
College of Occupational Therapists
Community Psychiatric Nurses' Association
Department of Health
Eli Lilly & Co. Ltd
General Medical Council
Health Technology Board of Scotland
Independent Healthcare Association
Inner Cities Mental Health Group, The
Ivax Pharmaceuticals UK (formerly Norton Healthcare Ltd)
Janssen-Cilag Ltd
Lundbeck Ltd

Manic Depression Fellowship
Mental Health Foundation
MIND
National Guidelines and Audit Patient Involvement Unit
National Institute for Mental Health in England (NIMHE)
National Voices Forum
Neurolink
Newcastle, North Tyneside and Northumberland Mental Health NHS Trust
NHS Information Authority (PHSMI Programme)
Novartis Pharmaceuticals UK Ltd
Nursing and Supportive Care Collaborating Centre
Pfizer Ltd
Pharmaceutical Schizophrenia Initiative
Primary Care Collaborating Centre
Prodigy
Rethink Severe Mental Illness (formerly National Schizophrenia Fellowship)
Royal College of General Practitioners
Royal College of Nursing
Royal College of Psychiatrists
Royal College of Speech and Language Therapists
Royal Pharmaceutical Society of Great Britain
Sainsbury Centre for Mental Health
SANE
Sanofi-Synthelabo
Schizophrenia Association of Great Britain
Scottish Intercollegiate Guidelines Network (SIGN)
Turning Point
UK Advocacy Network
UK Pain Society
UK Psychiatric Pharmacy Group
Welsh Assembly Government (formerly National Assembly for Wales)
Women's and Children's Collaborating Centre
Young Minds
Zito Trust

Systematic reviews used to evaluate the clinical evidence

The GDG would especially like to thank those members of the Cochrane Schizophrenia Group whose reviews were used during the production of this guideline.

Abbreviations

ACT	Assertive community treatment
AGREE	Appraisal of Guidelines for Research and Evaluation Instrument
AHA	American Hospital Association
AOT	Assertive outreach team
BNF	*British National Formulary*
BPRS	Brief Psychiatric Rating Scale
CBT	Cognitive–behavioural therapy
CCTR	Cochrane Controlled Trials Register
CDSR	Cochrane Database of Systematic Reviews
CEBMH	Centre for Evidence-based Mental Health (University of Oxford)
CGI	Clinical Global Impression
CI	Confidence interval
CM	Case management
CMHT	Community mental health team
CORE	Centre for Outcomes Research and Effectiveness (British Psychological Society)
CPA	Care programme approach
CPMP	Committee for Proprietary Medicinal Products
CPRS	Comprehensive Psychopathological Rating Scale
CRHTT	Crisis resolution and home treatment team
CRT	Cognitive remediation therapy
CRU	College Research Unit, Royal College of Psychiatrists
DARE	Database of Abstracts of Reviews of Effectiveness
DSM	*Diagnostic and Statistical Manual of Mental Disorders* (American Psychiatric Association)
DUP	Duration of untreated psychosis
eCPA	Enhanced care programme approach
ECG	Electrocardiogram
EED	Economic Evaluation Database
EIS	Early intervention service
EMBASE	Excerpta Medica Database
EPS	Extrapyramidal side-effect(s)/symptom(s)
GAS	Global Assessment Scale
GDG	Guideline Development Group
GP	General practitioner

GPP	Good practice point
HTA	Health Technology Assessment database
ICD	*International Statistical Classification of Diseases and Related Health Problems* (World Health Organization)
ICM	Intensive case management
IM	Intramuscular
IV	Intravenous
MADRS	Montgomery & Åsberg Depression Rating Scale
MAO	Monoamine oxidase
MSANS	Modified Scale for the Assessment of Negative Symptoms
NCCMH	National Collaborating Centre for Mental Health
NHS	National Health Service
NICE	National Institute for Clinical Excellence
NNH	Number needed to harm
NNT	Number needed to treat
NSF	National Service Framework
OHE HEED	Office of Health Economics Health Economic Evaluations Database
OR	Odds ratio
PEF	Psychiatric evaluation form
PANSS	Positive and Negative Symptom Scale
PSE	Present State Examination
QALY	Quality-adjusted life year
QT	The interval between Q and T waves in the electrocardiogram
RCT	Randomised controlled trial
RR	Relative risk (risk ratio)
SANS	Scale for the Assessment of Negative Symptoms
SMD	Standardised mean difference
SPC	Summary of Product Characteristics
SSRI	Selective serotonin reuptake inhibitor
TRS	Treatment-resistant schizophrenia
WMD	Weighted mean difference

Additional materials

There are two CD–ROMs that accompany this guideline. 'Schizophrenia: data on core intereventions in primary and secondary care' contains details of the evidence from which the guideline was developed. This includes tables of all clinical and health economics studies that were evaluated and either included or excluded for systematic review and meta-analysis, along with a master reference list, which includes primary-level studies referred to in randomised controlled trials. The meta-analyses from which guideline statements are drawn can be concisely visualised as forest plots; these visual representations are hyperlinked to each statement of evidence in the CD–ROM. An animated slide-show explaining how to use the Forest plots is also included.

A second CD–ROM, 'Using and understanding the NICE schizophrenia guideline: a training session', is primarily a training module on the use of the guidelines produced for NICE – *Schizophrenia: Core Interventions in the Treatment and Management of Schizophrenia in Primary and Secondary Care.* It also uses evidence from this full guideline. For ease of use, the training CD–ROM includes the electronic NICE guideline and the version for service users and the public: *Treating and Managing Schizophrenia (Core Interventions)*.

1 Introduction

This guideline has been developed to advise on the treatment and management of schizophrenia. The guideline recommendations have been arrived at by a team of health care professionals, service users, carers and researchers after careful consideration of the best available evidence. It is intended that the guideline should assist clinicians and others to provide high-quality care for people with schizophrenia and their families, while also emphasising the importance of the experience of care for service users and carers.

Schizophrenia is a mental illness with substantial short-term and long-term consequences for individuals, their families, the health service and society. About one in a hundred people will experience schizophrenia during their lifetime, although the highest incidence is in people in their early twenties. People with schizophrenia often suffer considerable distress and, not uncommonly, long-term disabilities and prejudice, which can have negative effects on employment, relationships and life satisfaction. Schizophrenia can disrupt home and family life, and impose a heavy burden on carers over long periods. Schizophrenia also costs the National Health Service more than any other mental illness, consuming more than 5% of the NHS in-patient budget. Combined with the loss of income and spending power that results from the illness, schizophrenia poses one of the most serious personal, medical, social and economic problems today.

Unfortunately, people with schizophrenia regularly encounter stigmatisation and discrimination. This may occur not only in wider society, where a diagnosis of schizophrenia can have serious implications for a person's career and social life, but also within the NHS, where service users with schizophrenia may receive sub-standard non-psychiatric care as a result of professional ignorance and prejudice. Moreover, the provision of effective psychiatric treatments, although excellent in some areas, is variable.

This guideline addresses the major treatments and services for people with schizophrenia. It is neither comprehensive nor definitive, and is necessarily limited given the size of the task. Future guidelines will cover other treatments and services, and update the scientific evidence base developed here.

As the ubiquity of mental ill health is now widely acknowledged, and as newer and more diverse treatments have become available, it is now more important than ever that clinicians, service users and carers become aware of the evidence for the different treatments available. We hope this guideline will help in that process.

1.1 National guidelines

1.1.1 What are clinical practice guidelines?

Clinical practice guidelines are 'systematically developed statements that assist clinicians and patients in making decisions about appropriate treatment for specific conditions' (NHS Executive, 1996). They are derived from the best available research evidence, using predetermined and systematic methods to identify and evaluate all the evidence relating to the specific condition in question. Where evidence is lacking, the guidelines will incorporate statements and recommendations based upon the consensus statements developed by the Guideline Development Group.

Clinical guidelines are intended to improve the process and outcomes of health care in a number of different ways. Clinical guidelines can:

- provide up-to-date, evidence-based recommendations for the management of conditions and disorders by health care professionals
- help in setting standards to assess the practice of health care professionals
- form the basis of education and training of health care professionals
- assist service users and carers in making informed decisions about their treatment and care
- improve communication between health care professionals, service users and carers
- help identify priority areas for further research.

1.1.2 Uses and limitations of clinical guidelines

Guidelines are not a substitute for professional knowledge and clinical judgement. Their usefulness and applicability can be limited by a number of different factors: the availability of high-quality research evidence; the quality of the methodology used in the development of the guideline; the generalisability of research findings; and the uniqueness of individual patients.

Although the quality of research in schizophrenia is variable, the methodology used here reflects current international understanding on the appropriate practice for guideline development (AGREE: Appraisal of Guidelines for Research and Evaluation Instrument; www.agreecollaboration.org), ensuring the collection and selection of the best research evidence available, and the systematic generation of treatment recommendations applicable to the majority of service users and situations. However, there will always be some patients and situations for which clinical guideline recommendations are not readily applicable. This guideline does not, therefore, override the individual responsibility of health professionals to make appropriate decisions in the circumstances of the individual service user, in consultation with the service user and/or carer.

In addition to the clinical evidence, cost-effectiveness information (where available) is taken into account in the generation of statements and recommendations. Although national guidelines are concerned with clinical and economic effectiveness, issues of affordability and implementation costs are to be determined by the NHS.

In using guidelines, it is important to remember that the absence of empirical evidence for the effectiveness of a particular intervention is not the same as evidence for ineffectiveness. In addition, of particular relevance in mental health, evidence-based treatments are often delivered within the context of an overall treatment programme including a range of activities, the purpose of which may be to help engage the service user, and provide an appropriate context for the delivery of specific interventions. It is important to maintain and enhance the service context in which these interventions are delivered, otherwise the specific benefits of effective interventions will be lost. Indeed, organising care in a manner that supports and encourages a good therapeutic relationship is at times more important than the specific treatments offered.

1.1.3 Why develop national guidelines?

The National Institute for Clinical Excellence (NICE) was established as a Special Health Authority for England and Wales in 1999, with a remit to provide a single source of authoritative and reliable guidance for patients, professionals and the public. This guidance is intended to improve standards of care, to diminish unacceptable variations in the provision and quality of care across the NHS, and to ensure that the health service is patient-centred. All guidance is developed in a transparent and collaborative manner using the best available evidence and involving all relevant stakeholders.

Guidance is generated by NICE in a number of different ways, two of which are relevant here. First, national guidance is produced by the Technology Appraisal Committee, who give robust advice about particular treatments, interventions, procedures and other health technology. Second, NICE commissions the production of national clinical practice guidelines focused upon the overall treatment and management of specific conditions, and with this objective NICE has established seven National Collaborating Centres in conjunction with a range of professional organisations involved in health care.

1.1.4 National Collaborating Centre for Mental Health

The National Collaborating Centre for Mental Health (NCCMH) is a collaboration of professional organisations involved in the field of mental health, national service user and carer organisations, academic institutions, and NICE. The NCCMH is funded by NICE and is led by a partnership between the Royal College of Psychiatrists' Research Unit and the British Psychological Society's equivalent unit, the Centre for Outcomes Research and Effectiveness (CORE). Members of the NCCMH reference group come from the following organisations:

- Royal College of Psychiatrists
- British Psychological Society
- Royal College of Nursing
- National Institute for Social Work
- College of Occupational Therapists, now replaced by the Clinical Effectiveness Forum for the Allied Health Professions
- Royal College of General Practitioners
- Royal Pharmaceutical Society
- Rethink Severe Mental Illness (formerly the National Schizophrenia Fellowship)
- Manic Depression Fellowship
- MIND
- Centre for Evidence-based Mental Health
- Centre for Economics in Mental Health
- Institute of Psychiatry.

The NCCMH reference group provides advice on a full range of issues relating to the development of guidelines, including the membership of experts, professionals, service users and carers within guideline development groups.

1.1.5 From national guidelines to local protocols

Once a national guideline has been published and disseminated, local health care groups will be expected to produce a plan and identify resources for implementation, along with appropriate timetables. It is recommended that a multi-disciplinary group involving commissioners of health care, primary care and specialist mental health professionals, service users and carers should subsequently undertake the translation of the implementation plan into local protocols. The nature and pace of the local plan will reflect local health care needs and the nature of existing services; full implementation may take a considerable time, especially where substantial training needs are identified.

1.1.6 Auditing the implementation of guidelines

This guideline identifies key areas of clinical practice and service delivery for local and national audit. Although the generation of audit standards is an important and necessary step in the implementation of this guidance, a more broadly based implementation strategy will be developed. Nevertheless, it should be noted that the Commission for Health Care, Audit and Improvement will monitor the extent to which primary care trusts, trusts responsible for mental health and social care, and health authorities have implemented these guidelines.

1.2 National schizophrenia guideline

1.2.1 Who has developed this guideline?

The Guideline Development Group (GDG) was convened by the NCCMH based upon advice from the Centre's reference group representatives, and is supported by funding from NICE. The GDG included representatives of the following professional groups: psychiatry, clinical psychology, nursing, psychiatric pharmacy and general practice. In addition, the GDG included a service user and a former service user representing Rethink and Voices Forum, as well as a carer representative, also from Rethink.

Staff from the NCCMH provided leadership and support throughout the process of guideline development, undertaking systematic searches, information retrieval, appraisal and systematic review of the evidence. Members of the GDG received training in the process of guideline development from the Centre for Evidence-based Mental Health and the Patient Involvement Unit of NICE. The National Guidelines Support and Research Unit, also established by NICE, provided advice and assistance regarding all aspects of the guideline development process.

All members of the GDG made formal declarations of interest at the outset, and these were updated at every meeting. The group members met a total of 23 times throughout the process of guideline development. For ease of evidence identification and analysis, members of the GDG formed subgroups (topic groups) covering identifiable treatment approaches. Topic groups were led by a national expert in the relevant field and supported by the NCCMH technical team, with additional expert advice from special advisers where necessary. Topic groups oversaw the production and synthesis of research evidence before presentation to the wider GDG. All statements and recommendations in this guideline have been generated and agreed by the whole GDG.

1.2.2 For whom is this guideline intended?

This guideline will be relevant to people with a diagnosis of schizophrenia with disease onset before 60 years of age, and who require treatment at any age. The guidance does not address either very early-onset (childhood-onset) or very late-onset schizophrenia (age of onset 60 years or greater); these may be the subject of a future guideline. Neither does it provide specific guidance on the management of schizophrenia for people with coexisting learning difficulties, substance misuse, or significant physical or sensory difficulties, or for those who are homeless. These may also be dealt with in a future guideline.

Although this guideline briefly addresses the issue of diagnosis, it does not make evidence-based recommendations or refer to evidence regarding diagnosis, primary prevention or assessment. In sum, this guideline is intended for use by:

- adults with a diagnosis of schizophrenia (onset before 60 years of age, without significant physical, sensory or learning difficulties) and their families and carers
- professional groups who share in the treatment and care of people with a diagnosis of schizophrenia, including psychiatrists, clinical psychologists, mental health nurses, community psychiatric nurses, social workers, practice nurses, occupational therapists, pharmacists, general practitioners and others
- professionals in other health and non-health sectors who may have direct contact with or are involved in the provision of health and other public services for those diagnosed with schizophrenia. These may include accident and emergency department staff, paramedical staff, prison doctors, the police, and professionals who work in the criminal justice and education sectors
- those with responsibility for planning services for people with a diagnosis of schizophrenia, and their carers, including directors of public health, NHS trust managers and managers in primary care trusts.

1.2.3 Specific aims of this guideline

The guideline sets out recommendations and good practice points for pharmacological treatments and the use of psychological and service-level interventions in combination with pharmacological treatments in the three phases of care. In particular, it aims to:

- evaluate the role of specific pharmacological agents in the treatment and management of schizophrenia
- evaluate the role of specific psychological interventions in the treatment and management of schizophrenia
- evaluate the role of specific service delivery systems and service-level interventions in the management of schizophrenia
- incorporate guidance generated by the NICE Technology Appraisal Committee on the use of atypical antipsychotic drugs
- integrate the above to provide best practice advice on the care of adults with a diagnosis of schizophrenia through the different phases of illness, including the initiation of treatment, the treatment of acute episodes and the promotion of recovery
- consider the cost-effectiveness of treatment and service options for people with schizophrenia.

2 Schizophrenia

This guideline is concerned with the treatment and management of schizophrenia and related disorders. Although the precise terminology used for these disorders has varied over the years, the guidance relates only to those identified by the tenth edition of the *International Statistical Classification of Diseases and Related Health Problems* (ICD–10; World Health Organization, 1992): namely, schizophrenia, schizoaffective disorder, schizophreniform disorder and delusional disorder. The guideline does not address the management of other psychotic disorders such as bipolar disorder, mania or depressive psychosis.

2.1 The disorder

2.1.1 Symptoms, presentation and patterns of illness

Schizophrenia is a term used to describe a major psychiatric disorder (or cluster of disorders) that alters an individual's perception, thoughts, affect and behaviour. The symptoms of schizophrenia are usually divided into positive symptoms, including hallucinations and delusions, and negative symptoms, such as emotional apathy, lack of drive, poverty of speech, social withdrawal and self-neglect. Nevertheless, individuals who develop schizophrenia will have their own unique combination of symptoms and experiences, the precise pattern of which will be influenced by their own particular circumstances.

Typically, schizophrenic illnesses are preceded by a prodromal period, characterised by early signs of deterioration in personal functioning. Impairments may include social withdrawal, peculiar and uncharacteristic behaviour, disturbed communication and affect, unusual ideation and perceptual experiences, poor personal hygiene, and reduced interest and motivation. During the prodromal period of illness, people with schizophrenia often feel that their world has changed. Their interpretation of this change is commonly at variance with others, with relatives frequently reporting that the person with schizophrenia has changed 'in themselves'. These changes may well affect the person's ability to hold down a job, attend to academic work, or relate to friends and family.

The prodromal period is followed by an acute phase marked by characteristic positive symptoms of hallucinations, delusions and behavioural disturbances. Following resolution of the acute phase, positive symptoms diminish or disappear for many people, sometimes leaving a number of negative symptoms not unlike the symptoms in the prodromal period. This third phase of illness, which may last many years, is often interrupted by acute exacerbations warranting additional treatment or interventions.

Although this pattern may be described as typical, the course of schizophrenia varies considerably. For example, although some people may experience the symptoms of schizophrenia only briefly, others may experience symptoms for much longer periods. A number of individuals experience no prodromal period, the disorder beginning with a sudden and often florid acute episode. Some have only occasional episodes of illness with more or less complete recovery between, while others have a greater frequency of episodes, with less than complete recovery between. In yet other cases, a schizophrenic illness will develop into a chronic disorder in which the person is never free of symptoms, although the severity of those symptoms may vary over time.

Whatever the pattern of illness, schizophrenic disorders have a strong tendency for recurrence: approximately half of people with schizophrenia treated in standard services will relapse and require readmission within the first 2 years, although about a quarter will have no further admissions (Mason *et al*, 1996). Recurrence, or relapse, can be affected by home circumstances: relapse rates can be higher for people living in stressful relationships, especially with family members (Vaughn & Leff, 1976; Bebbington & Kuipers, 1994). It is likely that relapse rates will also be affected by other life stresses, such as those related to finance and employment.

2.1.2 Impairment and disability

Although the symptoms and experience of schizophrenia are often distressing, the effects of the illness are more pervasive, with a significant number of people continuing to experience long-term disability (Harding *et al*, 1987). Schizophrenia can have a major detrimental effect on people's personal, social and occupational lives. The extent of continuing disability associated with schizophrenia can be seen from a recent UK survey, which found that nearly two-thirds of adults with schizophrenia had difficulty in at least one activity of daily living. Moreover, half of adults were classified as being unable to work, and less than a fifth were engaged in employment (Foster *et al*, 1996). It is worthy of note that one-third of service users in this study reported a severe lack of support. The high rate of cigarette smoking among people with schizophrenia may also contribute to their overall poor physical health.

The disabilities experienced by people with schizophrenia are not solely the result of the illness itself. The side-effects of treatments, social isolation, low income and homelessness all play a part in the disabilities faced by service users, difficulties not made any easier by the prejudice and stigma associated with the diagnosis of schizophrenia (Sartorius, 2002).

Worldwide, schizophrenia has been estimated to be one of 30 leading causes of disability (Murray & Lopez, 1997). Moreover, the excess mortality among people with schizophrenia is approximately 50% above that of the general population (Brown, 1997), partly as a result of an increased incidence of suicide (about 10% die by suicide) and violent death, and partly as a result of an increased risk of a range of physical diseases. The precise extent to which this excess mortality is, at least in part, a result of the treatments given for schizophrenia remains to be quantified. It is also unknown whether the difficulties experienced by people with schizophrenia in accessing general medical services, in both primary and secondary care, contribute to this excess mortality. We do know that the majority of people with schizophrenia smoke tobacco. The physical health of people with schizophrenia should be regularly monitored.

2.1.3 Course and prognosis

Historically, many psychiatrists and other health care professionals have taken a pessimistic view of the prognosis for schizophrenia, regarding it to be a severe, intractable and often deteriorating lifelong illness. This pessimistic view of schizophrenia has failed to find confirmation from long-term follow-up studies, which have demonstrated considerable variations in long-term outcome, with up to a third of people making a complete recovery, and only 10% deteriorating throughout their lives (Bleuler, 1978a). It should also be noted that some people who never experience complete recovery from their psychotic experiences nonetheless manage to sustain an acceptable quality of life if given adequate support and help.

The factors that influence the differential recovery from schizophrenia are not well known. However, recovery from schizophrenia may happen at any time during the illness, even after many years. Of those who make a full recovery, there are suggestions that involvement in a progressive therapeutic programme consisting of more than just medication might be an important factor (Bleuler, 1978b). Research has also suggested that delayed access to mental health services in early schizophrenia – often referred to as the duration of untreated psychosis – is associated with slower or less complete recovery (Loebel et al, 1992) and increased risk of relapse in the subsequent 2 years (Johnstone et al, 1996).

A number of social and economic factors also appear to affect the course of schizophrenia. For example, in developed countries it is well established that schizophrenia is more common in lower socio-economic groups. However, this appears to be partly reversed in some developing countries (Jablensky et al, 1992), suggesting that the relationship between incidence, recovery rates and cultural and economic factors is more complex than a simple correspondence with socio-economic deprivation (Warner, 1994).

The effects of schizophrenia on a person's life experience and opportunities are considerable; service users and carers need help and support to deal with their future and to cope with the changes the illness brings.

2.1.3.1   Health professionals should work in partnership with service users and carers, offering help, treatment and care in an atmosphere of hope and optimism. (GPP)

2.2 Diagnosis

A full and proper discussion of the diagnosis and classification of schizophrenia is outside the scope of this guideline. However, diagnosis and classification remain important issues in schizophrenia research and in clinical practice, and the impact of receiving a diagnosis of schizophrenia has considerable social and personal consequences for the individual.

The wide variation in presentation, course and outcome in schizophrenia may reflect an underlying variation in the nature of the disorder, or even that schizophrenia is a cluster of different disorders with variable courses and outcomes (Gelder et al, 1997). Equally, this variation may result from a complex interaction between biological, social, psychological, cultural and economic factors. Several models to explain this heterogeneity have been proposed, although none has been widely accepted. Moreover, prior to the establishment of diagnostic systems such as the *Diagnostic and Statistical Manual of Mental Disorders* (DSM; American Psychiatric Association, 1994) and the *International Statistical Classification of Diseases and Related Health Problems* (ICD; World Health Organization, 1992), large variations in the incidence and prevalence of the disorder were reported. While DSM, ICD and similar systems have improved the reliability and consistency of diagnosis, considerable controversy exists as to whether a diagnosis of schizophrenia really represents a single underlying disorder.

The uncertainty about diagnosis, and consequently its limited predictive validity, raises a number of important issues for service users. First, many clinicians in both primary and secondary care are reluctant to give this diagnosis, sometimes making it more difficult for people and their families to receive help early on. Second, some service users are reluctant to accept the diagnosis, and may reject suggestions that schizophrenia is an illness in need of treatment. Third, to receive a diagnosis of schizophrenia, with the stigma that this entails, seems to some a heavy price to pay given the diagnostic uncertainties that exist. Finally, some people diagnosed with schizophrenia object to receiving compulsory treatment for what they regard as no more than a putative illness.

That there are genuine problems with the diagnosis and classification of schizophrenia is not at question. However, for many people so diagnosed, the frequently painful and frightening experiences of schizophrenia and the disability often associated with the illness remain, with or without the diagnosis. Moreover, to improve treatments and services for this group of people would be difficult without an operational diagnostic category with which to undertake research, and to allocate resources on the basis of proven need. Despite this practical requirement for diagnostic categories, caution is necessary, to avoid making overly simplistic prognostications for individual service users. Professionals also have a duty to provide good, clear and honest information regarding the illness, and about the treatments and services available.

2.3 Incidence and prevalence

Schizophrenia is a relatively common illness, and it is certainly the most common form of psychotic disorder. The mean incidence of schizophrenia reported in epidemiological studies, when the diagnosis is limited to core criteria and corrected for age, is 0.11 per 1000 (range 0.07–0.17 per 1000); if broader criteria are used, this figure doubles to 0.24 per 1000 (range 0.07–0.52 per 1000) (Jablensky et al, 1992). Average rates for men and women are similar, although the mean age of onset is about 5 years greater in women (hence a lower female rate in adolescence), with a second smaller peak after the menopause. The lifetime prevalence of schizophrenia is between 0.4% and 1.4% (Cannon & Jones, 1996). The National Survey of Psychiatric Morbidity in the UK found a population prevalence of probable psychotic disorder of 5 per 1000 in the age group 16–74 years (Singleton et al, 2000).

Research into the epidemiology of schizophrenia has found a higher prevalence among individuals born in inner cities (van Os et al, 1996), and the diagnosis is applied more often to people of African–Caribbean origin living in the UK than would be expected (Harrison et al, 1988). It has been suggested that poverty and social isolation might trigger a schizophrenic psychosis in vulnerable individuals (Faris & Dunham, 1967). An alternative hypothesis is that people with schizophrenia might, as a result of their illness, be disadvantaged in terms of social functioning, and thus more likely to 'drift' into lower socio-economic circumstances, poor housing and unemployment (Jablensky et al, 1992). The impact of prejudice, stigma and social exclusion is also likely to have a significant role in the development of these negative social outcomes.

2.4 Aetiology of schizophrenia

The aetiology of schizophrenia is not well understood. Research has attempted to determine the aetiological role of specific biochemical variables, such as genetic and biochemical factors and brain pathology, as well as that of stressors such as low social class and family conflict. Some researchers have argued that schizophrenia covers a heterogeneous range of disorders, which may have a common underlying biological vulnerability (Gelder *et al*, 1997). This biological component, proposed to have a significant genetic basis, is seen as one vulnerability factor in the aetiology of schizophrenia, interacting with complex physical, environmental and psychological vulnerability factors. Biochemical theories have centred mainly on the 'dopamine hypothesis' (see Sedvall & Farde, 1995 for a review); that is, that schizophrenia might result from overproduction of the neurotransmitter dopamine, or an oversensitivity of dopamine receptors to dopamine.

Psychological factors such as problems with attention, executive functioning or reasoning and emotions have also been implicated in the development of symptoms of schizophrenia (Green, 1992; Nuechterlein & Subotnik, 1998; Garety *et al*, 2001). Social and environmental factors such as social isolation, urban birth or rearing, migration and stressful life events have all been argued to increase the risk of schizophrenia (Bramon *et al*, 2001). The idea that families have a causal role in the development of schizophrenia is controversial and is reviewed in section 6.5 on family interventions (Leff, 1978). However, the evidence that family members' attitudes can affect the outcome for people diagnosed with schizophrenia is now established (Smith & Birchwood, 1993; Bebbington & Kuipers, 1994; Barrowclough & Parle, 1997; Kuipers & Raune, 1999).

Much of the available research on the aetiology of schizophrenia is consistent with a 'stress-vulnerability' model of the illness (Nuechterlein & Dawson, 1984), a model that arguably best integrates current biological, psychological and social findings. This paradigm suggests that individuals possess different levels of vulnerability to schizophrenia, which are determined by a combination of biological, social and psychological factors. It is proposed that vulnerability would result in the development of problems only when environmental stressors are present. If the vulnerability is great, relatively low levels of environmental stress might be sufficient to cause problems. If the vulnerability is less, problems would develop only when higher levels of environmental stress are experienced. The model is consistent with a wide variety of putative causes of the disorder, as well as the differential relapse and readmission rates observed among people with schizophrenia.

2.5 Use of health service resources

Schizophrenia places a heavy burden on individuals and their carers, as well as potentially large demands on the health care system. The care of people with schizophrenia may consist of hospital care (in-patient, day patient and out-patient care), community health care (by community psychiatric nurses, community mental health teams and general practitioners) and social services (day care, home support and sheltered accommodation). Non-professional carers, usually relatives or friends, play an important part in the day-to-day support of people with schizophrenia. It is therefore important that carers themselves are given adequate support and are properly consulted in the formulation of care plans for service users. Some people with schizophrenia and their families receive care from the private sector; many more are recipients of at least part of their care from local voluntary sector organisations such as MIND and Rethink Severe Mental Illness (formerly the National Schizophrenia Fellowship). Many service users also find user-led and self-help groups helpful.

In England, a review estimated that 55% of service users receiving treatment lived at home, often with a family member, while 16% were housed in sheltered accommodation and a further 18% were hospital in-patients (Kavanagh et al, 1995). The most common points of contact were specialist hospital out-patient clinics, used by 44% of service users, and general practitioners, used by 55%. In addition, 21% had contact with community psychiatric nurses. People with schizophrenia also constitute 28.4% of the case-load of a consultant psychiatrist (Johnson, 1997).

In 1995 up to a quarter of people with schizophrenia received all or most of their psychiatric care from their general practitioner (Kendrick et al, 1995). While this may not always be desirable, it reflects the needs of some people, the current distribution of resources, and also the desire of some individuals not to receive most or all of their care from secondary care services. This guideline is therefore applicable to the management of people with schizophrenia in primary care and, where appropriate, refers to the interface between primary and secondary care services. In addition, many people when developing schizophrenia often present first to their general practitioner, who thus has an important role in the identification of schizophrenia (outside the scope of this guideline) and in its initial treatment and management.

The use of hospital beds by people with schizophrenia is substantial. In 1994 in England, 34 783 hospital admissions were for schizophrenia and related disorders, amounting to 50.2% of all admissions to psychiatric in-patient care. The mean length of stay was nearly 130 days, with a median duration of about 30 days, reflecting a highly skewed use of resources. Long-stay in-patient care is not just de-socialising for the patients; it is also by far the most costly health care component in the overall treatment of schizophrenia. Kavanagh et al (1995) found that 14% of all people with schizophrenia were in short-stay or long-stay hospitals, and yet the cost of this care accounted for 51% of the total expenditure on the treatment and care of people with schizophrenia. A more recent estimate suggested that in-patient care now accounts for 56.5% of the total treatment and care costs of schizophrenia, compared with 2.5% for out-patient care and 14.7% for day care (Knapp et al, 2002).

The cumulative cost of the care of individuals with schizophrenia is high. Davies & Drummond (1994) estimated that 1.6% of the total national health care budget, and 5.4% of National Health Service in-patient costs, were attributable to schizophrenia (Knapp, 1997). A cost-of-illness study estimated the total burden of schizophrenia in England in 1993 to be £2.6 billion (Knapp, 1997). Health and social services costs alone amounted to £810 million, of which in-patient care amounted to over £652 million. The estimated drugs bill for the treatment of schizophrenia is in the region of £38 million (Mason, 1999).

2.6 Other costs

The impact of schizophrenia falls upon the full range of public services and beyond, including health services, social services, the benefits system, the workplace and the legal system. The employment problems faced by many people with schizophrenia pose considerable direct and indirect costs. After the first episode of illness, 15–30% of service users are not in employment, a figure rising to over 65% following a second episode. Overall, the total employment impact of schizophrenia has been estimated to be £82.4 million in the UK (Guest & Cookson, 1999).

Carers also carry significant burdens that can affect health, leisure time, employment and financial status. Guest & Cookson (1999) estimated that 1.2–2.5% of carers gave up work to care for dependants with schizophrenia, which contributed to a total UK family impact cost of approximately £1.9 million in 1997. It is also the case that people with schizophrenia are over-represented in the criminal justice system (Kavanagh & Opit, 1994), at an estimated annual cost of £1.3 million in the UK (Guest & Cookson, 1999).

2.7 Treatment and management of schizophrenia in the NHS

Until the 1950s the treatment and management of schizophrenia generally took place in large asylums, where people remained confined for much of their lives. Although government policy initiated a programme of gradual closure of these large hospitals and the rehousing of the residents in the community, this process was greatly assisted by the introduction of chlorpromazine, thioridazine, haloperidol and other conventional antipsychotic drugs. Antipsychotic drugs would become the mainstay of treatment for the rest of the twentieth century.

2.7.1 Pharmacological treatment

Today, within both hospital and community settings, antipsychotic medicines remain the primary treatment for schizophrenia. There is well-established evidence for the efficacy of antipsychotic drugs in both the treatment of acute psychotic episodes and relapse prevention over time (Janicak et al, 1993). However, despite the effectiveness of these drugs, considerable problems remain. A significant proportion of service users, perhaps 40% (Klein & Davis, 1969; Kane et al, 1996), have a poor response to conventional antipsychotic drugs, and continue to show moderate to severe psychotic symptoms, both positive and negative.

In addition, conventional antipsychotic agents are associated with a high incidence and broad range of side-effects, including lethargy, weight gain, sexual dysfunction and sedation. Movement disorders, such as parkinsonism, akathisia and dystonia, often referred to as extrapyramidal side-effects (EPS), are common and can be disabling and distressing. Service users are most unhappy with sexual dysfunction, sedation and weight gain as well as EPS (www.rethink.org/information/research). A serious long-term side-effect is tardive dyskinesia, which develops in around 20% of people receiving conventional antipsychotic drugs (Kane et al, 1985). This is a late-onset EPS, characterised by abnormal involuntary movements of the lips, jaw, tongue and facial muscles, and sometimes the limbs and trunk. Although a person who develops tardive dyskinesia is initially usually unaware of the movements, they are clearly noticed by others, and the condition is rightly regarded as a severe social handicap.

In response to the limited effectiveness and extensive side-effects of conventional antipsychotic drugs, considerable effort has gone into developing pharmacological treatments for schizophrenia that produce fewer or less disabling side-effects. The main advantage of these newer, 'atypical' antipsychotics has been a lower liability to EPS. This is supported by a recent survey of individuals with schizophrenia, which suggested that service users find the side-effects associated with atypicals more acceptable than those of conventional antipsychotics (www.rethink.org/information/research). Moreover, it has also been argued that certain atypical drugs, particularly clozapine, can produce therapeutic gains in people with schizophrenia who do not respond well to conventional antipsychotics (Kane et al, 1988). However, a systematic review by Geddes et al (2000) suggested that for the atypical drugs more generally, claims for greater efficacy might be partly dependent upon the relative dosages used. Given the potential usefulness of the atypical antipsychotics, the NICE Technology Appraisal Committee has assessed this category of drugs, and the Committee's recommendations have been incorporated into this guideline.

2.7.2 Psychological interventions

Another relatively recent approach to helping people with schizophrenia is the use of specific psychological and psychosocial methods. Some of the earliest attempts included psychoanalysis (Fromm-Reichman, 1950), and a modification of psychoanalysis designed to enhance better integration into a hospital environment (Stack-Sullivan, 1947). Nevertheless, these pioneering efforts increased awareness of the psychological processes and personal impact of schizophrenia. Since then a number of psychological approaches have been introduced, including psychoeducation, family interventions, cognitive–behavioural therapy, cognitive remediation, social skills training, and counselling and supportive psychotherapy. These are described in Chapter 6.

2.7.3 Service-level interventions

New configurations in service delivery, such as the development of assertive outreach teams, have formed an increasingly important element in the management of all forms of severe mental illness. These interventions are new methods of directly and explicitly addressing the needs of people with serious mental health problems, principally those suffering from the psychoses. Although a number of studies suggest that these new service configurations have a positive impact, much of the research has been undertaken in countries other than the UK, in which the 'standard care' with which the new systems are compared may be substantially different from that in the UK, making the interpretation of these findings somewhat difficult.

Service-level interventions include the use of community mental health teams, crisis resolution and home treatment teams, assertive community treatment or outreach teams, case management, acute day hospital care, non-acute day hospital care, vocational rehabilitation, and early intervention services. Because of the impact of schizophrenia on employment status, some services have developed vocational rehabilitation schemes with the aim of improving employment and social functioning. The characteristics of these service systems are described in Chapter 7. It should be noted that although this guideline applies to both England and Wales, the configuration of services and the plans for further development of teams differ for each country.

2.7.4 Primary–secondary care interface

The large majority of people with a diagnosis of schizophrenia in the care of the NHS (about 85–90%) are treated by secondary care mental health services. Surveys suggest that about 10–15% of service users are managed solely in primary care (Johnstone, 1991; Jeffreys et al, 1997). This represents a significant shift from previous surveys (Johnstone et al, 1984; Pantelis et al, 1988) and may be an indication of the impact of recent changes in the structure and delivery of mental health services. This guideline therefore concentrates on the provision of care by secondary care services. It does not address the issue of the identification and initial diagnosis of schizophrenia, which is beyond its scope, although this is a key issue for primary care services.

Nevertheless, primary care services provide a vital service for people with schizophrenia. A small percentage of service users have all their mental health care needs provided by primary care; the majority receive significant monitoring, treatment and support for their mental health problems in collaboration with secondary care services; and the vast majority receive much, if not all, of their physical care from primary care. Where possible, the guideline addresses these issues in its evidenced-based recommendations; where this is not possible, they are addressed through a number of good practice points, particularly in relation to the interface between primary and secondary care. Guidance on this interface has been incorporated into Chapter 7 on service interventions as a number of good practice points, with the aim of assisting primary care professionals in the management and referral of people with schizophrenia.

2.7.5 Physical health care

The association between schizophrenia and poor physical health is well established (Phelan et al, 2001). Poor health results in higher standardised mortality rates and increased morbidity for individuals with schizophrenia. It is apparent from epidemiological work that this excess morbidity and mortality is the result, in significant part, of a range of physical disorders, and not simply due to the effects of long-term antipsychotic medication or other factors, such as substance misuse, which are also associated with schizophrenia.

Reports on the mortality of people with schizophrenia indicate that there is an increased risk of death from circulatory conditions, infections and endocrine disorders. Despite high reported rates of smoking in people with schizophrenia, rates of cancer do not appear to be raised (Gulbinat et al, 1992; Jeste et al, 1996; Harris & Barrowclough, 1998). People with schizophrenia have higher rates of cardiovascular disease, including myocardial infarction, than the general population (Tsaung et al, 1983; Harris, 1988).

Patients with schizophrenia are more likely than the general population to have lifestyle risk factors for cardiovascular disease and mortality (Kendrick, 1996; Brown et al, 1999). They were found to be more likely to smoke even when the study population was controlled for socio-economic class (Brown et al, 1999). It has been suggested that high smoking rates in people with schizophrenia can be explained by the therapeutic effect of nicotine on psychotic symptoms and the reduction in side-effects of antipsychotic medication due to the enhanced metabolism of antipsychotic drugs in smokers (Jeste et al, 1996). People with schizophrenia are also less likely to exercise and are more likely to have diets higher in fat and lower in fibre than the general population (Brown et al, 1999).

Antipsychotic medication may induce endocrine abnormalities (e.g. diabetes and galactorrhoea), neurological disorders (e.g. tardive dyskinesia) and cardiovascular side-effects (e.g. lengthening of the QT interval on electrocardiography) (Jeste et al, 1996; Koro et al, 2002). Newer antipsychotics are less toxic than the traditional drugs but are known to cause weight gain and diabetes.

The fact that this excess mortality and morbidity has a range of causes – including dietary and behavioural ones – suggests that lifestyle factors have a significant part to play. It could be that some of the problems associated with the development of schizophrenia impair or otherwise affect people's ability to manage their own physical health effectively. It is also likely that socio-economic factors, including social exclusion, have a significant role. Nevertheless, there is convincing evidence that psychiatrists and general practitioners are poor at recognising and treating physical conditions such as cardiovascular disorders in psychiatric patients (for a review see Osborn, 2001).

A number of suggestions, including the development of case registers and specific remuneration for general practitioners for the monitoring of physical health problems, have been made about how to address this problem (Osborn, 2001). As yet, the evidence for such interventions remains uncertain, although some early findings suggest that quite simple interventions might have some impact on the lifestyle factors associated with increased morbidity, for example group interventions for smoking cessation (Addington *et al*, 1998). There is also evidence to suggest that people with schizophrenia have relatively high levels of contact with their general practitioners (Jablensky *et al*, 2000). Given this, careful consideration should be given to the role of general practitioners in the management of physical health problems. This is discussed further in section 7.10.

The higher physical morbidity and mortality of service users with schizophrenia must be considered in all assessments. Particular attention should be paid to the risk of metabolic and cardiovascular disease, and attention should be given to the promotion of lifestyle and dietary changes that might promote better health outcomes. Although this would normally be expected to be the responsibility of primary care services, secondary care professionals should nevertheless monitor these matters, especially where they believe a service user might have little regular contact with primary care.

2.7.5.1   Primary and secondary care services, in conjunction with the service user, should jointly identify which service will take responsibility for assessing and monitoring the physical health care needs of the service user. This should be documented in both primary and secondary care notes and care plans, and clearly recorded by care coordinators for those assigned to an enhanced care programme approach. (GPP)

2.8 Assessment

The purpose of this guideline is to help improve the experience and outcomes of care for people with schizophrenia. These outcomes include the degree of symptomatic recovery, quality of life, degree of personal autonomy, ability and access to work, stability and quality of living accommodation, degree and quality of social integration, degree of financial independence, and the experience and impact of side-effects.

2.8.1   The assessment of needs for health and social care of people with schizophrenia should be comprehensive and should address medical, social, psychological, occupational, economic, physical and cultural issues. (GPP)

In addition, the possible presence of comorbid conditions, including substance and alcohol misuse or physical illness, or the existence of a forensic history, will necessitate the development of treatment and care plans outside the scope of this guideline. Nevertheless, full assessment of these issues must be included.

2.8.2   A full assessment of health and social care needs should be undertaken regularly, including assessment of accommodation and quality of life. The frequency of these assessments should be based upon clinical need and discussed with the service user. The agreed frequency of assessment should be documented in the care plan. (GPP)

2.8.3   All non-professional carers who provide regular care for a person as part of the care programme approach should have a regular assessment of their own caring, physical and mental health needs, at a frequency agreed with the carer and recorded in the carer's own care plan. (GPP)

2.8.4   People with schizophrenia experience considerable difficulty in obtaining employment and many remain unemployed for long periods. The assessment of people with schizophrenia should include assessment of their occupational status and potential, which should be recorded in their notes and care plans. (GPP)

Considerations regarding supported employment are dealt with in Chapter 7.

Given the uncertainties surrounding the diagnosis of schizophrenia, it is important that following a full needs assessment, a comprehensive care plan is implemented whenever this diagnosis is suspected. Reaching a definitive diagnosis is often difficult in the early stages; nevertheless, assessment and treatment should not be delayed. When a diagnosis has been reached and fully discussed with the service user (and with the carer where appropriate), the service user (and carer) may want this reviewed by a second opinion, as many people following the first episode are unsure about their diagnosis and may need help with this.

2.8.5   A decision by the service user, and carer where appropriate, to seek a second opinion on the diagnosis should be supported, particularly in view of the considerable personal and social consequences of being diagnosed with schizophrenia. (GPP)

2.9 Engagement, consent and the therapeutic alliance

Whatever treatments are offered, it is essential to engage the service user in a collaborative, trusting and caring working relationship at the earliest opportunity. Professionals should take into full account the particular nature of schizophrenia: namely, that the illness may affect people's ability to make judgements, to recognise that they are ill, to comprehend clearly what professionals might say to them, and to make informed decisions about their treatment and care.

2.9.1   Health professionals should make all efforts necessary to ensure that a service user can give meaningful and properly informed consent before treatment is initiated, giving adequate time for discussion and the provision of written information. (GPP)

It is also important to convey to service users that their problems, as they experience them, are being taken seriously. Wherever appropriate and possible, carers or advocates should also be involved in the decision-making process at the earliest opportunity.

If compulsory treatment proves necessary, additional efforts will be required to ensure proper protection of the service user's human rights. In these circumstances, individuals have the right to expect that the most skilled staff available manage their assessment and treatment, including a consultant psychiatrist. These rights include having access to the same type and quality of treatments as those who are treated voluntarily.

2.9.2   Although there are limitations with advance directives regarding the choice of treatment for individuals with schizophrenia, it is recommended that they are developed and documented in individuals' care programmes whenever possible. (NICE 2002)

2.9.3   When advance directives have been agreed, copies should be placed in both primary and secondary care case notes and care plans, and copies given to the service user and the user's care coordinator. If appropriate, and subject to agreement with the service user, a copy should be given to the carer. (GPP)

For most people experiencing a schizophrenic breakdown, the level of distress, anxiety and subjective confusion, especially during first episodes, leads to difficulty in accessing services. They may feel suspicious of friends, relatives and professionals, and their distressed state can alarm others who may respond in a less than helpful way. Many people breaking down do not agree with others around them about the events and experiences they are having, nor with the explanations other people give. In these circumstances, many service users are vulnerable to exploitation and abuse, not only by other members of the public, but also by professionals and other service users. It is important that service users and carers receive help early to minimise unnecessary suffering.

2.9.4   Service users and their relatives seeking help should be assessed and receive treatment at the earliest possible opportunity. (GPP)

Given the particular problems encountered in the treatment and care of people with schizophrenia, professionals must work sensitively and respectfully, sometimes in the face of challenging and disturbing behaviour, to communicate and engage in a trusting and meaningful way. Without being able to engage the person sufficiently to form a working therapeutic alliance, providing specific psychological and psychosocial treatments will be impossible. It is also probable that other treatments will be less effective, and people will be less likely to adhere to treatment plans.

2.9.5   Health professionals involved in the routine treatment and management of schizophrenia should take time to build a supportive and empathic relationship with service users and carers; this should be regarded as an essential element of the routine care offered. (GPP)

Within mental health services, service users commonly feel their account of their experience is not given much credence, and they are rarely given the opportunity to offer a contribution to the understanding of their illness. This may hinder the development of a good working alliance.

2.9.6   Consideration should be given, where practicable, to encouraging service users to write their own account of their illness in their notes. (GPP)

Bearing in mind the recurrent nature of schizophrenic illness, and the fact that many people with such disorders will require services over a number of years, the need to form and sustain an effective therapeutic alliance must be a central aim for all services and personnel involved in the care of people with schizophrenia. For the same reasons, every attempt should be made to ensure the continuity of care for individuals and their carers. It is also essential to maintain good communication between the different professionals and services in the context of the care programme approach, and to help service users and carers develop community-based supports through voluntary organisations such as MIND and Rethink. Special support will need to be provided for people whose first language is not English. A key objective is to develop an equal partnership, based on shared information, empathy and encouraged participation, between the user, carer and professionals, without compromising user confidentiality.

2.10 Language, stigma and blame

Until recently the history of the treatment and care of people with schizophrenia was characterised by varying levels of social exclusion for the individual, enforced treatment by professionals, fear among the public, and shame or embarrassment within the families of those affected. Although new treatments were introduced in the 1950s and 1960s, which resulted in an increased discharge of patients into the community, the public perception of people with schizophrenia often remains one based upon fear and ignorance, partly because of the disproportionate media coverage given to tragic events associated with this illness. People with a diagnosis of schizophrenia live with the stigma of an illness often seen as dangerous and best dealt with away from the rest of society. In this regard, research has shown that while the number of psychiatrically unrelated homicides rose between 1957 and 1995, homicides by people sent for psychiatric treatment did not, suggesting that the public fear of violence arising from people with schizophrenia is misplaced (Taylor & Gunn, 1999).

The stigma experienced by people with schizophrenia is also partly the result of health care systems and professionals. The socially disabling effects of extrapyramidal side-effects, the less than careful use of diagnostic labels, and the fact that psychiatric service users are subject to different legislation from other service users, all contribute to singling out people with schizophrenia, marking them as different. In an editorial for the *British Medical Journal*, Norman Sartorius claimed that 'stigma remains the main obstacle to a better life for the many hundreds of millions of people suffering from mental disorders', a stigma professionals have inadvertently made worse (Sartorius, 2002).

In the view of many service users, clinical language is not always used in a helpful way, and may contribute to the stigma of schizophrenia. For example, calling someone a 'schizophrenic' or a 'psychotic' gives the impression that the person has been wholly taken over by an illness, such that no recognisable or civilised person remains. Many non-psychiatric health workers and many employers continue to approach people with schizophrenia in this way. In addition, people with schizophrenia prefer to be described as 'service users' or as 'people with schizophrenia' rather than as 'patients'.

It is important that professionals are careful and considerate, but clear and thorough in their use of clinical language and in the explanations they provide, not just to service users and carers, but also to other health workers.

2.10.1   When talking to service users and carers, health professionals should avoid using clinical language or keep it to a minimum. Where clinical language is used, service users and carers should have access to written explanations. (GPP)

Also, services should ensure that all clinicians are sensitive to the needs and differences of other cultures.

2.10.2   All services should provide written material in the language of the service user, and interpreters should be sought for people who have difficulty in speaking English. (GPP)

The families of people with schizophrenia often play an essential part in the treatment and care of their relative, and with the right support and help can positively contribute to promoting recovery. Parents of people with schizophrenia often feel to blame, either because they have 'passed on the genes' causing schizophrenia, or because they are 'bad parents'.

2.10.3   Clear and intelligible information should be made available to service users and their families about schizophrenia and its possible causes, and about the possible role families can have in promoting recovery and reducing relapse. (GPP)

3 Methods used to develop this guideline

3.1 Overview

The development of this guideline drew upon methods outlined by the National Institute for Clinical Excellence (Eccles & Mason, 2001; NICE, 2002). A team of experts, professionals, service users and a carer, known as the Guideline Development Group (GDG), with the support of staff from the National Collaborating Centre for Mental Health (NCCMH), undertook the development of a patient-centred, evidence-based guideline. There are five steps in the process of developing a guideline:

1. define clinical questions considered important for practitioners and service users
2. develop criteria for evidence searching and search for evidence
3. design validated protocols for systematic review and apply to evidence recovered by search
4. synthesise and (meta-)analyse data retrieved, guided by the clinical questions
5. answer clinical questions with evidence-based recommendations for clinical practice.

The clinical practice recommendations made by the GDG are therefore derived from the most up-to-date and robust evidence base for the clinical and economic effectiveness of the treatments and services used in the management of schizophrenia. In addition, to ensure a service user and carer focus, the concerns of service users and carers regarding clinical practice have been highlighted and addressed by good practice points and recommendations agreed by the whole GDG. The evidence-based recommendations and good practice points are the core of this guideline.

3.2 Guideline Development Group

The Schizophrenia Guideline Development Group was composed of professionals in psychiatry, nursing, pharmacy and general practice; academic experts in psychiatry and psychology; a service user; a former service user; and a carer. The guideline development process was supported by staff from the National Collaborating Centre for Mental Health (NCCMH), who undertook the clinical and health economics literature searches, reviewed and presented the evidence to the GDG, managed the process, and contributed to the drafting of the guideline.

3.2.1 Guideline Development Group meetings

Twenty-three Schizophrenia GDG meetings were held between April 2001 and November 2002. During each day-long meeting, in a plenary session, clinical questions and clinical evidence were reviewed and assessed, statements developed and recommendations formulated. At each meeting, every GDG member declared any potential conflict of interest, and service user and carer concerns were routinely discussed as part of a standing agenda.

3.2.2 Topic groups

The GDG divided its workload along clinically relevant lines to simplify the guideline development process, and GDG members formed smaller topic groups to undertake guideline work in that area of clinical practice. Topic groups covered pharmacological, service-level and psychological interventions. These groups were designed to organise the large volume of evidence appraisal prior to presenting it to the GDG as a whole. Each topic group was chaired by a health care professional with expert knowledge of that particular topic. Topic groups refined the clinical definitions of treatment interventions, identified relevant clinical questions, reviewed and prepared the evidence with the systematic reviewer before presenting it to the GDG as a whole, and helped the GDG to identify further expertise in the topic. Topic group leaders reported the status of the group's work as part of the standing agenda. They also introduced and led the GDG discussion of the evidence review for that topic, and assisted the GDG Chair in drafting the relevant section of the guideline.

3.2.3 Service users and carers

Group members with direct experience of services gave an integral service user focus to the GDG and the guideline. The current and former service users and the carer contributed to writing the clinical questions, helping to ensure that the evidence addressed their views and preferences, highlighting sensitive issues and terminology associated with schizophrenia, and bringing service-user research to the attention of the GDG. They edited the first draft of the guideline's introduction and identified good practice points from the service user and carer perspective; their suggestions were incorporated before the draft was distributed to the GDG for further review.

3.2.4 Special advisers

Special advisers who had specific expertise in one or more aspects of the treatment and management of schizophrenia assisted the guideline development process, commenting on specific aspects of the guideline, fine-tuning clinical questions, and sometimes making presentations to the GDG. In particular, special advisers discussed the clinical questions with the Pharmacological Interventions Topic Group, and commented on drafts of narrative reviews on rapid tranquillisation, depot antipsychotic treatment and antipsychotic dosage. The changing role of psychodynamic psychotherapies, both in the UK and in other countries, was presented to the GDG by a special adviser. Appendix 2 lists those who agreed to act as special advisers.

3.2.5 National and international experts

National and international experts in schizophrenia research were identified through the literature search and through the experience of the GDG members. These experts were contacted to recommend unpublished or soon-to-be published studies in order to ensure that up-to-date evidence on the management of schizophrenia was included in the development of the guideline. They informed the group about completed trials at the pre-publication stage, systematic reviews in the process of being published, studies relating to the cost-effectiveness of treatment, and trial data if the GDG could be provided with full access to the complete trial report. Appendix 5 lists the researchers who were contacted.

3.3 Clinical questions

Clinical questions were used to guide the identification and interrogation of the evidence base relating to the use of psychological interventions, service-level interventions, and pharmacological interventions in the treatment and management of schizophrenia. The GDG necessarily had to limit the number of questions to those they regarded as essential. Questions were developed for each clinical topic area. Appendix 6 lists the clinical questions and Appendix 7 the drug names and clinical definitions of interventions reviewed.

3.4 Systematic clinical literature review strategies

The aims of the clinical literature review were the systematic identification and synthesis of relevant evidence from the published literature in order to answer specific clinical questions developed by the GDG. Thus, clinical practice recommendations are evidence-based, where possible; the absence of evidence identified gaps where future research is needed.

3.4.1 Methodology

A stepwise, hierarchical approach was taken to locating and presenting evidence to the GDG. This process was developed by the NCCMH review team after considering recommendations from several sources. These included:

- National Guidelines Support and Research Unit (NICE)
- Centre for Clinical Policy and Practice of the New South Wales Health Department, Australia
- Clinical Evidence Online
- Cochrane Collaboration
- New Zealand Guideline Group
- NHS Centre for Reviews and Dissemination
- Oxford Centre for Evidence-based Medicine
- Scottish Intercollegiate Guidelines Network
- United States Agency for Health Research and Quality.

3.4.2 Review process

The initial evidence base was formed from high-quality, recently published or updated, randomised controlled trials (RCTs) that addressed at least one of the clinical questions developed by the GDG. Systematic reviews were selected on predetermined quality criteria. Further searches for new RCTs were undertaken. New RCTs meeting inclusion criteria set by the GDG were incorporated into existing systematic reviews and fresh analyses performed. If no systematic review was available, the review team located all relevant high-quality RCTs for review and, where appropriate, conducted meta-analyses. The review process is illustrated in Figure 3.1.

Given the size of the evidence base for the treatment and management of schizophrenia, the GDG elected to limit the collection and analysis of data to systematic reviews and RCTs. Although there are a number of difficulties with the use of RCTs in the evaluation of interventions in mental health, some of which also apply to the use of RCTs in any health research, the RCT remains the most important method for establishing efficacy. However, in some cases it was not possible to identify high-quality systematic reviews or a substantial body of RCTs that directly addressed a clinical question. In this situation, an informal consensus process was adopted (see section 3.4.8). Future guidelines on the treatment and management of schizophrenia will be able to update and extend the usable evidence base from the evidence collected, synthesised and analysed for this guideline.

3.4.3 Difficulties in RCT research into mental health treatments

There are several difficulties in undertaking, evaluating and interpreting research into interventions in mental health. The RCT is widely recognised as the 'gold standard' for evaluating treatment efficacy, but some methodological problems exist for research into mental health treatments generally, some of which may apply more specifically to pharmacological, psychological or service-level interventions. For example, there are difficulties in the choice of the control condition: there may be problems interpreting results when an intervention is compared with 'standard care', since standard care may include a range of forms of psychological help (including, sometimes, aspects of the intervention studied); thus as standard care improves, the apparent effects of the treatment investigated may diminish. Also, standard care will differ from country to country, limiting the usefulness of research from non-UK countries that use standard care as a comparator.

On the other hand, when an intervention is compared with another intervention instead of standard care, with the aim of controlling for the general benefits of time and attention to the individual's concerns, real benefits may accrue to the control, again reducing the apparent effects of the intervention under study. Moreover, the benefits gained in terms of time and attention for all participants in an RCT may generate improvements for experimental and control groups that dwarf the additional effects of the experimental intervention.

Psychological and service-level interventions in particular are rarely simple technical interventions and usually demand flexibility in their application. This is especially the case in psychological treatments for people with schizophrenia. Although studies can build flexibility into their treatment manuals, it is likely that the approach would be more constrained by, for example, a stricter adherence to a therapeutic model than would be the case in ordinary clinical practice. This raises questions of generalisability.

Financial and methodological considerations also typically necessitate time-limited interventions and shorter RCTs, rather than the longer, more flexible therapeutic programmes that may be found in routine clinical practice. Schizophrenia may affect people for much of their lives, with treatment extending sometimes over many years.

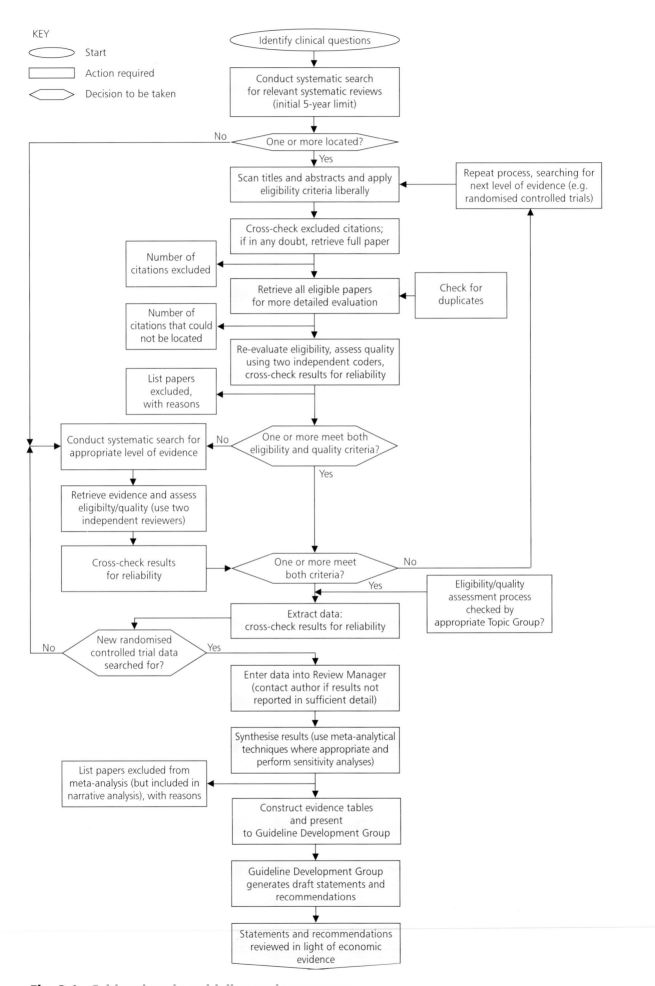

KEY

⬭ Start

▭ Action required

⬡ Decision to be taken

Identify clinical questions

Conduct systematic search
for relevant systematic reviews
(initial 5-year limit)

One or more located? — No

Yes

Scan titles and abstracts and apply
eligibility criteria liberally

Repeat process, searching for
next level of evidence (e.g.
randomised controlled trials)

Cross-check excluded citations;
if in any doubt, retrieve full paper

Number of
citations excluded

Retrieve all eligible papers
for more detailed evaluation

Check for
duplicates

Number of
citations that could
not be located

Re-evaluate eligibility, assess quality
using two independent coders,
cross-check results for reliability

List papers
excluded,
with reasons

Conduct systematic search for
appropriate level of evidence — No — One or more meet both
eligibility and quality criteria?

Yes

Retrieve evidence and assess
eligibilty/quality (use two
independent reviewers)

Cross-check results
for reliability

One or more meet
both criteria? — No

Yes

Eligibility/quality
assessment process
checked by
appropriate Topic Group?

New randomised
controlled trial data
searched for? — No

Yes

Extract data:
cross-check results for reliability

Enter data into Review Manager
(contact author if results not
reported in sufficient detail)

Synthesise results (use meta-analytical
techniques where appropriate and
perform sensitivity analyses)

List papers excluded from
meta-analysis (but included in
narrative analysis), with reasons

Construct evidence tables
and present
to Guideline Development Group

Guideline Development Group
generates draft statements and
recommendations

Statements and recommendations
reviewed in light of economic
evidence

Fig. 3.1 Schizophrenia guideline review process

Short interventions and short trials will generate only a limited understanding of the impact of an intervention.

Other differences from routine practice include participant selection by specific criteria (e.g. levels of certain symptoms); high rates of participant refusal (e.g. because of reluctance to undergo randomisation or assessments); and the fact that the clinicians conducting the trial are often more highly trained, or therapists more carefully supervised in the case of psychological interventions research.

These factors may compromise the generalisability of the findings of research to the ordinary treatment setting. Nevertheless, it is still recognised that RCTs are an indispensable first step in the evaluation of interventions in mental health and provide the most valid method for determining the impact of two contrasting treatment conditions (treatment efficacy), while controlling for a wide range of participant factors, including the effects of spontaneous remission. Once an approach has been demonstrated as efficacious under the stringent conditions of an RCT, a next step is to examine its effectiveness in ordinary treatment conditions, including large-scale effectiveness studies (very few of which are currently available), which may add to our understanding of the pharmacological, psychological and service-level interventions in the treatment and management of schizophrenia.

In addition to the methodological issues described above, the use of RCTs and other studies in the evaluation of interventions in the treatment and management of schizophrenia is limited in many cases by the absence of important outcome measures. For example, few trials report evidence on quality of life or satisfaction with services, despite the fact that services users and carers view these measures as very important.

3.4.4 Search strategies

In conducting the review, the team searched the literature for all English-language systematic reviews relevant to the schizophrenia scope (see Appendix 1) that were published or updated after 1995 (see Appendix 8 for a detailed description of the review process). Search filters consisted of a combination of subject headings and free text phrases. The filter for schizophrenia was adapted from that suggested by the Cochrane Schizophrenia Group (May 2001). The search filters can be found in Appendix 9.

Electronic searches were made of the major bibliographic databases (Medline, EMBASE, PsycINFO, CINAHL), in addition to the Cochrane Database of Systematic Reviews, the NHS R&D Health Technology Assessment database, Evidence-Based Mental Health, Medical Matrix, and Clinical Evidence (Issue 5). Ineligible articles were excluded, and a second independent reviewer cross-checked these for relevance. The remaining references were acquired in full and re-evaluated for eligibility. The most recently published reviews that appropriately addressed a clinical question were selected. For each systematic review used, a search was made for new RCTs, and the papers for these and for existing RCTs were retrieved.

The search for further evidence included RCTs published after each review's search date, in-press papers identified by experts, and reviews of reference lists and recent contents of selected papers. All reports that were retrieved but later excluded were listed with reasons for exclusion in the appropriate evidence table. Where no relevant systematic review was located, the review team asked the GDG to decide whether a fresh systematic review should be undertaken. Eligible reviews were critically appraised for methodological quality and the reliability of this procedure was confirmed by parallel independent assessment. The eligibility and quality assessment was tested on a representative sample of papers. The GDG topic groups checked this process and made adjustments to the guideline review's focus or eligibility criteria as necessary. Appendix 10 provides the eligibility checklist.

Out of 2153 articles that were initially identified from database searches, 49 met the guideline eligibility and quality criteria. For the psychological topic area, 4 existing reviews were used and 1 new review was conducted. Twenty-one individual RCTs contributed new data to the analyses (2 papers reported follow-up data to existing trials) and 7 RCTs that were used in existing reviews were excluded. For the service topic area, 7 existing reviews were used, 9 new individual RCTs were found and 9 RCTs that were used in existing reviews were excluded. For the pharmacological topic area, 11 existing reviews were used and 11 new reviews were conducted. Thirty-four individual RCTs contributed new data and 131 RCTs used in existing reviews were excluded.

3.4.5 Synthesising the evidence

Outcome data were extracted directly from all eligible RCTs that met accepted quality criteria into Review Manager 4.1 (Cochrane Collaboration, 2000). Where appropriate, data from the existing trials were synthesised with that from new trials using meta-analytic techniques in Metaview 4.1 (Build 0600; Update Software, 1999). Where necessary, reanalyses of the data or sensitivity analyses were used to answer clinical questions not addressed in the original review.

General information about each eligible systematic review and the included and excluded trials was entered into an evidence table. Consultation was used to overcome difficulties with coding. Data from trials included in existing systematic reviews were extracted independently by one reviewer directly into Review Manager and cross-checked with the existing data-set. Two independent reviewers extracted data from new RCTs, and disagreements were resolved with discussion. Where consensus could not be reached, a third reviewer resolved the disagreement. Masked assessment (i.e. masked with regard to the journal that published the article, the authors, the institution, and the magnitude of the effect) was not used since it is unclear that doing so reduces bias (Jadad *et al*, 1996; Berlin, 2001).

3.4.6 Presenting the data to the GDG

In presenting data to the GDG, forest plots were organised so that display of data in the area to the left of the 'line of no effect' indicated a 'favourable' outcome for the treatment in question. Dichotomous outcomes were presented as a standard estimation of the odds ratio and its 95% confidence interval. The relative risk and, where appropriate, the number needed to treat or number needed to harm, were also calculated on an intention-to-treat basis (i.e. a 'once randomised, always analyse' basis). This assumes that participants who ceased to engage in the study – from whatever group – had an unfavourable outcome (with the exception of the outcome of 'death'). Numbers needed to treat were reported for all statistically significant end-of-treatment outcomes where available, but were not reported for follow-up periods where the length of follow-up differed between studies.

The chi-squared test of heterogeneity ($P<0.10$) was used, as well as visual inspection of graphs, to look for the possibility of heterogeneity. Where no heterogeneity was detected, a fixed-effects model was used to summarise the results. Where heterogeneity was present, an attempt was made to explain the variation. If studies with heterogeneous results were found to be comparable, a random-effects model was used to synthesise the results (DerSimonian & Laird, 1986). In the random-effects analysis, heterogeneity is accounted for both in the width of confidence intervals and the estimate of the treatment effect. With decreasing heterogeneity the random-effects approach moves asymptotically towards a fixed-effects model.

3.4.7 Forming and grading the recommendations

The GDG was presented with the available research evidence that was relevant to its clinical questions. The systematic reviewer presented evidence tables on each clinical question to the GDG with the results displayed graphically in forest plots. The group reviewed and analysed the evidence tables and forest plots, which formed the basis for developing statements and recommendations. Evidence was classified according to an accepted hierarchy (Box 3.1). Recommendations were then graded A to C based on the level of associated evidence, or noted as a good practice point (Box 3.2).

In order to facilitate consistency in generating and drafting the clinical statements arising from RCTs and meta-analyses of RCTs, the GDG adopted the following decision tree.

3.4.7.1 Level 1a evidence

Evidence was classified as '1a' if it came from a single trial with at least 150 participants in any single arm of the trial or from three or more randomised trials.

Box 3.1 Hierarchy of evidence

Level	Type of evidence
Ia	Evidence obtained from a single, large randomised trial or a meta-analysis of at least three randomised controlled trials
Ib	Evidence obtained from a small randomised controlled trial or a meta-analysis of fewer than three randomised controlled trials
IIa	Evidence obtained from at least one well-designed controlled study without randomisation
IIb	Evidence obtained from at least one other well-designed quasi-experimental study
III	Evidence obtained from well-designed, non-experimental descriptive studies, such as comparative studies, correlation studies and case studies
IV	Evidence obtained from expert committee reports or opinions and/or clinical experiences of respected authorities

Adapted from Eccles, M. & Mason, J. (2001) How to develop cost-conscious guidelines. Health Technology Assessment, *5, 8.*

Box 3.2   Grading of recommendations

A	At least one randomised controlled trial as part of a body of literature of overall good quality and consistency addressing the specific recommendation (evidence levels Ia and Ib) without extrapolation
B	Well-conducted clinical studies but no randomised clinical trials on the topic of recommendation (evidence levels IIa, IIb, III); or extrapolated from level I evidence
C	Expert committee reports or opinions and/or clinical experiences of respected authorities. This grading indicates that directly applicable clinical studies of good quality are absent (evidence level IV), or with extrapolation from higher levels of evidence
NICE 2002	Recommendation drawn from the NICE Technology Appraisal of the use of the newer (atypical) antipsychotic drugs for schizophrenia (NICE, 2002)
GPP	Good practice point: recommended good practice based on the clinical experience of the GDG and arrived at through consensus

Based on a scheme from: NHS Executive (1996) Clinical Guidelines: Using Clinical Guidelines to Improve Patient Care Within the NHS. London: Department of Health.

3.4.7.2 Level 1b evidence

Evidence was classified as '1b' if it came from a single trial with fewer than 150 participants in any single arm of the trial or from fewer than three trials. For the purpose of generating statements, level 1a evidence was regarded as 'strong evidence' and level 1b evidence was regarded as 'limited evidence'.

3.4.7.3 Statistically significant findings

Where a statistically significant result was obtained, the GDG considered whether this finding was of clinical significance (i.e. was it likely to be of benefit to service users), taking into account the trial population, the nature of the outcome and the size of the effect. On the basis of this consideration results were characterised as either 'clinically significant' or 'unlikely to be clinically significant'.

3.4.7.4 Non-statistically significant findings

Where a non-statistically significant result was obtained, the GDG reviewed the results, the trial population, the nature of the outcome and size of the effect, and in particular the confidence intervals surrounding the result. Where the confidence intervals were narrow, this was seen as indicating evidence of no clinically significant difference; where they were wide, this was seen as indicating insufficient evidence to determine whether there was a clinically significant difference.

The complete decision tree is set out in Figure 3.2.

Grading the recommendations allowed the GDG to distinguish between the level of evidence and the strength of the associated recommendation. It is possible that a statement of evidence would cover only one part of an area in which a recommendation

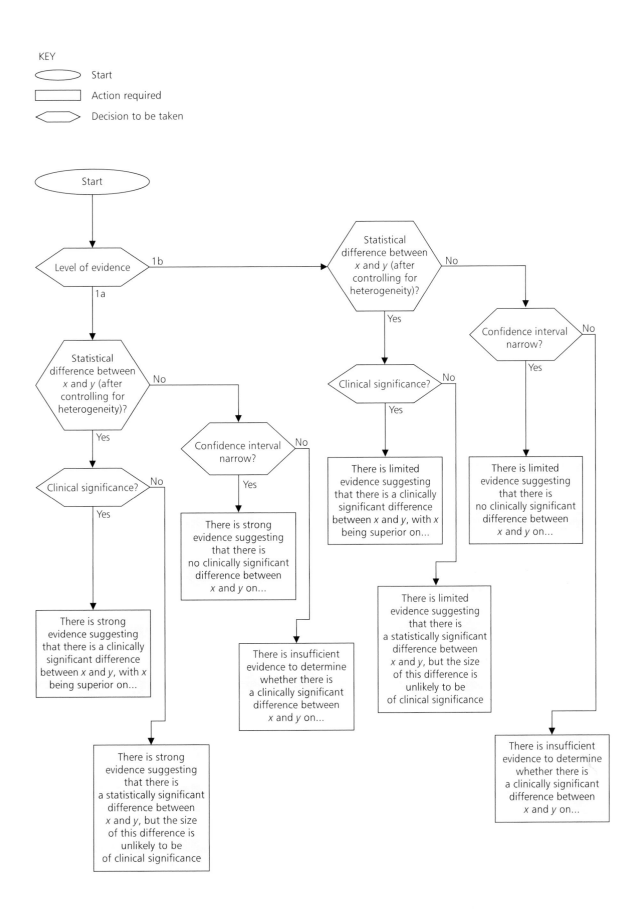

KEY

⬭ Start

▭ Action required

⬡ Decision to be taken

Start

Level of evidence

1b

1a

Statistical difference between *x* and *y* (after controlling for heterogeneity)?

No

Statistical difference between *x* and *y* (after controlling for heterogeneity)?

No

Yes

Yes

Confidence interval narrow?

No

Clinical significance?

No

Confidence interval narrow?

Yes

Clinical significance?

No

Yes

Confidence interval narrow?

No

Yes

There is strong evidence suggesting that there is no clinically significant difference between *x* and *y* on...

There is limited evidence suggesting that there is a clinically significant difference between *x* and *y*, with *x* being superior on...

There is limited evidence suggesting that there is no clinically significant difference between *x* and *y* on...

There is strong evidence suggesting that there is a clinically significant difference between *x* and *y*, with *x* being superior on...

There is insufficient evidence to determine whether there is a clinically significant difference between *x* and *y* on...

There is limited evidence suggesting that there is a statistically significant difference between *x* and *y*, but the size of this difference is unlikely to be of clinical significance

There is strong evidence suggesting that there is a statistically significant difference between *x* and *y*, but the size of this difference is unlikely to be of clinical significance

There is insufficient evidence to determine whether there is a clinically significant difference between *x* and *y* on...

Fig. 3.2 Schizophrenia guideline statement decision tree

29

was to be made or would cover it in a way that would conflict with other evidence. In order to produce more comprehensive recommendations, the GDG had to extrapolate from the available evidence. This led to a weaker level of recommendation (i.e. B, as data were based upon level I evidence). In addition, it is possible to have methodologically sound (level I) evidence about an area of practice that is of little direct clinical relevance or has such a small effect that it is of little practical importance. In this case, the evidence would attract a lower strength of recommendation (i.e. there would be necessity for extrapolation). 'NICE 2002' indicates a recommendation drawn from the NICE Technology Appraisal of the use of the newer (atypical) antipsychotic drugs for the treatment of schizophrenia (NICE, 2002).

The process also allowed the GDG to moderate recommendations based on factors other than the strength of evidence. Such considerations include the applicability of the evidence to people with schizophrenia, economic considerations, values of the development group and society, and the group's awareness of practical issues (Eccles *et al*, 1998).

3.4.8 Method used to answer the clinical question in the absence of high-quality systematic reviews or RCTs

Where it was not possible to identify at least one high-quality systematic review (e.g. one based on a substantial body of RCTs) or where the GDG was of the opinion (on the basis of previous searches) that there were unlikely to be RCTs that directly addressed the clinical question, an informal consensus process was adopted. This process focused on questions that the GDG considered a priority.

The starting point for this process of informal consensus was that a member of the topic group identified, with help from the systematic reviewer, a narrative review that most directly addressed the clinical question. Where this was not possible a new brief review of the literature was initiated. This existing narrative review or new review was used as a basis for identifying any level of evidence relevant to the clinical question. This was then presented for discussion to the GDG. On the basis of this, additional information was sought and added to the information collected. This might include RCTs that did not directly address the clinical question but were thought to contain relevant data. This led to the development of an initial draft report through the following process.

- A description of what was known about the issues concerning the clinical question was compiled.
- The existing evidence, including RCTs, non-randomised controlled studies, cohort studies and other studies that addressed the issue, was briefly reviewed.
- The summary of the evidence thus far obtained was presented in narrative form to the GDG, and further comments were sought about the evidence and its perceived relevance to the clinical question.
- If, during the course of preparing the report, a significant body of RCTs were identified, a new systematic review was undertaken.
- At this time, subject possibly to further reviews of the evidence, a series of statements that directly addressed the clinical question were developed.
- Following this, on occasion and as deemed appropriate by the development group, the report was sent to appointed experts outside the GDG for peer review and comment. The information from this process was then fed back to the GDG for further discussion of the statements.

- Recommendations were then developed and could also be sent for further external peer review.
- After this final stage of comment, the statements and recommendations were again reviewed and agreed upon by the GDG.

3.5 Health economics review strategies

The aim of the health economics literature review was to contribute evidence on cost and cost-effectiveness to the GDG's statement and recommendation formulation process.

3.5.1 Method

A separate systematic literature review was conducted to assess the state of the economic evidence concerning pharmacological, psychological and service-level interventions that the GDG had primarily classified as having evidence-based clinical effectiveness. Only information that could be generalised to the UK context was used in the review. For interventions directly addressed by the NICE Technology Appraisal of atypical antipsychotics (NICE, 2002), the economic evidence provided in the appraisal was used as the basis for the economic evidence in the guideline.

Since cross-national differences in medical practice, health care settings, social system structures, and financing systems greatly influence the results of economic studies, and between-country adjustments are often misleading, the results of the economic evidence review were not summarised in the form of meta-analyses. A general descriptive overview of the studies, their qualities, and conclusions were presented, and summarised in the form of a short narrative review.

3.5.2 Review process

A general search was carried out for economic studies of interventions for schizophrenia. Cost or cost-offset analyses were also included in the review, owing to the limited number of economic evaluations such as cost-effectiveness (including cost–consequence and cost-minimisation analyses), cost–utility and cost–benefit studies.

Computerised databases were first systematically searched for studies. Ineligible articles were excluded, and a sample of these were cross-checked for relevance by a second independent reviewer. All potentially eligible studies were then tested against a set of standard inclusion criteria. Only primary economic evidence was eligible; thus, secondary sources such as existing reviews and guidelines were excluded, except for the NICE Technology Appraisal (NICE, 2002). The eligible papers were not subjected to systematic quality review and selection, but all included papers were checked for validity and assessed for risk of bias. The search for further evidence included papers identified from reference lists of eligible studies and relevant reviews. Known experts in the field of mental health economics were also contacted to identify relevant published and unpublished studies. Studies in the clinical literature review were also checked for economic evidence, and stakeholders' submissions were screened for relevant data.

3.5.3 Search strategy

The search strategy for economic evidence was based on the schizophrenia spectrum disorders search filter, developed for the clinical literature search, and an economic search filter used by the Centre for the Economics of Mental Health at the Institute of Psychiatry in London. Appendix 12 lists the search strategy. No restriction was placed on language or publication status of the papers, but only studies published after 1985 were identified by the search strategy. This restriction was deemed appropriate on account of the continuous methodological development in health economics and the greater risk of bias in earlier studies. An exception was made if a study published before 1985 was included in the clinical literature review and contained economic evidence.

Bibliographic electronic databases (Medline, PreMedline, EMBASE, PsycINFO, CINAHL, the Cochrane Database of Systematic Reviews (CDSR), the Database of Abstracts of Reviews of Effectiveness (DARE), the Cochrane Controlled Trials Register, the NHS R&D Health Technology Assessment programme and special health economic databases (Office of Health Economics Health Economic Evaluations Database and the NHS Economic Evaluation Database) were searched. The details of the electronic search (interfaces, dates) are reported in Appendix 13.

Upon completion of the database searches, titles and abstracts of all references were screened for relevance to the scope of the guideline. The health economist then assessed relevant papers against the standard inclusion criteria (Appendix 14).

Economic studies based on RCTs, controlled studies with concurrent controls, and modelling where most of the background clinical information was derived from a meta-analysis or RCTs (levels Ia and Ib of clinical evidence) were considered for inclusion. Where no such evidence was available, economic evaluations based on high-quality mirror-image studies or controlled studies with historical controls were also considered. Only studies from OECD countries were considered for inclusion (see section 3.5.1).

The selection criteria for types of participants, treatment definitions and settings were identical to those used in the clinical literature review. Results of studies that were conducted in a mixed population of patients with mental illness were also used, provided that they included a majority of people with schizophrenia spectrum disorder, or the economic information could be estimated separately for this subgroup. The expression 'severely mentally ill' was used as a proxy for schizophrenia.

Besides economic evaluations, cost or cost-offset studies were considered for inclusion if they contained a clear description of the applied resource costing method. Full texts of papers considered relevant and eligible were obtained. Where eligibility was not clear from the abstract, full reports were obtained.

Papers eligible for inclusion were subsequently assessed for validity with the widely used 'checklist' compiled by Drummond & Jefferson (1996). Different checklists were used for economic evaluations and for costing studies. Papers were classified as having a low risk of bias if they fulfilled at least 50% of the validity criteria, and as having a high risk of bias if they fulfilled less than 50% of the validity criteria. Appendix 15 lists the checklist for economic evaluations and Appendix 16 lists the checklist for costing studies.

Data were abstracted using a standard form based on the Economic Evaluation Abstraction form used in the Guide to Community Preventive Services (Carande-Kulis *et al*, 2000). Given the time and resource frame of the guideline, a proportion of papers were double-checked for eligibility and validity assessments by a second reviewer. Disagreements were discussed and a common decision was reached. The economic data abstraction form is presented in Appendix 17.

3.5.4 Results of the search

The electronic database search resulted in 995 hits. After the exclusion of obviously non-relevant articles, 68 papers were identified for possible inclusion in the psychological economic evidence review, 151 potentially relevant papers were found for the service economic review and 208 papers were selected for consideration for the pharmacology economic review. An additional 65 papers across all topic areas were identified by hand searching and recommendations from experts. After more detailed inspection of the abstracts, 26 full trial reports were retrieved for the psychological topic, 88 for the service topic and 77 for the pharmacological topic. Multiple trial reports reporting the same results were excluded. Ultimately 7 psychological, 36 service-related and 15 pharmacological papers, excluding those used in the NICE Technology Appraisal (NICE, 2002), were deemed eligible for inclusion in this review. Six articles were not available. See accompanying CD–ROM for more details.

3.5.5 Synthesising the evidence

The results of the review process were presented as qualitative analyses. Economic evidence tables were created to present the main results and characteristics of the included studies. The available economic estimations of the same intervention were synthesised in the form of a narrative summary and statements.

Upon completion of the health economics review and synthesis, the GDG reconsidered their drafted clinical statements, taking into account the available efficiency information. Thus, the final guideline recommendations were based on both clinical and economic evidence. Where no economic evidence was available, the guideline highlighted the necessity for further high-quality economic evaluations in those areas.

3.5.6 Presentation of data and statements in the guideline

The GDG examined all relevant outcomes for all studies included for review and analysis, and relevant data where available were presented in the statements with associated statistics. Where data were not available, no statement could be made. For reasons of space, the absence of data is indicated by its absence from the statements. In other words, non-reporting reflects the absence of data. This includes outcomes such as relapse, symptom reduction, suicide rates, costs and health economic data.

3.6 Stakeholder contributions

Professionals, service users and companies have contributed to and commented on the schizophrenia guideline at key stages in its development. Stakeholders for this guideline include:

- service-user and carer stakeholders: the national service-user and carer organisations representing people whose care is described in this guideline

- professional stakeholders: the national organisations representing health care professionals who are providing services to people with schizophrenia
- commercial stakeholders: the companies that manufacture medicines used in the treatment of schizophrenia
- primary care trusts
- Department of Health and Welsh Assembly Government.

Stakeholders have been involved in the guideline's development at the following points:

- commenting on the initial scope of the guideline and attending a briefing meeting held by NICE
- contributing lists of evidence to the GDG
- commenting on the first and second drafts of the guideline.

3.7 Validation of this guideline

This guideline has been validated through two consultation exercises. The first consultation draft was submitted to the NICE Guidelines Advisory Committee Panel, and circulated to stakeholders and other reviewers nominated by GDG members.

After taking into account comments from stakeholders, the NICE Guidelines Advisory Committee, a number of health authority and trust representatives and a wide range of national and international experts from this round of consultation, the GDG responded to all comments and prepared a final consultation draft which was submitted to NICE, circulated to all stakeholders for final comments and posted on the website for public consultation. The final draft was then submitted to the NICE Guidelines Advisory Committee for review prior to publication.

4 Summary of recommendations

For the purposes of this guideline, the treatment and management of schizophrenia have been divided into three phases:

- the initiation of treatment at the first episode
- the acute phase
- the promotion of recovery.

This guideline sets out good practice points and evidence-based recommendations for pharmacological, psychological and service-level interventions in these three phases, for both primary and secondary care, to be applied in an integrated mental health service focused on service users and carers.

4.1 Care across all phases

4.1.1 Optimism

The effects of schizophrenia on a person's life experience and opportunities are considerable; service users and carers need help and support to deal with their future and to cope with the changes the illness brings.

4.1.1.1 Health professionals should work in partnership with service users and carers, offering help, treatment and care in an atmosphere of hope and optimism. (GPP)

4.1.2 Getting help early

For most people experiencing a schizophrenic breakdown, the level of distress, anxiety and subjective confusion, especially during first episodes, leads to difficulty in accessing services.

4.1.2.1 Service users and their relatives seeking help should be assessed and receive treatment at the earliest possible opportunity. (GPP)

4.1.3 Assessment

The purpose of this guideline is to help improve the experience and outcomes of care for people with schizophrenia. These outcomes include the degree of symptomatic recovery, quality of life, degree of personal autonomy, ability and access to work, stability and quality of living accommodation, degree and quality of social integration, degree of financial independence, and experience and impact of side-effects of treatment.

4.1.3.1 The assessment of the needs for health and social care of people with schizophrenia should be comprehensive and should address medical, social, psychological, occupational, economic, physical and cultural issues. (GPP)

4.1.4 Working in partnership with service users and carers

4.1.4.1   Health professionals involved in the routine treatment and management of schizophrenia should take time to build a supportive and empathic relationship with service users and carers; this should be regarded as an essential element of the routine care offered. (GPP)

The families of people with schizophrenia often play an essential part in the treatment and care of their relative, and with the right support and help, can positively contribute to promoting recovery. Parents of people with schizophrenia often feel to blame, either because they have 'passed on the genes' causing schizophrenia, or because they are 'bad parents'.

4.1.4.2   Clear and intelligible information should be made available to service users and their families about schizophrenia and its possible causes, and about the possible role families can have in promoting recovery and reducing relapse. (GPP)

4.1.5 Consent

Whatever treatments are offered, it is essential to engage the service user in a collaborative, trusting and caring working relationship at the earliest opportunity. Professionals should take into full account the particular nature of schizophrenia: namely, that the illness may affect people's ability to make judgements, to recognise that they are ill, to comprehend clearly what professionals might say to them, and to make informed decisions about their treatment and care.

4.1.5.1   Health professionals should make all efforts necessary to ensure that a service user can give meaningful and properly informed consent before treatment is initiated, giving adequate time for discussion and the provision of written information. (GPP)

4.1.6 Providing information and mutual support

4.1.6.1   Health professionals should provide accessible information about schizophrenia and its treatment to service users and carers; this should be considered an essential part of the routine treatment and management of schizophrenia. (GPP)

4.1.6.2   In addition to the provision of good-quality information, families and carers should be offered the opportunity to participate in family or carer support programmes, where these exist. (GPP)

4.1.7 Language and culture

4.1.7.1   When talking to service users and carers, health professionals should avoid using clinical language, or at least keep it to a minimum. Where clinical language is used, service users and carers should have access to written explanations. (GPP)

4.1.7.2 All services should provide written material in the language of the service user, and interpreters should be sought for people who have difficulty in speaking English. (GPP)

4.1.8 Advance directives

4.1.8.1 Although there are limitations with advance directives regarding the choice of treatment for individuals with schizophrenia, it is recommended that they are developed and documented in individuals' care programmes whenever possible. (NICE 2002)

4.1.8.2 When advance directives have been agreed, copies should be placed in both primary care and secondary care case notes and care plans, and copies given to the service user and the care coordinator. If appropriate, and subject to agreement with the service user, a copy should be given to the carer. (GPP)

4.2 Initiation of treatment (first episode)

4.2.1 Early referral

It is most likely that the first point of contact for people who may be developing schizophrenia for the first time will be a primary care professional. Rapid identification, early referral and good liaison with secondary services are a priority.

4.2.1.1 In primary care, all people with suspected or newly diagnosed schizophrenia should be referred urgently to secondary mental health services for assessment and development of a care plan. If there is a presumed diagnosis of schizophrenia, then part of the urgent assessment should include an early assessment by a consultant psychiatrist. (GPP)

4.2.2 Early intervention services

4.2.2.1 Because many people with actual or possible schizophrenia have difficulty in getting help, treatment and care at an early stage, it is recommended that early intervention services are developed to provide the correct mix of specialist pharmacological, psychological, social, occupational and educational interventions at the earliest opportunity. (GPP)

4.2.2.2 Where the needs of the service user or carer exceed the capacity of early intervention services, referral to crisis resolution and home treatment teams, acute day hospitals or in-patient services should be considered. (GPP)

4.2.3 Early treatment

4.2.3.1 When there are acute symptoms of schizophrenia, the general practitioner should consider giving an atypical antipsychotic drug at the earliest opportunity – before the individual is seen by a psychiatrist, if necessary.

Wherever possible, this should be following discussion with a psychiatrist, and referral should be a matter of urgency. (GPP)

4.2.4 Pharmacological intervention

4.2.4.1   It is recommended that the oral atypical antipsychotic drugs amisulpride, olanzapine, quetiapine, risperidone and zotepine are considered in the choice of first-line treatments for individuals with newly diagnosed schizophrenia. (NICE 2002)

4.2.4.2   Pharmacotherapy with an atypical antipsychotic drug at a dosage at the lower end of the standard range is the preferred treatment for a person experiencing a first episode of schizophrenia. (C)

4.2.5 Second opinion

After the first episode, many people are unsure about their diagnosis and may need help with this.

4.2.5.1   A decision by the service user, and carer where appropriate, to seek a second opinion on the diagnosis should be supported, particularly in view of the considerable personal and social consequences of being diagnosed with schizophrenia. (GPP)

4.3 Treatment of the acute episode

4.3.1 Service-level interventions

The services most likely to help people who are acutely ill include crisis resolution and home treatment teams, early intervention teams, community mental health teams and acute day hospitals. If these services are unable to meet the needs of a service user, or the Mental Health Act is used, in-patient treatment may prove necessary for a time. Whatever services are available, a broad range of social, group and physical activities are essential elements of the services provided.

4.3.1.1   Community mental health teams are an acceptable way of organising community care and may have the potential for effectively coordinating and integrating other community-based teams providing services for people with schizophrenia. However, there is insufficient evidence of their advantages to support any recommendation that precludes or inhibits the development of alternative service configurations. (C)

4.3.1.2   Crisis resolution and home treatment teams should be used as a means of managing crises for service users, and as a means of delivering high-quality acute care. In this context, teams should pay particular attention to risk monitoring as a high-priority routine activity. (B)

4.3.1.3   Crisis resolution and home treatment should be considered for people with schizophrenia who are in crisis, to augment the services provided by early intervention services and assertive outreach teams. (C)

4.3.1.4 Crisis resolution and home treatment should be considered for people with schizophrenia who might benefit from early discharge from hospital following a period of in-patient care. (C)

4.3.1.5 Acute day hospitals should be considered as a clinically and economically effective option for the provision of acute care, both as an alternative to acute admission to in-patient care and to facilitate early discharge from hospital. (A)

4.3.1.6 Social, group and physical activities are an important aspect of comprehensive service provision for people with schizophrenia as the acute phase recedes, and afterwards. All care plans should record the arrangements for such activities. (GPP)

4.3.2 Pharmacological interventions

During an acute episode, antipsychotic drugs are necessary. Wherever possible, service users should make an informed choice as to the medication they prefer. If a service user is unable to make a preference known, an atypical antipsychotic drug should be prescribed. It is best to use a single drug, with doses within the *British National Formulary* (BNF) dose range, and not to use high or loading doses. Clinical response and side-effects should be monitored routinely and regularly. If treatment with conventional antipsychotics gives rise to troublesome side-effects or symptom control is inadequate, an atypical drug should be offered. During an acute episode, some service users become behaviourally disturbed and may need rapid tranquillisation. The recommendations for this are given in section 4.5.

4.3.2.1 The choice of antipsychotic drug should be made jointly by the individual and the clinician responsible for treatment, based on an informed discussion of the relative benefits of the drugs and their side-effect profiles. The individual's advocate or carer should be consulted where appropriate. (NICE 2002)

4.3.2.2 Antipsychotic therapy should be initiated as part of a comprehensive package of care that addresses the individual's clinical, emotional and social needs. The clinician responsible for treatment and the keyworker should monitor both therapeutic progress and tolerability of the drug on an ongoing basis. Monitoring is particularly important when individuals have just changed from one antipsychotic to another. (NICE 2002)

4.3.2.3 The dosage of conventional antipsychotic medication for an acute episode should be in the range 300–1000 mg chlorpromazine equivalents per day for a minimum of 6 weeks. Reasons for dosage outside this range should be justified and documented. The minimum effective dose should be used. (C)

4.3.2.4 In the treatment of acute episodes of schizophrenia, massive loading doses of antipsychotic medication, referred to as 'rapid neuroleptisation', should not be used. (C)

4.3.2.5 The oral atypical antipsychotic drugs (amisulpride, olanzapine, quetiapine, risperidone, zotepine) should be considered as treatment options for individuals currently receiving conventional antipsychotic drugs who, despite adequate symptom control, are experiencing unacceptable side-effects, and for those in relapse who have previously experienced unsatisfactory management or unacceptable side-effects with conventional antipsychotic drugs. The decision as to what constitutes unacceptable side-effects should be taken following discussion between the patient and the clinician responsible for treatment. (NICE 2002)

4.3.2.6 When full discussion between the clinician responsible for treatment and the individual concerned is not possible, in particular in the management of an acute schizophrenic episode, the oral atypical drugs should be considered as the treatment options of choice because of the lower potential risk of extrapyramidal symptoms (EPS). In these circumstances, the individual's carer or advocate should be consulted where possible and appropriate. Although advance directives regarding the choice of treatment for individuals with schizophrenia have limitations, it is recommended that they are developed and documented in individuals' care programmes whenever possible. (NICE 2002)

4.3.2.7 It is not recommended that, in routine clinical practice, individuals change to one of the oral atypical antipsychotic drugs if they are achieving good control of their condition without unacceptable side-effects with a conventional antipsychotic drug. (NICE 2002)

4.3.2.8 Antipsychotic drugs, atypical or conventional, should not be prescribed concurrently, except for short periods to cover changeover. (C)

4.3.2.9 When prescribed chlorpromazine, individuals should be warned of a potential photosensitive skin response, as this is an easily preventable side-effect. (B)

4.3.2.10 Where a potential to cause weight gain or diabetes has been identified (or is included in the Summary of Product Characteristics) for the atypical antipsychotic being prescribed, there should be routine monitoring in respect of these potential risks. (B)

4.3.3 Early post-acute period

Towards the end of an acute episode of schizophrenia, service users should be offered help in understanding the period of illness, and given the opportunity to write their own account of the episode in their notes. Carers may also need help in understanding the experience. Assessment for further help to minimise disability, reduce risk and improve quality of life should be routinely undertaken during recovery from the acute phase. In particular, psychological and family help, contingency planning and identifying local resources and services are important. Advice about drug treatment to maintain recovery is also important.

Service user focus

4.3.3.1 Consideration should be given, where practicable, to encouraging service users to write their own account of their illness in their notes. (GPP)

4.3.3.2 Psychoanalytic and psychodynamic principles may be considered to help health professionals to understand the experience of individual service users and their interpersonal relationships. (GPP)

Assessment

The purpose of this guideline is to help improve the experience and outcomes of care for people with schizophrenia. These outcomes include the degree of symptomatic recovery, quality of life, degree of personal autonomy, ability and access to work, stability and quality of living accommodation, degree and quality of social integration, degree of financial independence and the experience and impact of side-effects.

4.3.3.3   The assessment of needs for health and social care of people with schizophrenia should be comprehensive and should address medical, social, psychological, occupational, economic, physical and cultural issues. (GPP)

Psychological treatments

4.3.3.4   Cognitive–behavioural therapy should be available as a treatment option for people with schizophrenia. (A)

4.3.3.5   Family interventions should be available to the families of people with schizophrenia who are living with or who are in close contact with the service user. (A)

4.3.3.6   Counselling and supportive psychotherapy are not recommended as discrete interventions in the routine care of people with schizophrenia where other psychological interventions of proven efficacy are indicated and available. However, service user preferences should be taken into account, especially if other more efficacious psychological treatments are not locally available. (C)

Medication advice

4.3.3.7   Given the high risk of relapse following an acute episode, the continuation of antipsychotic drugs for up to 1–2 years after a relapse should be discussed with service users, and with carers where appropriate. (GPP)

4.3.3.8   Withdrawal from antipsychotic medication should be undertaken gradually while regularly monitoring signs and symptoms for evidence of potential relapse. (GPP)

4.3.3.9   Following withdrawal from antipsychotic medication, monitoring for signs and symptoms of potential relapse should continue for at least 2 years after the last acute episode. (GPP)

4.4 Promoting recovery

There are a number of options for promoting and maintaining recovery. The general principles for all phases apply equally in this situation. Early intervention to provide early additional treatment and care should the need arise remains important.

4.4.1 Primary care

Primary care professionals have an important part to play in the physical and mental health care of people with schizophrenia. They are best placed to monitor the physical health of people with schizophrenia and should do so regularly. Case registers will be an important means of providing such checks. In addition, primary care workers should monitor the mental health and treatment of their service users, work closely with secondary services and refer before crises arise wherever possible.

4.4.1.1   The setting up of practice case registers is recommended as an essential step in monitoring the physical and mental health of people with schizophrenia in primary care. (GPP)

4.4.1.2   General practitioners and other primary health care workers should regularly monitor the physical health of people with schizophrenia registered with their practice. The frequency of checks will be a clinical decision made jointly between the service user and clinician. The agreed frequency should be recorded in the patient's notes. (GPP)

4.4.1.3   Physical health checks should pay particular attention to endocrine disorders such as diabetes and hyperprolactinaemia, cardiovascular risk factors such as blood pressure and lipid levels, side-effects of medication, and lifestyle factors such as smoking. These must be recorded in the notes. (GPP)

4.4.1.4   The decision to refer a service user from primary care back to the mental health services is a complex clinical judgement that should take account of the views of the service user and, where appropriate, carers. Issues of confidentiality should be respected when involving carers. Referral may be considered in a number of circumstances, including the following:
- if treatment adherence is a problem, referral is usually indicated
- if response to treatment is poor, referral is a higher priority
- if comorbid substance misuse is suspected, referral is indicated
- if the level of risk to self or others is increased, referral is indicated
- if a person with schizophrenia has newly joined a general practice list, referral to secondary services for assessment and care programming is indicated, subject to the full agreement of the service user. (GPP)

4.4.2 Secondary services

Secondary services should undertake regular and full assessment of the mental and physical health of their service users, addressing all the issues relevant to a person's quality of life and well-being. When a service user chooses not to receive physical care from a general practitioner, this should be monitored by doctors in secondary care. Carers should be contacted routinely, subject to the agreement of the service user, and should be provided with a care plan.

The possible presence of comorbid conditions, including substance and alcohol misuse or physical illness, or the existence of a forensic history, will necessitate the development of treatment and care plans outside the scope of this guideline. Nevertheless, full assessment of these issues should be included.

4.4.2.1   A full assessment of health and social care needs should be undertaken regularly, including assessment of accommodation and quality of life. The frequency of these assessments should be based upon clinical need, and discussed with the service user. The agreed frequency of assessment should be documented in the care plan. (GPP)

The higher physical morbidity and mortality of service users with schizophrenia should be considered in all assessments. While this would normally be expected to be the role of primary care services, secondary care services should nevertheless monitor these matters where they believe a service user may have little regular contact with primary care.

4.4.2.2   Primary and secondary care services, in conjunction with the service user, should jointly identify which service will take responsibility for assessing and monitoring the physical health care needs of service users. This should be documented in both primary and secondary care notes and care plans, and clearly recorded by care coordinators for those assigned to an enhanced care programme approach. (GPP)

4.4.2.3   All non-professional carers who regularly look after a person on the care programme approach should have assessments of their own caring, physical and mental health needs, at a frequency agreed in conjunction with the carer and recorded in the carer's own plan. (GPP)

4.4.3 Service interventions

The range of services required for people with schizophrenia are diverse and need to be tailored to individual circumstances and current local resources. However, some people with schizophrenia have exceptional needs for care and tend to be lost from ordinary services. Assertive outreach teams (assertive community treatment) are an effective way of helping to meet those needs and are better at staying in touch than ordinary services. Also, most people with schizophrenia will need rapid access to help in crises. Services need to plan how best to deliver help and treatment, ensuring that teams are functionally integrated.

4.4.3.1   Assertive outreach teams should be provided for people with serious mental disorders, including schizophrenia. (B)

4.4.3.2   Assertive outreach teams should be provided for people with serious mental disorders, including schizophrenia, who make extensive use of in-patient services and who have a history of poor engagement with services, leading to frequent relapse or social breakdown (as manifested by homelessness or seriously inadequate accommodation). (B)

4.4.3.3   Assertive outreach teams should be provided for people with schizophrenia who are homeless. (B)

4.4.3.4   Where the needs of the service user or carer exceed the capacity of the assertive outreach team, referral to crisis resolution and home treatment teams, acute day hospitals or in-patient services should be considered. (GPP)

4.4.3.5   Crisis resolution and home treatment should be considered for people with schizophrenia who are in crisis, to augment the services provided by early intervention services and assertive outreach teams. (C)

4.4.3.6   Integrating the care of people with schizophrenia who receive services from community mental health teams, assertive outreach teams, early intervention services, and crisis resolution and home treatment teams should be carefully considered. The care programme approach should be the main mechanism by which the care of individuals across services is properly managed and integrated. (GPP)

4.4.4 Psychological interventions

Psychological treatments should be an indispensable part of the treatment options available for service users and their families in the effort to promote recovery. Those with the best evidence of effectiveness are cognitive–behavioural therapy and family interventions. These should be used to prevent relapse, to reduce symptoms, increase insight and to promote adherence to medication regimens.

4.4.4.1   Cognitive–behavioural therapy should be available as a treatment option for people with schizophrenia. (A)

4.4.4.2   In particular, cognitive–behavioural therapy should be offered to people with schizophrenia who are experiencing persisting psychotic symptoms. (A)

4.4.4.3   Cognitive–behavioural therapy should be considered as a treatment option to assist in the development of insight. (B)

4.4.4.4   Cognitive–behavioural therapy may be considered as a treatment option in the management of poor treatment adherence. (C)

4.4.4.5   Longer treatments with cognitive–behavioural therapy are significantly more effective than shorter ones, which may improve depressive symptoms but are unlikely to improve psychotic symptoms. An adequate course of cognitive–behavioural therapy to generate improvements in psychotic symptoms in these circumstances should be of more than 6 months' duration and include more than ten planned sessions. (B)

4.4.4.6   Family interventions should be available to families who are living with or who are in close contact with a relative with schizophrenia. (A)

4.4.4.7   Family interventions should be offered to the families of people with schizophrenia who have recently relapsed or who are considered at risk of relapse. (A)

4.4.4.8   Family interventions should be offered to the families of people with schizophrenia who have persisting symptoms. (A)

4.4.4.9   The duration of a family intervention programme should normally be longer than 6 months, and it should include more than ten sessions of treatment. (B)

4.4.4.10 The service user should normally be included in family intervention sessions, as doing so significantly improves the outcome. Sometimes, however, this is not practicable. (B)

4.4.4.11 Service users and their carers may prefer single family interventions rather than multi-family group interventions. (A)

4.4.5 Pharmacological interventions

Antipsychotic drugs are an indispensable treatment option for most people in the recovery phase of schizophrenia. The main aim is to prevent relapse and to keep the person stable enough to live as normal a life as possible. Drugs are also necessary for psychological treatments to be effective.

The service user and clinician should jointly decide on the drug to be used, but the service user's preferences are central. Oral or depot preparations can be used. Follow *British National Formulary* (BNF) guidance on dosage and test dosing. If conventional antipsychotics have been used and are not effective, or are causing unacceptable side-effects, change to an atypical drug. If an atypical antipsychotic is causing diabetes or excessive weight gain, this must be monitored, or consider changing to a different atypical or a conventional antipsychotic. Always monitor and record clinical response, side-effects and service user satisfaction. If the person is satisfied with a drug, make no changes. Do consider the use of psychological interventions if a person has persisting symptoms or frequent relapses.

If a service user has taken two antipsychotic drugs (including one atypical) each for 6–8 weeks without significant improvement, check the possible reasons for the lack of response and consider prescribing clozapine. In some circumstances it may be supportable to add a second antipsychotic drug to clozapine if there has been a suboptimal response at standard doses. Do not use more than one antipsychotic drug in other situations, except when changing from one drug to another. Other adjunctive treatments are outside the scope of this guideline.

Relapse prevention: oral antipsychotics

4.4.5.1 The choice of antipsychotic drug should be made jointly by the individual and the clinician responsible for treatment, based on an informed discussion of the relative benefits of the drugs and their side-effect profiles. The individual's advocate or carer should be consulted where appropriate. (NICE 2002)

4.4.5.2 The oral atypical antipsychotic drugs (amisulpride, olanzapine, quetiapine, risperidone and zotepine) should be considered as treatment options for individuals currently receiving typical antipsychotic drugs who, despite adequate symptom control, are experiencing unacceptable side-effects, and for those in relapse who have previously experienced unsatisfactory management or unacceptable side-effects with typical antipsychotic drugs. The decision as to what constitutes unacceptable side-effects should be taken following discussion between the patient and the clinician responsible for treatment. (NICE 2002)

4.4.5.3 It is not recommended that, in routine clinical practice, individuals change to one of the oral atypical antipsychotic drugs if they are currently achieving good control of their condition without unacceptable side-effects with typical antipsychotic drugs. (NICE 2002)

4.4.5.4 Antipsychotic therapy should be initiated as part of a comprehensive package of care that addresses the individual's clinical, emotional and social needs. The clinician responsible for treatment and the keyworker should monitor both therapeutic progress and tolerability of the drug on an ongoing basis. Monitoring is particularly important when individuals have just changed from one antipsychotic to another. (NICE 2002)

4.4.5.5 Targeted, intermittent dosage maintenance strategies should not be used routinely in lieu of continuous dosage regimens because of the increased risk of symptom worsening or relapse. However, these strategies may be considered for service users who refuse maintenance or for whom some other contraindication to maintenance therapy exists, such as side-effect sensitivity. (C)

4.4.5.6 Antipsychotic drugs, atypical or conventional, should not be prescribed concurrently, except for short periods to cover changeover. (C)

4.4.5.7   A risk assessment should be performed by the clinician responsible for treatment and the multi-disciplinary team regarding concordance with medication, and depot preparations should be prescribed when appropriate. (NICE 2002)

4.4.5.8   Depot preparations should be a treatment option where a service user expresses a preference for such treatment because of its convenience, or as part of a treatment plan in which the avoidance of covert non-adherence to an antipsychotic drug regimen is a clinical priority. (B)

4.4.5.9   For optimum effectiveness in preventing relapse, depot preparations should be prescribed within the standard recommended dosage and interval range. (A)

4.4.5.10 Following full discussion between the responsible clinician and the service user, the decision to initiate depot antipsychotic injections should take into account the preferences and attitudes of the service user towards the mode of administration and organisational procedures (for example, home visits and location of clinics) related to the delivery of regular intramuscular injections. (GPP)

4.4.5.11 Test doses should normally be used as set out in the BNF; full licensed prescribing information on depot antipsychotics is available from the Summary of Product Characteristics, which can be found in the electronic Medicines Compendium (www.emc.vhn.net). (GPP)

4.4.5.12 As with oral antipsychotic therapy, people receiving depot preparations should be maintained under regular clinical review, particularly in relation to the risks and benefits of the drug regimen. (GPP)

Treatment-resistant schizophrenia

4.4.5.13 The first step in the clinical management of treatment-resistant schizophrenia (TRS) is to establish that antipsychotic drugs have been adequately tried in terms of dosage, duration and adherence. Other causes of non-response should be considered in the clinical assessment, such as comorbid substance misuse, poor treatment adherence, the concurrent use of other prescribed medicines, and physical illness. (GPP)

4.4.5.14 If the symptoms of schizophrenia are unresponsive to conventional antipsychotic therapy, the prescribing clinician and service user may wish to consider an atypical antipsychotic in advance of a diagnosis of treatment-resistant schizophrenia and a trial of clozapine. In such cases, olanzapine or risperidone may be worth considering. Service users should be informed that while these drugs may possibly be beneficial, the evidence for improvement in this situation is more limited than for clozapine. (C)

4.4.5.15 In individuals with evidence of TRS, clozapine should be introduced at the earliest opportunity. Treatment resistance is suggested by a lack of satisfactory clinical improvement despite the sequential use of the recommended doses for 6–8 weeks of at least two antipsychotic drugs, at least one of which should be an atypical. (NICE 2002)

4.4.5.16 Antipsychotic drugs, atypical or conventional, should not be prescribed concurrently, except for short periods to cover changeover. (C)

4.4.5.17 The addition of a second antipsychotic drug to clozapine may, however, be considered for people with TRS in whom clozapine alone has proved insufficiently effective. (C)

4.4.6 Employment

The overall aim of mental health services is to help service users return to living an ordinary life as far as possible. Assessment should be comprehensive, and includes assessing a person's work potential. Mental health and social care services also need to help support the development of employment opportunities for people with schizophrenia.

4.4.6.1 People with schizophrenia experience considerable difficulty in obtaining employment and many remain unemployed for long periods. The assessment of people with schizophrenia should include assessment of their occupational status and potential. This should be recorded in their notes and care plans. (GPP)

4.4.6.2 Supported employment programmes should be provided for people with schizophrenia who wish to return to work or gain employment. However, it should not be the only work-related activity offered when individuals are unable to work or are unsuccessful in their attempts to find employment. (C)

4.4.6.3 Mental health services, in partnership with social care providers and other local stakeholders, should enable people to use local employment opportunities, including a range of employment schemes to suit the different needs and level of skills, for people with severe mental health problems, including people with schizophrenia. (GPP)

4.5 Rapid tranquillisation

During an acute illness, some service users can become behaviourally disturbed and may need help to calm down; for the majority of service users, however, rapid tranquillisation is unnecessary and should not be resorted to routinely. It is important to ensure that the environment is properly adapted for the needs of the acutely ill, and that communication between staff and service users is clear and therapeutic to minimise frustration and misunderstandings. Staff on psychiatric in-patient units should be trained in how to assess and manage potential and actual violence using de-escalation techniques, restraint, seclusion and rapid tranquillisation. Staff should also be trained to undertake cardiopulmonary resuscitation.

If drugs are needed to calm an individual, an oral preparation should be offered first. If intramuscular injection proves necessary, lorazepam, haloperidol or olanzapine are the preferred drugs. If two drugs are needed, consider lorazepam and haloperidol. If haloperidol is used, anticholinergics should be administered. Vital signs and side-effects should be regularly monitored and full physical and mental health assessment undertaken at the earliest opportunity. Rapid tranquillisation may be traumatic – patients will need debriefing with full explanation, discussion and support.

4.5.1.1   Health professionals should identify and take steps to minimise the environmental and social factors that might increase the likelihood of violence and aggression during an episode, particularly during periods of hospitalisation. Factors to be routinely identified, monitored and corrected include overcrowding; lack of privacy; lack of activities; long waiting times to see staff; poor communication between patients and staff; and weak clinical leadership. (C)

4.5.2 Aims of rapid tranquillisation

The aim of drug treatment in situations requiring rapid tranquillisation is to calm the person, and reduce the risk of violence and harm, rather than treat the underlying psychiatric condition. An optimal response would be a reduction in agitation or aggression without sedation, allowing the service user to participate in further assessment and treatment. Ideally, the drug should have a rapid onset of action and a low level of side-effects.

4.5.2.1   Staff who use rapid tranquillisation should be trained in the assessment and management of service users specifically in this context: this should include assessing and managing the risks of drugs (benzodiazepines and antipsychotics), using and maintaining the techniques and equipment needed for cardiopulmonary resuscitation, prescribing within therapeutic limits, and using flumazenil (benzodiazepine antagonist). (C)

4.5.3 Training for behavioural control and rapid tranquillisation

4.5.3.1   Staff need to be trained to anticipate possible violence and to de-escalate the situation at the earliest opportunity, and physical means of restraint or seclusion should be resorted to 'only after the failure of attempts to promote full participation in self-care'. (C)

4.5.3.2   Training in the use and the dangers of rapid tranquillisation is as essential as training in de-escalation and restraint. Health professionals should be as familiar with the properties of benzodiazepines as they are with those of antipsychotics. (C)

4.5.3.3   Specifically, health professionals should:
- be able to assess the risks associated with rapid tranquillisation, particularly when the service user is highly aroused and may have been misusing drugs or alcohol, be dehydrated or possibly be physically ill
- understand the cardiorespiratory effects of the acute administration of these drugs and the need to titrate dosage to effect
- recognise the importance of nursing, in the recovery position, people who have received these drugs and also of monitoring pulse, blood pressure and respiration
- be familiar with, and trained in, the use of resuscitation equipment; this is essential, as an anaesthetist or experienced 'crash team' may not be available

- undertake annual retraining in resuscitation techniques
- understand the importance of maintaining an unobstructed airway. (C)

4.5.4 Principles of rapid tranquillisation

4.5.4.1   The psychiatrist and the multi-disciplinary team should, at the earliest opportunity, undertake a full assessment, including consideration of the medical and psychiatric differential diagnoses. (C)

4.5.4.2   Drugs for rapid tranquillisation, particularly in the context of restraint, should be used with caution because of the following risks:
- loss of consciousness instead of sedation
- oversedation with loss of alertness
- possible damage to the therapeutic partnership between service user and clinician
- specific issues in relation to diagnosis. (C)

4.5.4.3   Resuscitation equipment and drugs, including flumazenil, must be available and easily accessible where rapid tranquillisation is used. (C)

4.5.4.4   Because of the serious risk to life, service users who are heavily sedated or using illicit drugs or alcohol should not be secluded. (C)

4.5.4.5   If a service user is secluded, the potential complications of rapid tranquillisation should be taken particularly seriously. (C)

4.5.4.6   Violent behaviour can be managed without the prescription of unusually high doses or 'drug cocktails'. The minimum effective dose should be used. The BNF recommendations for maximum doses should be adhered to unless exceptional circumstances arise. (C)

4.5.4.7   Because of growing awareness that involuntary procedures produce traumatic reactions in the recipient, following the use of rapid tranquillisation, service users should be offered the opportunity to discuss their experiences and should be provided with a clear explanation of the decision to use urgent sedation. This should be documented in their notes. (GPP)

4.5.4.8   Service users should be given the opportunity to write their own account of the experience of rapid tranquillisation in their notes. (GPP)

4.5.5 Route of drug administration

4.5.5.1   Oral medication should be offered before parenteral medication. (C)

4.5.5.2   If parenteral treatment proves necessary, the intramuscular route is preferred to the intravenous one from a safety point of view. Intravenous administration should be used only in exceptional circumstances. (C)

4.5.5.3   Vital signs must be monitored after parenteral treatment is administered. Blood pressure, pulse, temperature and respiratory rate should be recorded at regular intervals (agreed by the multi-disciplinary team) until the service user becomes active again. If the service user appears to be or is asleep, more intensive monitoring is required. (C)

4.5.6 Pharmacological agents used in rapid tranquillisation

4.5.6.1   The intramuscular (IM) preparations recommended for use in rapid tranquillisation are lorazepam, haloperidol and olanzapine. Wherever possible, a single agent is preferred to a combination. (C)

4.5.6.2   When rapid tranquillisation is urgently needed, a combination of IM haloperidol and IM lorazepam should be considered. (C)

4.5.6.3   Intramuscular diazepam is not recommended for the pharmacological control of behavioural disturbances in people with schizophrenia. (C)

4.5.6.4   Intramuscular chlorpromazine is not recommended for the pharmacological control of behavioural disturbances in people with schizophrenia. (C)

4.5.6.5   When using IM haloperidol (or any other IM conventional antipsychotic) as a means of behavioural control, an anticholinergic agent should be given to reduce the risk of dystonia and other extrapyramidal side-effects. (C)

4.6 Algorithms and pathways to care

The algorithms and pathways to care in Figures 4.1–4.6 summarise the way in which the recommendations might work in practice.

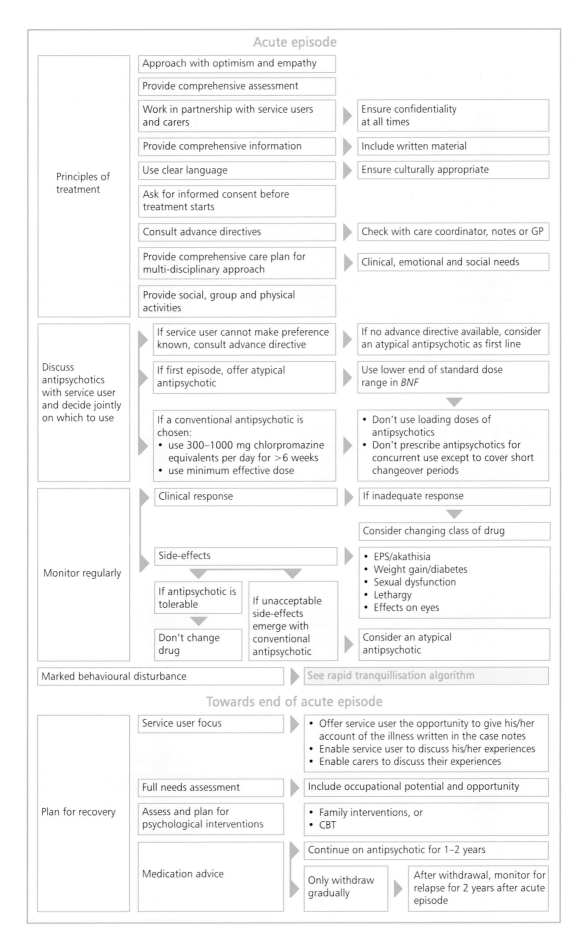

Fig. 4.1 Management of the acute episode of schizophrenia and management in the early-post-acute phase

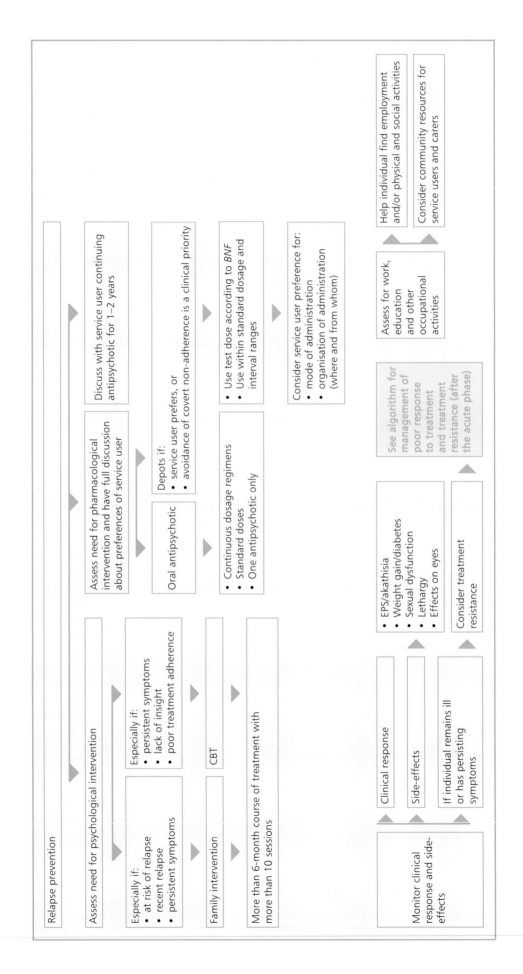

Fig. 4.2 **Promoting recovery**

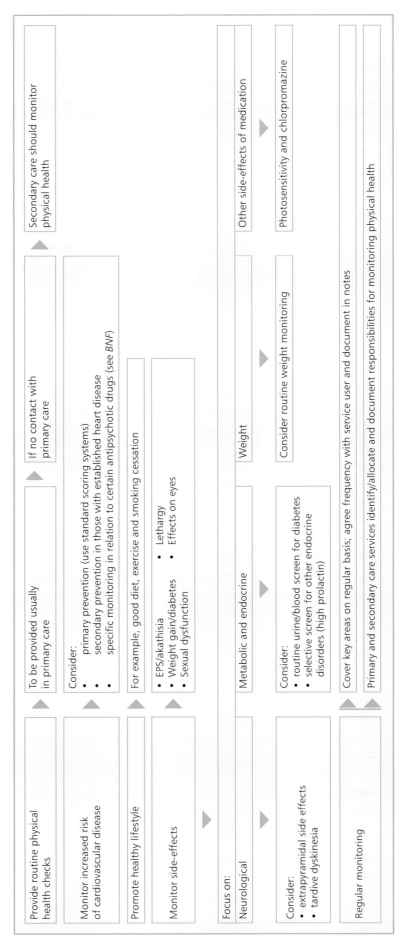

Fig. 4.3 Physical care

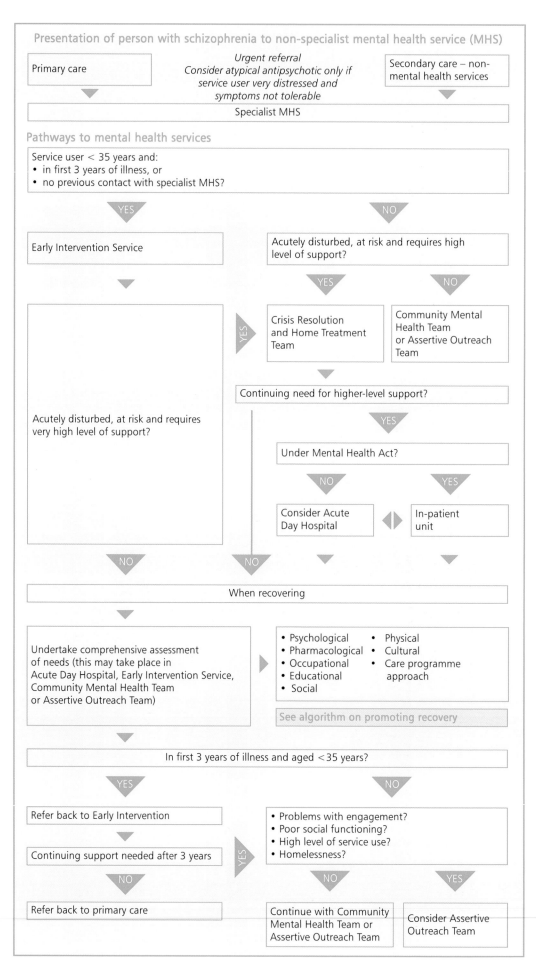

Fig. 4.4 Pathways to care

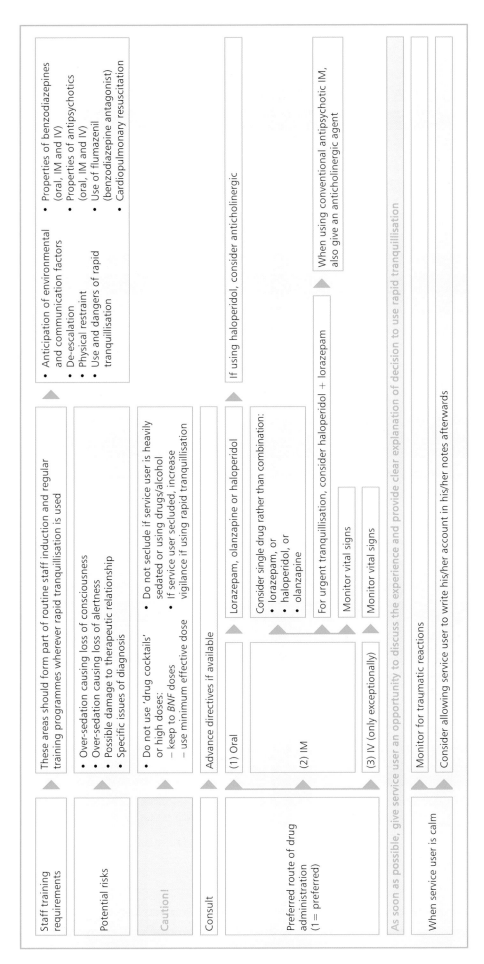

Fig. 4.5 Rapid tranquillisation in schizophrenia

Staff training requirements
→ These areas should form part of routine staff induction and regular training programmes wherever rapid tranquillisation is used
→ • Anticipation of environmental and communication factors
  • De-escalation
  • Physical restraint
  • Use and dangers of rapid tranquillisation
→ • Properties of benzodiazepines (oral, IM and IV)
  • Properties of antipsychotics (oral, IM and IV)
  • Use of flumazenil (benzodiazepine antagonist)
  • Cardiopulmonary resuscitation

Potential risks
→ • Over-sedation causing loss of consciousness
  • Over-sedation causing loss of alertness
  • Possible damage to therapeutic relationship
  • Specific issues of diagnosis

Caution!
→ • Do not use 'drug cocktails' or high doses:
  – keep to BNF doses
  – use minimum effective dose
  • Do not seclude if service user is heavily sedated or using drugs/alcohol
  • If service user secluded, increase vigilance if using rapid tranquillisation

Consult
Advance directives if available

Preferred route of drug administration (1 = preferred)
(1) Oral → Lorazepam, olanzapine or haloperidol
(2) IM → Consider single drug rather than combination:
  • lorazepam, or
  • haloperidol, or
  • olanzapine
→ For urgent tranquillisation, consider haloperidol + lorazepam
→ Monitor vital signs → If using haloperidol, consider anticholinergic
(3) IV (only exceptionally) → Monitor vital signs → When using conventional antipsychotic IM, also give an anticholinergic agent

As soon as possible, give service user an opportunity to discuss the experience and provide clear explanation of decision to use rapid tranquillisation

When service user is calm
→ Monitor for traumatic reactions
→ Consider allowing service user to write his/her account in his/her notes afterwards

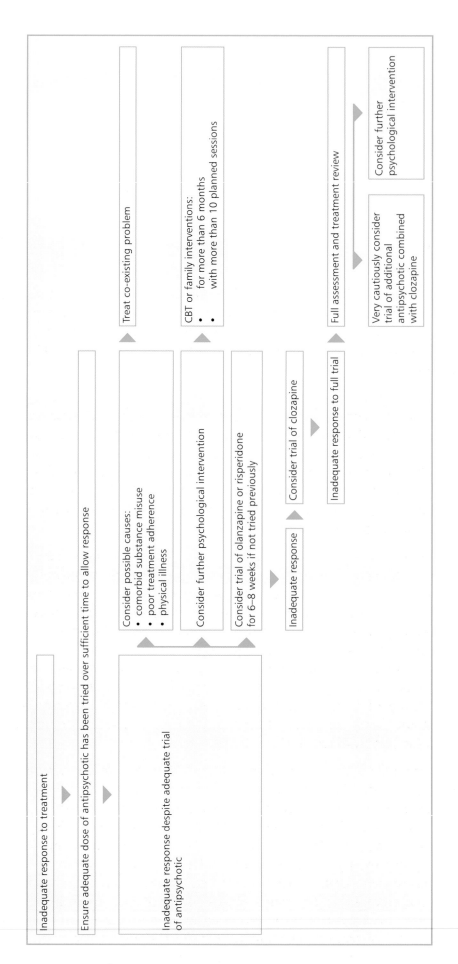

Fig. 4.6 Management of poor response to treatment and treatment resistance (after the acute phase)

5 Pharmacological interventions in the treatment and management of schizophrenia

5.1 Introduction

Antipsychotic drugs have been the mainstay of treatment of schizophrenia since the 1950s. Initially used for the treatment of acute psychotic states, their subsequent use to prevent relapse led to these drugs being prescribed for long-term maintenance treatment, either as oral preparations or in the form of long-acting injectable preparations ('depots').

Although a number of different classes of drugs have antipsychotic activity, the primary pharmacological action of antipsychotic drugs is their antagonistic effect on the D2 dopamine receptors. Indeed, the potency of a drug's antipsychotic effect is, at least in part, determined by its affinity for the D2 receptor (Snyder *et al*, 1974; Kapur & Remington, 2001), an association that informed the dopamine hypothesis of schizophrenia. It is worth noting, however, that antipsychotic drugs are also of use in the treatment of other psychotic disorders, their dopamine-blocking activity probably again central to their pharmacological efficacy.

Blockade of D2 receptors is also responsible for extrapyramidal side-effects (EPS) such as parkinsonism, dystonia and dyskinesia, but the antipsychotic effect may occur at a lower level of D2 receptor occupancy than the level associated with the emergence of EPS (Farde *et al*, 1992). Antipsychotic drugs also have strong affinity for a range of other receptors, including histaminergic, serotonergic, cholinergic and alpha-adrenergic types, which may produce a number of other effects such as sedation, weight gain and low blood pressure. As the various antipsychotic drugs possess different relative affinities for each receptor type, each drug will have its own specific profile of side-effects. However, all the older antipsychotic drugs tend to have a high incidence of side-effects, including acute EPS, and with long-term use all have the risk of causing late-onset and often persistent EPS (tardive dyskinesia) (Kane, 1992).

The antipsychotic clozapine was introduced in the 1970s, only to be withdrawn soon after because of the risk of potentially fatal agranulocytosis. However, after further research revealed the drug's efficacy in treatment-resistant schizophrenia (e.g. Kane *et al*, 1988), clozapine was reintroduced in the 1980s with requirements for appropriate haematological monitoring. Clozapine was considered to have a novel mode of action, with a relatively low affinity for D2 receptors and a much higher affinity for D4 dopamine receptors and for subtypes of serotonin receptors, although it is not clear exactly which structure–activity relationships are responsible for its antipsychotic effect. Its unusual mode of action, in that the drug's antipsychotic activity does not appear to correlate with its D2 receptor-blocking activity, led to clozapine being dubbed an 'atypical' antipsychotic, in contrast to the older, predominantly D2-blocking 'conventional' antipsychotics.

The discovery of clozapine heralded the development of a number of other new drugs for the treatment of schizophrenia (risperidone, olanzapine, quetiapine, zotepine and amisulpride), generally known as 'atypicals' on the grounds of their clozapine-like properties, specifically a lower liability to cause EPS. However, the distinction between conventional and atypical antipsychotic drugs is now somewhat blurred, as some older conventional drugs resemble some of the newer atypicals, either in their pharmacological properties or in their mode of action. The term 'atypical' is now virtually synonymous with newer antipsychotics.

The atypical antipsychotics do have different side-effect profiles compared with the older drugs, however, and some are claimed to induce less damaging long-term effects. Claims have also been made for the greater clinical efficacy of some atypicals over conventional pharmacological treatments. In particular, attention has focused on the possible role of atypicals in the treatment of people with schizophrenia whose illness is resistant to standard treatments. However, since the efficacy and many of the side-effects of antipsychotic drugs are highly dose-dependent, the results from trials comparing different antipsychotics have also been highly dependent upon dose. This is complicated still further by changes in the perceptions of the effective dosage ranges for individual drugs, and a lack of agreement regarding dose equivalence. There is considerable variation in the published equivalence tables, with some (Dewan & Koss, 1995) estimating a 500% variation in reported antipsychotic dose equivalents, with most variation occurring around the 'high potency' drugs such as haloperidol. Nevertheless, equivalence tables produced in the UK by the British Medical Association and the Royal Pharmaceutical Society have gained reasonable consensus for the conventional antipsychotics, though not for depot preparations or the atypical antipsychotics.

5.1.1 Antipsychotic dose

The current *British National Formulary* (BNF) is the most widely used reference for the prescription of medicines and the pharmacy industry within the UK, and a complete Summary of Product Characteristics (SPC) for all the drugs referred to in this guideline can be found in the Electronic Medicines Compendium (www.emc.vhn.net). The recommended dose range listed in the BNF normally reflects the information contained in the manufacturers' SPC, as well as advice from an external panel of experts to ensure that the SPC recommendations on issues such as dose range reflect current good practice ('standard dosing'). 'Standard doses' are identified as doses that fall within the range likely to achieve the best balance between therapeutic gain and dose-related adverse effects. However, with about 40% of individuals not responding effectively to antipsychotic medication, there has been a general trend for clinicians to prescribe increasingly large doses of these drugs, making standard dosing difficult to define.

By the early 1970s it had become common practice to exceed BNF maximum doses ('high doses') for those who did not respond to standard doses, and by the late 1970s and early 1980s 'megadoses' (doses several orders of magnitude greater than BNF limits) of antipsychotics were being tested as a means of controlling symptoms in people who would otherwise be considered resistant to treatment (Aubree & Lader, 1980). By the 1990s, despite occasional reports of people responding to these high-dose regimens, controlled studies had failed to demonstrate the value of this practice (Hirsch & Barnes, 1995). However, surveys of prescribing practice suggest that doses of antipsychotics exceeding BNF limits, either for a single drug or through combining antipsychotics, continue to be commonly used (Peralta *et al*, 1994; Lehman *et al*, 1998; Harrington *et al*, 2002).

In people with an established disorder, low-dose prescribing and the use of intermittent dosing strategies (with identification of early signs of relapse) designed to minimise side-effects have also been recommended in the past. However, when these were tested in controlled trials, the risks, particularly in terms of increased relapse, outweighed any benefits (Dixon *et al*, 1995; Hirsch & Barnes, 1995).

> "Targeted, intermittent dosage maintenance strategies should not be used routinely in lieu of continuous dosage regimens because of the increased risk of symptom worsening or relapse. These strategies may be considered for service users who refuse maintenance or for whom some other contraindication to maintenance therapy exists, such as side-effect sensitivity" (Schizophrenia Patient Outcomes Research Team, 1998).

In an attempt to increase the rate or extent of response, 'loading doses' and rapid dose escalation strategies have been employed (Kane & Marder, 1993); studies have failed to show improvements in terms of speed or degree of treatment response (Dixon *et al*, 1995).

In the treatment of acute episodes of schizophrenia, 'massive loading doses of antipsychotic medication, referred to as "rapid neuroleptisation", should not be used' (Schizophrenia Patient Outcomes Reseach Team, 1998).

Evidence suggests that drug-naïve patients may respond to relatively lower doses of antipsychotic drugs (McEvoy *et al*, 1991; Oosthuizen *et al*, 2001; Tauscher & Kapur, 2001; Cookson *et al*, 2002). This may have particular implications in the treatment of people experiencing their first episode of schizophrenia. Lehman *et al* (1998) have suggested that the maximum dose should be 500 mg chlorpromazine equivalents per day for drug-naïve patients. This contrasts with the recommended optimal oral dose of an antipsychotic in non-drug-naïve patients of 300–1000 mg chlorpromazine equivalents per day for the routine treatment of an acute episode. Although these dose equivalents are established for the conventional antipsychotics, this is not the case for atypical antipsychotics. It is suggested that doses at the lower end of the dose range in the SPC be adopted for drug-naïve patients treated with an atypical antipsychotic.

Persons experiencing their first episode of schizophrenia should be treated with an antipsychotic medication at the lower end of the recommended dose range in the SPC.

The dosage of conventional antipsychotic medication for an acute episode should be in the range 300–1000 mg chlorpromazine equivalents per day for a minimum of 6 weeks. Reasons for dosage outside this range should be justified and documented. The minimum effective dose should be used (Schizophrenia Patient Outcomes Research Team, 1998).

For prophylactic treatment evidence is available about the optimal dose range for those with continuing schizophrenic illness. Following a meta-analysis of 22 randomised clinical trials of the use of conventional antipsychotic drugs, Bollini *et al* (1994) suggested that the optimum dose range of antipsychotics is between 165 mg and 375 mg chlorpromazine equivalents per day. More recently, as part of their systematic review of atypical antipsychotics in the treatment of schizophrenia, Geddes *et al* (2000) investigated the doses of haloperidol and chlorpromazine used in 23 trials and 7 trials respectively, each compared with an atypical antipsychotic. They found the mean daily dose range used in these mainly short-term trials to be between 6 mg and 22 mg for haloperidol, and between 375 mg and 1000 mg for chlorpromazine. Although a significant advantage in terms of EPS was found for the atypical antipsychotics against all doses of the comparator drugs, the authors suggested that doses above 12 mg haloperidol per day produced no additional therapeutic benefit. Again, no such evidence is currently available for atypical antipsychotics. Citing Barbui *et al* (1996), the Health Evidence Bulletins stated that "Low dose antipsychotic therapy (equivalent to 50–100 mg chlorpromazine) was not as effective as standard doses (equivalent to 200–500 mg chlorpromazine) in preventing relapse [pooled odds ratio was 2.08 (95% CI: 1.3–3.3, $P<0.005$) at 12 months and 1.09 (95% CI: 0.55–2.1) at 24 months]. The relative risk reduction was −47% (95% CI: −15, −88%) at 12 months and −5% (95% CI: 28%, −52%) at 24 months (on an intention to treat analysis)" (Health Evidence Bulletins, 1998).

5.1.2 Antipsychotic dose equivalents (chlorpromazine equivalents)

Chlorpromazine dose equivalents were devised in order to compare the use of antipsychotic drug combinations within a particular research setting. The concept has commonly been used to describe prescribing patterns or trends in antipsychotic drug use (Atkins & Bauer, 1992–93). In a clinical setting, an awareness of dose equivalents may also help to avoid inadvertently increasing or decreasing the amount of antipsychotic medication when switching between different drugs. Dose equivalence does not, however, equate with equivalence of tolerability, and should be considered as a general concept rather than a precise clinical guide.

5.1.3 Antipsychotic prophylaxis

Antipsychotic prophylaxis has been the subject of considerable debate. Placebo-controlled studies have demonstrated that up to 60% of individuals who are not given prophylactic antipsychotics will relapse within 1 year of their first episode of psychosis. Consensus guidelines (Kissling, 1991) recommend 1–2 years of prophylaxis for all people diagnosed with schizophrenia.

5.1.4 Antipsychotics reviewed

All conventional antipsychotics available in the UK were reviewed through an evaluation of comparator trials by the Guideline Development Group (GDG). The GDG used the National Institute for Clinical Excellence Technology Appraisal of atypical antipsychotics as the basis for their consideration of the evidence for these drugs (NICE, 2002). The technology appraisal was supplemented by more detailed reviews where appropriate. These reviews, on which the guideline was based, took into account all antipsychotics licensed for use in the UK up to May 2002. Thus, drugs that were due to be introduced (or reintroduced) after this date were not included. However, it is anticipated that future updates of the guideline will review any drugs introduced in the interim. Only evidence that identified key clinical findings is presented in the text of the guideline.

5.1.5 Uses of antipsychotics

In the treatment and management of schizophrenia, antipsychotics are currently used for the treatment of acute episodes, for relapse prevention, for the emergency treatment of acute behavioural disturbance (rapid tranquillisation) and for symptom reduction.

Antipsychotics are available as oral, intramuscular (IM) and intravenous (IV) preparations, or as medium- or long-acting depot IM preparations. Clozapine is only licensed for use for schizophrenia in people unresponsive to, or intolerant of, conventional antipsychotics.

Antipsychotics are used either alone, or in combination with other antipsychotic agents when a single drug proves to be ineffective, and increasingly they are used alongside psychological treatments. Antipsychotics are also used in combination with a range of other classes of drugs, such as anticonvulsants, mood stabilisers, anticholinergics, antidepressants and benzodiazepines. Augmenting antipsychotics with these other classes of drugs may be appropriate when there is a lack of effective response to antipsychotics alone, for behavioural control, for the treatment of the side-effects of antipsychotics, or for the treatment of secondary problems such as depression and anxiety. Although treatment augmentation strategies are commonly used in clinical practice, they are outside the scope of this guideline. It is anticipated that a future guideline will address the evidence base for these interventions. Given the volume of studies to consider, the GDG elected to strictly limit the evidence review to the following areas:

- treatment with oral antipsychotics
- treatment with depot antipsychotic preparations
- relapse prevention
- rapid tranquillisation for behavioural disturbance
- treatment-resistant schizophrenia
- combined antipsychotics
- side-effects focusing on EPS, weight gain, and diabetes, as these were considered a priority by the GDG and were also highlighted as areas of concern by service users.

Clinical issues relating to the last area and other side-effects were well summarised by NICE (2002), as follows:

> "The *British National Formulary* (BNF) currently lists amisulpride (Solian, Sanofi-Synthelabo), olanzapine (Zyprexa, Lilly), quetiapine (Seroquel, AstraZeneca), risperidone (Risperdal, Janssen-Cilag, Organon), sertindole (Serdolect, Lundbeck) and zotepine (Zoleptil, Orion) as atypical antipsychotics. In 2001, the Committee for Proprietary Medicinal Products (CPMP) recommended that the marketing authorisation for sertindole be reinstated. Because of ongoing concerns over cardiovascular safety, the CPMP recommended that sertindole should only be used in individuals with schizophrenia who are intolerant to at least one other antipsychotic agent (typical or atypical). It is only available direct from the manufacturers through registered centres and ongoing monitoring is a prerequisite of its use. All individuals receiving sertindole will therefore be required to enrol in post-marketing studies. It is anticipated that the CPMP will review this requirement in 2003, giving consideration to the new safety data; prescribers should therefore consult the manufacturers for further information.

> All antipsychotic agents are associated with side-effects but the profile and clinical significance of these varies among individuals and drugs. These may include EPS (such as parkinsonism, acute dystonic reactions, akathisia and tardive dyskinesia), autonomic effects (such as blurring of vision, increased intra-ocular pressure, dry mouth and eyes, constipation and urinary retention), increased prolactin levels, seizures, sedation and weight gain. Cardiac safety is also an issue because several

antipsychotics have been shown to prolong ventricular repolarisation, which is associated with an increased risk of ventricular arrhythmias. Routine monitoring is a pre-requisite of clozapine use because of the risk of neutropenia and agranulocytosis. Prescribers are therefore required to ensure that effective ongoing monitoring is maintained if alternative brands of clozapine become available.

Individuals with schizophrenia consider the most troublesome side-effects to be EPS, weight gain, sexual dysfunction and sedation. EPS are easily recognised, but their occurrence cannot be predicted accurately and they are related to poor prognosis. Akathisia is also often missed or misdiagnosed as agitation. Of particular concern is tardive dyskinesia (orofacial and trunk movements), which may not be evident immediately, is resistant to treatment, may be irreversible, and may worsen on treatment withdrawal. Sexual dysfunction can result from drug-induced hyperprolactinaemia; it is likely to be an underreported side-effect of antipsychotic treatment, as discussion of this issue is often difficult to initiate." (NICE, 2002)

5.2 Oral antipsychotics in the treatment of the acute episode

5.2.1 Introduction

Chlorpromazine, introduced in the mid-1950s, is considered to have been the first antipsychotic drug. The introduction of chlorpromazine was followed by a series of other antipsychotic drugs, all initially referred to as 'major tranquillisers'. Subsequently, clinical studies established that these drugs were effective in the treatment of acute schizophrenic episodes (Davis & Garver, 1978), although they proved to be more effective at alleviating positive symptoms than negative symptoms. However, no consistent difference between the early antipsychotic drugs was demonstrated in terms of antipsychotic efficacy or effects on individual symptoms, syndromes or schizophrenia subgroups. Accordingly, the choice of drug for an individual was largely dependent on differences in side-effect profiles (Hollister, 1974; Davis & Garver, 1978).

The limitations of these antipsychotic drugs included heterogeneity of response in acute episodes, with a proportion of individuals showing little improvement (Kane, 1987), and a range of undesirable acute and long-term side-effects, with perhaps the greatest burden being EPS. The search for better-tolerated and more effective drugs eventually generated a series of second-generation atypical drugs, characterised by a lower liability to EPS (Barnes & McPhillips, 1999; Geddes *et al*, 2000; Cookson *et al*, 2002). The older drugs began to be labelled as 'conventional' in their propensity to cause EPS.

5.2.2 Drugs included for this review

The following drugs were considered: amisulpride, benperidol, chlorpromazine hydrochloride, haloperidol, flupentixol, fluphenazine hydrochloride, loxapine, olanzapine, oxypertine, pericyazine, perphenazine, pimozide, prochlorperazine, promazine hydrochloride, quetiapine, risperidone, sulpiride, thioridazine, trifluoperazine, zotepine and zuclopenthixol dihydrochloride.

5.2.3 Studies considered for review

The GDG used six existing systematic reviews of oral antipsychotics: the review of atypical antipsychotics produced for the NICE Technology Appraisal (NICE, 2002) and the Cochrane reviews of benperidol (Leucht & Hartung, 2002), loxapine (Fenton *et al*, 2002*b*), pimozide (Sultana & McMonagle, 2002), sulpiride (Soares *et al*, 2002) and thioridazine (Sultana *et al*, 2002). New systematic reviews were undertaken by the guideline review team of chlorpromazine, flupentixol, fluphenazine, oxypertine,[1] pericyazine, perphenazine, prochlorperazine, promazine, trifluoperazine, and zuclopenthixol dihydrochloride.

For the purposes of the guideline, data from 122 trials, included in the existing reviews named above, were excluded from the data analysis because they were based on comparisons either between a single drug and placebo, or with a drug currently unavailable in the UK. In addition, a small number of studies were excluded because they failed to meet quality criteria.

Data from the remaining trials (*n* = 146) were synthesised with data from 34 new trials. A further 37 new trials were excluded because they failed to meet eligibility or quality criteria. This resulted in 85 head-to-head comparisons of an oral antipsychotic with haloperidol and 54 comparisons involving chlorpromazine. The studies were categorised as short-term (<12 weeks), medium-term (12–51 weeks) and long-term (52 weeks or more).

In considering the evidence for conventional antipsychotics, the GDG focused on comparisons with haloperidol and chlorpromazine, as these were used as the main comparators in most head-to-head clinical trials. Studies included varied in the following ways:

- method (allocation, masking)
- dose
- duration
- inclusion criteria
- participants (age, mean duration of illness, diagnostic criteria used)
- site of treatment (hospital, community)
- outcomes recorded.

5.2.4 Results

The conclusions that can be drawn from the majority of the studies are limited because of the lack of long-term follow-up, high attrition rates and the inadequacy of collection and reporting of adverse events. In addition, haloperidol (which may be associated with a higher incidence of EPS than other conventional antipsychotics) was used as the comparator in many of the trials. The generalisability of individual study results was limited by the exclusion of elderly people, as well as of individuals with treatment-

---

1. 'Oxypertine 10 mg capsules and oxypertine 40 mg tablets are being discontinued because of manufacturing problems (Sanofi-Synthelabo). Sanofi-Synthelabo will provide a three-month supply of oxypertine 10 mg capsules on an "as needed basis" only until 31 May. After this the 10 mg capsules will no longer be available. Oxypertine 40 mg tablets will be discontinued from 31 August' (*Pharmaceutical Journal*, 2002, vol. 268, no. 7188, p. 323).

resistant schizophrenia, predominantly negative symptoms, learning disabilities, comorbid depression and substance misuse disorders.

The evidence considered suggests that the atypical antipsychotics are at least as efficacious as the conventional drugs in terms of overall response rates. There is also evidence to suggest that they may vary in their relative effects on positive and negative symptoms and relapse rates. However, there are inadequate data to permit separate evaluation of the overall impact of individual atypicals for people with schizophrenia.

The following statements emerged from a further consideration of the evidence reviewed for conventional and atypical antipsychotics. Owing to the large number of comparisons, only the results deemed to be clinically important by the GDG are presented here.

In head-to-head comparisons between chlorpromazine and other conventional antipsychotics at the end of treatment:

- there is limited evidence that a higher proportion of participants receiving pimozide needed anticholinergic drugs compared with those taking chlorpromazine ($n=40$, RR=0.47, 95% CI 0.27 to 0.83; NNT=3, 95% CI 2 to 6) (Ib)
- there is strong evidence that a higher proportion of participants receiving loxapine needed anticholinergic drugs compared with those taking chlorpromazine ($n=192$, RR=0.56, 95% CI 0.37 to 0.83; NNT=6, 95% CI 4 to 15) (Ia)
- there is limited evidence for fewer EPS with chlorpromazine compared with pimozide (Simpson Angus scale: $n=20$; WMD=−9.37, 95% CI −11.71 to −7.03) (Ib)
- there is limited evidence that chlorpromazine is associated with more short-term sedation than haloperidol ($n=28$, RR=15.00, 95% CI 0.94 to 239.82; NNH=2, 95% CI 2 to 5) (Ib); pimozide ($n=60$, RR=1.64, 95% CI 1.07 to 2.53; NNH=4, 95% CI 2 to 19) (Ib); and oral fluphenazine ($n=471$, RR=1.73, 95% CI 1.73 to 2.33; NNH=7, 95% CI 5 to 15) (Ib)
- there is limited evidence that the use of chlorpromazine is associated with photosensitivity when compared with thioridazine ($n=69$, RR=14.71, 95% CI 2.07 to 104.77; NNH=3, 95% CI 2 to 4). (Ib)

Comparative studies of chlorpromazine and thioridazine yielded findings on cardiovascular variables and adverse electrocardiographic changes that were compatible with current recommendations in the BNF relating to the restricted use of thioridazine. For example, at the end of treatment:

- thioridazine was significantly more likely to produce a cardiovascular adverse event ($n=74$, RR=3.17, 95% CI 1.43 to 7.02; NNH=3, 95% CI 2 to 7) (Ib) and adverse ECG changes ($n=234$, RR=2.11, 95% CI 1.39 to 3.21; NNH=5, 95% CI 3 to 10). (Ib)

In head-to-head comparisons between haloperidol and other conventional antipsychotics, at the end of treatment:

- there is limited evidence suggesting that haloperidol produces less EPS than pimozide (tremor: $n=52$, RR=0.46, 95% CI 0.24 to 0.88; NNT=3, 95% CI 2 to 10) (Ib) and less use of anticholinergic drugs ($n=50$, RR=0.48, 95% CI 0.32 to 0.72; NNT=2, 95% CI 2 to 4). (Ib)

In head-to-head comparisons between atypical antipsychotics and conventional antipsychotics, at the end of treatment:

- there is strong evidence suggesting that atypical antipsychotics as a group are associated with lower numbers leaving the study early in the short to medium term ($n=11\ 668$, RR=0.73, 95% CI 0.69 to 0.77; NNT=10, 95% CI 10 to 13) (Ia)

- there is strong evidence suggesting that atypical antipsychotics as a group are associated with a lower risk of EPS when compared with haloperidol in the short to medium term (n=4890; random effects RR=0.57, 95% CI 0.47 to 0.69; NNT=5, 95% CI 4 to 8) (Ia)

- there is strong evidence suggesting that olanzapine is associated with greater weight gain in the medium term (n=128, WMD=5.40; 95% CI 0.63 to 10.18), but the evidence is inconsistent in short-term studies (n=2162, WMD=0.91, 95% CI –0.56 to 2.38) (Ia), and there are no long-term data

- there is strong evidence suggesting that risperidone is associated with greater risk of weight gain in the short term (n=1652, RR=1.37, 95% CI 1.10 to 1.71; NNH=13, 95% CI 8 to 34) (Ia); however, there are no medium or long-term data

- there is limited evidence suggesting that amisulpride is associated with greater risk of weight gain in the long term (n=440, RR=1.80, 95% CI 1.18 to 2.73; NNH=7, 95% CI 5 to 17) (Ib)

- however, the evidence is insufficient to determine the effect in the short term (n=132, RR=0.95, 95% CI 0.50 to 1.81) or in the medium term (n=199, RR=16.74, 95% CI 0.97 to 289.15). (Ib)

No consistent or relevant data from comparator trials reviewed in this guideline provided information on an association between diabetes and the use of antipsychotics. Nevertheless, a data-mining study (Sernyak *et al*, 2002) reported a relative increase of 9% in the prevalence of diabetes in individuals receiving atypical compared with conventional antipsychotics (age-adjusted OR 1.09, 95% CI 1.03 to 1.15; P=0.002). Emerging evidence suggests that antipsychotics vary in their propensity to cause diabetes (Koro *et al*, 2002) and weight gain (Allison *et al*, 1999).

5.2.5 Clinical summary

The further analysis of oral antipsychotics undertaken for this guideline suggested that chlorpromazine has a lower propensity to produce EPS than some other conventional antipsychotics (pimozide and loxapine), but is associated with greater sedation and increased photosensitivity. The results also supported current BNF recommendations concerning the restricted use of thioridazine.

There is strong evidence suggesting that atypical antipsychotics as a group are associated with a lower risk of EPS than conventional antipsychotics such as haloperidol. The atypical antipsychotics are also associated with fewer people stopping treatment. With regard to increased weight gain, relevant data from clinical trials were only available for olanzapine, risperidone and amisulpride, and provided evidence for differential weight gain with these individual drugs. Preliminary evidence suggests that some atypical antipsychotics may be associated with a higher prevalence of diabetes.

5.2.6 Health economic evidence

This guideline addressed the question of the cost-effectiveness of atypical antipsychotic drugs, using the NICE Technology Appraisal of atypical antipsychotics (NICE, 2002), and uncovered some additional papers that had not been identified by the original appraisal. Ten new studies were found to be eligible, while three papers were not available. The results of the new studies were analysed and compared with those of the Technology Appraisal's literature review.

The following conclusions are based on all available published evidence on the cost-effectiveness of atypical antipsychotics. Additional conclusions regarding the use of atypical antipsychotics for treatment-resistant schizophrenia and chronic schizophrenia are presented in the section on treatment resistance (section 5.6.6).

- It is difficult to draw any firm conclusion about the cost-effectiveness of atypical antipsychotics compared with haloperidol or chlorpromazine in the acute episode, because of the lack of available evidence.

- It is also difficult to draw any firm conclusion about the comparative cost-effectiveness of different atypical antipsychotic drugs in the acute episode because of the lack of available evidence, or ambiguous results.

5.2.7 Clinical practice recommendations

5.2.7.1   The choice of antipsychotic drug should be made jointly by the individual and the clinician responsible for treatment, based on an informed discussion of the relative benefits of the drugs and their side-effect profiles. The individual's advocate or carer should be consulted where appropriate. (NICE 2002)

5.2.7.2   Antipsychotic therapy should be initiated as part of a comprehensive package of care that addresses the individual's clinical, emotional and social needs. The clinician responsible for treatment and the keyworker should monitor both therapeutic progress and tolerability of the drug on an ongoing basis. Monitoring is particularly important when individuals have just changed from one antipsychotic to another. (NICE 2002)

5.2.7.3   The dosage of conventional antipsychotic medication for an acute episode should be in the range 300–1000 mg chlorpromazine equivalents per day for a minimum of 6 weeks. Reasons for dosage outside this range should be justified and documented. The minimum effective dose should be used. (C)

5.2.7.4   In the treatment of acute episodes of schizophrenia, massive loading doses of antipsychotic medication, referred to as 'rapid neuroleptisation', should not be used. (C)

5.2.7.5   Targeted, intermittent dosage maintenance strategies should not be used routinely in lieu of continuous dosage regimens because of the increased risk of symptom worsening or relapse. However, these strategies may be considered for service users who refuse maintenance or for whom some other contraindication to maintenance therapy exists, such as side-effect sensitivity. (C)

5.2.7.6   The oral atypical antipsychotic drugs (amisulpride, olanzapine, quetiapine, risperidone and zotepine) should be considered as treatment options for individuals currently receiving conventional antipsychotic drugs who, despite adequate symptom control, are experiencing unacceptable side-effects, and for those in relapse who have previously experienced unsatisfactory management or unacceptable side-effects with conventional antipsychotic drugs. The decision as to what are unacceptable side-effects should be taken following discussion between the patient and the clinician responsible for treatment. (NICE 2002)

5.2.7.7   It is recommended that the oral atypical antipsychotic drugs amisulpride, olanzapine, quetiapine, risperidone and zotepine are considered in the choice of first-line treatments for individuals with newly diagnosed schizophrenia. (NICE 2002)

5.2.7.8 Atypical antipsychotics at the lower end of the standard dose range are the preferred treatments for a person experiencing a first episode of schizophrenia. (C)

5.2.7.9 When full discussion between the clinician responsible for treatment and the individual concerned is not possible, in particular in the management of an acute schizophrenic episode, the oral atypical drugs should be considered as the treatment options of choice because of the lower potential risk of extrapyramidal side-effects. In these circumstances, the individual's carer or advocate should be consulted where possible and appropriate. Although there are limitations with advance directives regarding the choice of treatment for individuals with schizophrenia, it is recommended that they are developed and documented in individuals' care programmes whenever possible. (NICE 2002)

5.2.7.10 It is not recommended that, in routine clinical practice, individuals change to one of the oral atypical antipsychotic drugs if they are currently achieving good control of their condition without unacceptable side-effects with conventional antipsychotic drugs. (NICE 2002)

5.2.7.11 Antipsychotic drugs, whether atypical or conventional, should not be prescribed concurrently, except for short periods to cover changeover. (C)

5.2.7.12 When prescribed chlorpromazine, individuals should be warned of a potential photosensitive skin response, as this is an easily preventable side-effect. (B)

5.2.7.13 Where a potential to cause weight gain or diabetes has been identified (or included in the Summary of Product Characteristics) for the atypical antipsychotic being prescribed, there should be routine monitoring in respect of these potential risks. (B)

5.2.7.14 Given the high risk of relapse following an acute episode, the continuation of antipsychotic drugs for up to 1–2 years after a relapse should be discussed with service users, and carers where appropriate. (GPP)

5.2.7.15 Withdrawal from antipsychotic medication should be undertaken gradually while regularly monitoring signs and symptoms for evidence of potential relapse. (GPP)

5.2.7.16 Following withdrawal from antipsychotic medication, monitoring for signs and symptoms of potential relapse should continue for at least 2 years after the last acute episode. (GPP)

5.2.8 Research recommendations

5.2.8.1 More long-term, head-to-head, randomised controlled trials (RCTs) of the atypical antipsychotic drugs are required, especially trials that include individuals in their first episode of schizophrenia, younger individuals and the elderly. (NICE 2002)

5.2.8.2 Direct comparisons between atypical antipsychotics are needed to establish their respective risk/long-term benefit, including effects upon relapse rates and persisting symptoms. Trials should pay particular attention to the long-term benefits and risks of the drugs, including diabetes, weight gain, EPS (including tardive dyskinesia), sexual dysfunction, lethargy and quality of life.

5.2.8.3   Further RCTs investigating the cost-effectiveness of atypical antipsychotics compared with each other and with depot preparations are necessary.

5.2.8.4   Large-scale, observational, survey-based studies, including qualitative components, of the experience of drug treatment (with both conventional and atypical antipsychotics) should be undertaken. Studies should include data on service-user satisfaction, side-effects, preferences, provision of information and quality of life.

5.2.8.5   Further work is required on the nature and severity of antipsychotic drug discontinuation phenomena, including the re-emergence of psychotic symptoms, and their relationship to different antipsychotic withdrawal strategies.

5.3 Pharmacological relapse prevention

5.3.1 Introduction

Since their introduction in the 1950s, conventional antipsychotic drugs such as chlorpromazine and haloperidol have been used to treat people experiencing acute psychotic symptoms and to prevent relapse (Davis *et al*, 1993; Gilbert *et al*, 1995; Hirsch & Barnes, 1995). A meta-analysis of 35 double-blind studies (Davis *et al*, 1993) compared maintenance treatment using conventional antipsychotics with placebo in over 3500 service users. Relapse was reported in 55% of those who were randomised to receive placebo, but in only 21% of those receiving active drugs. Gilbert *et al* (1995) reviewed 66 antipsychotic withdrawal studies, published between 1958 and 1993, and involving over 4000 service users. The mean cumulative rate of relapse in the medication withdrawal groups was 53% (follow-up period 6–10 months) compared with 16% (follow-up 8 months) in the antipsychotic maintenance groups. Over a period of several years, continuing treatment with conventional antipsychotics appears to reduce the risk of relapse by about two-thirds (Kissling, 1991).

When the effects of stopping antipsychotic drugs after an acute psychotic episode or after long-term maintenance treatment were examined, the subsequent rate of relapse seemed to be similar in both situations. Individuals who are well stabilised on maintenance medication show high rates of relapse when their antipsychotic therapy is discontinued (Kane, 1990) or switched to placebo (Hogarty *et al*, 1976). A meta-analysis of data from several large collaborative studies (Davis *et al*, 1993) suggested that the number of people who survive without relapse after discontinuing drug treatment declines exponentially by around 10% a month.

Whether maintenance drug treatment is required for all people with schizophrenia is uncertain. Around 20% of individuals will only experience a single episode (Möller & van Zerssen, 1995), while a similar percentage will experience a relapse despite continued antipsychotic drug treatment. It is unclear whether those in the latter group benefit from an increase in antipsychotic dosage during episodes of psychotic exacerbation (Steingard *et al*, 1994). Nevertheless, given that there is no reliable predictor of prognosis or drug response, pharmacological relapse prevention should be considered for every patient diagnosed with schizophrenia. Possible exceptions are people with very brief psychotic episodes without negative psychosocial consequences, and the uncommon patient for whom all available antipsychotics pose a significant health risk (Fleischhacker & Hummer, 1997).

It is clear from the placebo-controlled RCTs and discontinuation studies cited above that the efficacy of antipsychotics in relapse prevention is established. Indeed, all the antipsychotics identified for review have established supremacy over placebo in the prevention of relapse, although whether one antipsychotic has greater efficacy or better tolerability than another is uncertain, especially with regard to the atypical antipsychotic drugs. The aim of antipsychotic drug development has been the creation of new agents with superior efficacy and fewer side-effects. Studies of the newer, atypical drugs have suggested that their short-term efficacy is at least equal to that of conventional antipsychotic agents, but with fewer extrapyramidal side-effects, and although the difference in the incidence of side-effects is highly dose-dependent for the latter (Geddes *et al*, 2000; NICE, 2002), the degree to which EPS are dose-dependent with the atypical antipsychotics varies between the individual drugs. Also, long-term follow-up of treatment with these newer drugs is essential to establish their value for relapse prevention for people with schizophrenia. The GDG therefore decided that the evidence review would be limited to trials comparing the efficacy of the atypical antipsychotics with conventional drugs in the prevention of relapse in schizophrenia.

5.3.2 Definitions

The definitions of relapse used in this review were those adopted by the individual studies. This definition varied between studies. For example, four studies (Essock *et al*, 1996; Tran *et al*, 1998*a,b,c*) defined relapse as hospitalisation for psychopathology; one study (Speller *et al*, 1997) required an increase of three or more positive symptom items on the Brief Psychiatric Rating Scale (BPRS) which did not respond to a dose increase; while another study (Csernansky & Okamoto, 2000) required one of the following: hospitalisation for schizophrenia; increased level of care and a 20% increase in the Positive and Negative Symptom Scale (PANSS) score; self-injury, suicide or homicidal ideation or violent behaviour; or a Clinical Global Impression (CGI) rating of above 6. These varying definitions require that caution be exercised in the interpretation of the results.

5.3.3 Studies considered for review[2]

A systematic review and meta-analysis by Leucht *et al* (2003) of ten RCTs involving an atypical antipsychotic compared with a conventional antipsychotic for a period of 6 months or more was identified by the review team. For the purposes of this guideline, studies that did not report treatment adherence data or that involved antipsychotics not available in the UK were excluded from the evidence review. Thus, nine RCTs involving 1656 patients were reanalysed (TAMMINGA 1994; ESSOCK 1996; SPELLER 1997; TRAN 1997; TRAN 1998*a,b,c*; ROSENHECK 1999; CSERNANSKY 2000). The trials incorporated compared the atypical antipsychotics with haloperidol – except that of Essock (1996),

---

2. Here and elsewhere in the guideline, each primary-level study included for review is referred to using a study ID (i.e. surname of the first author in upper-case letters and, where appropriate, the date of primary report). Full details of each study can be found on the data CD–ROM distributed with this book.

which used a range of conventional antipsychotics including haloperidol. The atypical antipsychotic drugs reviewed were amisulpride, clozapine, olanzapine and risperidone. Studies included varied in the following ways:

- method (allocation, masking)
- definition of relapse (see below)
- dose (haloperidol range 3–30 mg/day)
- duration (range 22 weeks to 2.5 years)
- inclusion criteria
- participants (age, mean duration of illness, diagnostic criteria used)
- site of treatment (hospital, community)
- outcomes recorded.

5.3.4 Results

As stated above, the definition of relapse differed between studies, limiting the validity of these results and preventing the GDG from reaching firm conclusions. Also, the number of treatment failures tended to be high in both the treatment and comparator groups, and the average daily dose of haloperidol tended to be high (10–20 mg) in most studies, with only one study (SPELLER 1997) using doses of haloperidol below 5 mg daily. Individually, the studies tended to show limited superiority in relapse prevention for the atypical antipsychotics over haloperidol, but given the above it was not possible to determine whether this was related to the enhanced efficacy, greater tolerability or better treatment adherence for the atypicals, or a combination of these factors.

When data were pooled across the atypical antipsychotics, there was strong evidence that, at the end of treatment, atypical drugs were superior to haloperidol in terms of:

- overall risk of relapse (*n*=1444, RR=0.65, 95% CI 0.53 to 0.80; NNT=8, 95% CI 5 to 20) (Ia)
- overall treatment failure including relapse (*n*=1232, RR=0.80, 95% CI 0.73 to 0.87; NNT=8, 95% CI 5 to 12). (Ia)

There is insufficient evidence to determine whether there is a clinically significant difference, at the end of treatment, between the newer drugs and haloperidol in terms of treatment acceptability:

- leaving the study early because of adverse events (*n*=1271, RR=0.81, 95% CI 0.58 to 1.13). (Ia)

5.3.5 Clinical summary

In the absence of head-to-head trials of sufficiently long duration, the relative efficacy for relapse prevention of conventional antipsychotics against atypicals remains uncertain.

5.3.6 Clinical practice recommendations

5.3.6.1 The choice of antipsychotic drug should be made jointly by the individual and the clinician responsible for treatment, based on an informed discussion of the relative benefits of the drugs and their side-effect profiles. The individual's advocate or carer should be consulted where appropriate. (NICE 2002)

5.3.6.2   The oral atypical antipsychotic drugs (amisulpride, olanzapine, quetiapine, risperidone and zotepine) should be considered as treatment options for individuals receiving typical antipsychotic drugs who, despite adequate symptom control, are experiencing unacceptable side-effects, and for those in relapse who have previously experienced unsatisfactory management or unacceptable side-effects with typical antipsychotic drugs. The decision as to what are unacceptable side-effects should be taken following discussion between the patient and the clinician responsible for treatment. (NICE 2002)

5.3.6.3   It is not recommended that, in routine clinical practice, individuals change to one of the oral atypical antipsychotic drugs if they are currently achieving good control of their condition without unacceptable side-effects with typical antipsychotic drugs. (NICE 2002)

5.3.6.4   A risk assessment should be performed by the clinician responsible for treatment and the multi-disciplinary team regarding concordance with medication, and depot preparations should be prescribed when appropriate. (NICE 2002)

5.3.6.5   Antipsychotic therapy should be initiated as part of a comprehensive package of care that addresses the individual's clinical, emotional and social needs. The clinician responsible for treatment and the keyworker should monitor both therapeutic progress and tolerability of the drug on an ongoing basis. Monitoring is particularly important when individuals have just changed from one antipsychotic to another. (NICE 2002)

5.3.6.6   Antipsychotic drugs, whether atypical or conventional, should not be prescribed concurrently, except for short periods to cover changeover. (C)

5.3.6.7   Targeted, intermittent dosage maintenance strategies should not be used routinely in lieu of continuous dosage regimens because of the increased risk of symptom worsening or relapse. However, these strategies may be considered for service users who refuse maintenance or for whom some other contra-indication to maintenance therapy exists, such as side-effect sensitivity. (C)

5.4 Depot antipsychotic treatment

5.4.1 Introduction

The introduction of depot antipsychotic formulations in the 1960s was heralded as a major advance in the treatment of chronic schizophrenia outside hospital. Depot preparations could guarantee consistent drug delivery, overcome the bioavailability problems that occur with oral preparations (such as gut wall and hepatic first-pass metabolism) and eliminate the risk of deliberate or inadvertent overdose. In the subsequent decades, the main practical clinical advantage has been the avoidance of covert non-adherence to drug treatment, where there is close nursing supervision and documentation of clinic attendance (Barnes & Curson, 1994). Service users who are receiving depot treatment and who decline their injection or fail to receive it through forgetfulness (or any other reason) will be immediately identified, allowing appropriate intervention. However, the use of depot drugs does not guarantee good treatment adherence. Around a third of those who are prescribed maintenance treatment with depot preparations after discharge from hospital will fail to become established on the injections.

Figures on the use of depot treatments are sparse. Some years ago, Crammer & Eccleston (1989) reported a survey of the use of depot antipsychotics in the north of England. Out of a catchment population of 3 million, about 2000 persons were regularly receiving depot injections – that is, about 1 in every 1500. The authors calculated that if this were a generalisable finding for the UK, then approximately 32 000 people in England and Wales would be receiving depot injections, a quarter of whom would be over 60 years old. More recently, a UK national household survey found that approximately 29% of 390 non-hospitalised individuals with psychotic disorders were receiving depot treatment (Foster *et al*, 1996).

5.4.2 Depots: uses and disadvantages

Depot antipsychotic formulations generally consist of an ester of the drug in an oily solution, which is administered by deep intramuscular injection. The drug is slowly released from the injection site, giving relatively stable plasma drug levels over long periods, allowing the injections to be given every few weeks. However, this also represents a potential disadvantage, as there is a lack of flexibility of administration, with adjustment to the optimal dosage being a protracted and uncertain process. The controlled studies of low-dose maintenance treatment with depot preparations suggest that any increased risk of relapse consequent upon a dose reduction may take months or years to become manifest. Another disadvantage is that, for some people, receiving the depot injection is a rather ignominious and passive experience. Further, there have been reports of pain, oedema, pruritus and sometimes a palpable mass at the injection site. Nevertheless, there is evidence from a systematic review (Walburn *et al*, 2001) suggesting that some people receiving depot antipsychotics prefer them to oral therapy, largely because they consider them to be more convenient.

5.4.3 Studies considered for review

The GDG relied heavily on the recent Health Technology Assessment of depot antipsychotics (David & Adams, 2001) in examining the evidence. The assessment was a meta-review of nine systematic reviews. The GDG excluded studies involving antipsychotics not currently available in the UK and reanalysed the trial data. No information was available on the newer atypical depot preparations. The review therefore incorporated 92 RCTs involving five depot preparations (flupentixol decanoate, fluphenazine decanoate, haloperidol decanoate, pipotiazine palmitate and zuclopenthixol decanoate) and including data on 5522 individuals. The studies included varied in the following ways:
- method (allocation, masking)
- dose (e.g. haloperidol decanoate range 15–900 mg per 2–4 weeks)
- duration of treatment (range 2 weeks to 3 years)
- participants (age, mean duration of illness, diagnostic criteria used)
- site of treatment (hospital, community)
- outcomes recorded.

Interpretation of the results of comparative studies of depot and oral antipsychotics should take account of the relatively short duration of these studies, and the likelihood that individuals in whom an advantage might be anticipated, such as those who comply poorly with their medication, are unlikely to have been included in the trials.

5.4.4 Results

There is strong evidence suggesting that there is no clinically significant difference between depot antipsychotics (fluphenazine decanoate, pipotiazine palmitate) and conventional oral antipsychotics in terms of:

- relapse rates (*n*=808, RR=0.97, 95% CI 0.81 to 1.16) (Ia)
- leaving the study early (*n*=774, RR=1.13, 95% CI 0.88 to 1.44). (Ia)

There is strong evidence suggesting that depot antipsychotics (fluphenazine decanoate, haloperidol decanoate, pipotiazine palmitate) do not increase the risk of movement disorders compared with conventional oral antipsychotics:

- tardive dyskinesia (*n*=272, RR=0.66, 95% CI 0.34 to 1.30) (Ia)
- use of anticholinergic drugs (*n*=301, RR=1.00, 95% CI 0.86 to 1.16). (Ia)

There is limited evidence suggesting that, at the end of treatment, there is a clinically significant difference between depot (fluphenazine decanoate, haloperidol decanoate) and oral antipsychotics, favouring depots:

- on a measure of global functioning (no clinically important change on CGI: *n*=96, RR=0.67, 95% CI 0.53 to 0.85; NNT=4, 95% CI 3 to 7). (Ib)

Generally, there is little or insufficient evidence suggesting superiority of one conventional antipsychotic depot over another. However, there are two clinically important findings:

- there is limited evidence suggesting that, at the end of treatment, zuclopenthixol decanoate carries a lower risk of relapse when compared with a control depot (flupentixol decanoate, haloperidol decanoate) (*n*=124, RR=0.24, 95% CI 0.07 to 0.82; NNT=8, 95% CI 4 to 34) (Ib)
- there is strong evidence suggesting that, at the end of treatment, fluphenazine decanoate has a higher risk of producing a movement disorder (as measured by the use of anticholinergic drugs) when compared with a control depot (*n*=727, RR=1.26, 95% CI 1.11 to 1.42; NNH=8, 95% CI 5 to 17). (Ia)

There is some evidence that the dosage of conventional depots, at the end of treatment, may influence relapse rates:

- there is strong evidence that low doses are less effective than standard doses (*n*=639, RR=1.52; 95% CI 1.21 to 1.91; NNH=8, 95% CI 5 to 17) (Ia)
- there is insufficient evidence to determine whether high doses show an advantage over standard doses (*n*=68, RR=0.83, 95% CI 0.29 to 2.37). (Ib)

5.4.5 Clinical summary

Depot antipsychotics do not appear to be significantly different from oral conventional antipsychotics in terms of relapse rates, numbers of participants leaving the study early, and side-effects. Depots do not appear to be associated with an increased risk of movement disorders over oral conventional antipsychotics. There is some limited evidence to suggest that depots, compared with oral conventional antipsychotics, may confer some advantages in terms of global functioning. There is no convincing evidence for the superiority of any one type of depot, although some limited evidence suggests zuclopenthixol decanoate may carry a lower risk of relapse than either flupentixol decanoate or haloperidol decanoate. In addition, the use of fluphenazine decanoate may be associated with a greater risk of movement disorders (as indicated by the use of anticholinergic drugs) relative to the other depots. The use of low-dose depot preparations appears to be less effective than standard-dose depots. There is insufficient evidence to suggest that high-dose depots are more effective.

5.4.6 Health economic evidence

It has been hypothesised that depot antipsychotics might demonstrate an advantage over conventional oral antipsychotics by improving adherence to drug treatment, leading to a reduction in readmission costs and assorted social costs (e.g. housing costs, legal costs). More recently, attention has focused on the cost-effectiveness of depot antipsychotics compared with oral atypical antipsychotics.

The economic review identified four eligible studies. Only one study was conducted in the UK (Hale & Wood, 1996). Three studies used modelling methods (Glazer & Ereshefsky, 1996; Hale & Wood, 1996; Oh *et al*, 2001), while the fourth study based its calculations on a controlled trial with concurrent controls (Moore *et al*, 1998). The quality of the studies was mixed. All authors investigated costs only narrowly, which made estimation of the broader cost consequences of depot preparations impossible.

Two studies compared oral conventional atypicals with depots. Glazer & Ereshefsky (1996) concluded that haloperidol decanoate is less costly than oral haloperidol. The other study examined the effect of switching 10% more people with schizophrenia to depot antipsychotic drugs in the UK, and demonstrated substantial cost savings (Hale & Wood, 1996). However, both studies used decision analytic modelling, and the results are valid only under certain assumptions. Two studies addressed the question of the cost-effectiveness of different depot preparations. Both studies compared haloperidol decanoate with fluphenazine decanoate. The modelling study by Oh *et al* (2001) found haloperidol decanoate to be dominant over fluphenazine decanoate, while Moore *et al* (1998) showed the two drugs to be equally effective, and fluphenazine decanoate to be less costly. Three studies compared risperidone, an atypical antipsychotic, to haloperidol decanoate. Glazer & Ereshefsky (1996) found haloperidol decanoate to be the cheaper option, whereas the other two studies concluded that risperidone was more cost-effective (Moore *et al*, 1998; Oh *et al*, 2001).

5.4.6.1 Health economic conclusions

Despite the widespread use of depot antipsychotics in the treatment of schizophrenia, the quantity and the quality of the available evidence are poor, and it is difficult to draw any firm conclusion about the cost-effectiveness of depot antipsychotic therapy on the basis of this evidence.

5.4.7 Clinical practice recommendations

5.4.7.1   Depot preparations should be offered as a treatment option where a service user expresses a preference for such treatment because of its convenience, or as part of a treatment plan in which the avoidance of covert non-adherence to the antipsychotic drug regimen is a clinical priority. (B)

5.4.7.2   For optimum effectiveness in preventing relapse, depot preparations should be prescribed within the standard recommended dosage and interval range. (A)

5.4.7.3   A risk assessment should be performed by the clinician responsible for treatment and the multi-disciplinary team regarding concordance with medication, and depot preparations should be prescribed when appropriate. (NICE 2002)

5.4.7.4   Following full discussion between the responsible clinician and the service user, the decision to initiate depot antipsychotic injections should take into account the preferences and attitudes of the service user towards the mode of administration and organisational procedures (for example, home visits and location of clinics) related to the delivery of regular intramuscular injections. (GPP)

5.4.7.5   Test doses should normally be used as set out in the BNF, and full licensed prescribing information on depot antipsychotics is available from the Summary of Product Characteristics, which can be found in the Electronic Medicines Compendium (www.emc.vhn.net). (GPP)

5.4.7.6   As with oral antipsychotic therapy, people receiving depot preparations should be maintained under regular clinical review, particularly in relation to the risks and benefits of the drug regimen. (GPP)

5.4.8 Research recommendations

5.4.8.1   Further RCT-based cost-effectiveness studies are needed to establish the clinical and economic effectiveness of depot and similar preparations of both conventional and atypical antipsychotics, in particular their safety, efficacy, side-effect profile and impact upon quality of life.

5.5 Rapid tranquillisation

5.5.1 Introduction

Acute behavioural disturbances in the context of schizophrenia typically occur during periods of hospitalisation, but may arise at any time during the course of the illness, as part of an exacerbation. A person may be agitated, aggressive or violent towards others, as a result of psychotic symptoms (e.g. persecutory delusions, command hallucinations) or non-psychotic symptoms (e.g. high levels of anxiety). However, in the Royal College of Psychiatrists' guideline on the *Management of Imminent Violence* (1998), environmental factors, including overcrowding, lack of privacy, lack of activities and long waiting times to see staff, are identified as playing an important part in increasing the likelihood of aggression or violence. Also, social factors, such as poor communication between service users and staff, and weak clinical leadership, may contribute to feelings of frustration and tension among all parties. Dealing with these issues in advance may reduce the risk of violence and aggression (Royal College of Psychiatrists, 1998).

The initial response should be to provide structure, to reduce stimulation and to try to verbally reassure and calm the person (Osser & Sigadel, 2001). Staff need to be trained to anticipate possible violence and to de-escalate the situation at the earliest opportunity. Physical means of restraint or seclusion should be resorted to 'only after the failure of attempts to promote full participation in self-care'. In this context, the use of drugs to control disturbed behaviour (rapid tranquillisation) is often seen as a last resort, for use where appropriate psychological and behavioural approaches have failed or are inappropriate. However, service users who participated in discussion groups on this topic have expressed the view that when they behaved violently, their preference was for medication rather than seclusion or prolonged physical restraint (Royal College of Psychiatrists, 1998).

The aim of drug treatment in such circumstances is to calm the person and reduce the risk of violence and harm, rather than treat the underlying psychiatric condition. An optimal response would be a reduction in agitation or aggression without sedation, allowing the service user to participate in further assessment and treatment. Ideally, the drug should have a rapid onset of action and a low level of side-effects. Psychiatrists and the multi-disciplinary teams who use rapid tranquillisation should be trained in the assessment and management of service users specifically in this context: this should include assessing and managing the risks of drugs (benzodiazepines and antipsychotics), using and maintaining the techniques and equipment needed for cardiopulmonary resuscitation, and prescribing within therapeutic limits and using flumazenil (a benzodiazepine antagonist).

5.5.1.1 Current practice

In clinical practice in the UK, the most common choice of drug for rapid tranquillisation has been an antipsychotic such as haloperidol, chlorpromazine or droperidol, often in combination with a benzodiazepine such as diazepam or lorazepam (Pilowsky *et al*, 1992; Cunnane, 1994; Simpson & Anderson, 1996; Mannion *et al*, 1997). Zuclopenthixol acetate, a short-acting depot antipsychotic, has also been commonly used, although doubts as to its value have recently been raised (Fenton *et al*, 2002a). Previously published guidelines have generally recommended that drug treatment should be administered orally, if the person is willing to accept this (Atakan & Davies, 1987; Kerr & Taylor, 1997; Royal College of Psychiatrists, 1997). Liquid or rapidly dissolving preparations may be particularly useful.

However, current practice is not underpinned by a strong evidence base. There are relatively few controlled studies on which to base prescribing decisions. Further, in studies of drug treatment of acute behavioural disturbance, there may be some doubt about the generalisability of the patient samples, in that many of the individuals who require rapid tranquillisation would be too disturbed to give informed consent to participate. Placebo-controlled studies would be necessary to assess the overall advantage of treatment using the various drug regimens, but such studies are likely to be regarded as unethical given that rapid tranquillisation is usually indicated only after other non-pharmacological approaches have failed. In any event, a major concern in this situation is to minimise the risk of harm to the individual, the staff and others.

5.5.1.2 Safety considerations

The benefit of reducing the risk of harm to the individual or others must be balanced against the risk of adverse effects associated with such drug regimens. In a survey of around a hundred incidents of rapid tranquillisation, Pilowsky *et al* (1992) found few adverse events, although those reported were potentially serious cardiovascular and cardiorespiratory events. The cardiovascular effects of antipsychotics in such situations have become a source of growing concern. Osser & Sigadel (2001) recommend that chlorpromazine should be avoided because of its greater risk of hypotension. Droperidol, an antipsychotic widely used for rapid tranquillisation, was voluntarily withdrawn in 2001 because of reports of QT prolongation, serious ventricular arrhythmia and sudden death. A change in the rate-corrected QT interval (QT_c) on the ECG associated with an antipsychotic may be an indicator of cardiotoxicity. An increased risk of QT interval prolongation has been reported with several antipsychotic drugs (Royal College of Psychiatrists, 1997). In a naturalistic study in the UK (Reilly *et al*, 2000), a prolonged QT_c was associated with both thioridazine and droperidol. Partly on the basis that QT_c prolongation may be a marker of risk of arrhythmia, the use of thioridazine has been restricted in the UK since the end of 2000, and would not be appropriate for rapid tranquillisation.

Acute extrapyramidal side-effects, such as akathisia, parkinsonism and dystonia, are commonly observed with intramuscular conventional antipsychotic drugs. Dystonic reactions can be particularly severe and unpleasant (Royal College of Psychiatrists, 1997), and both akathisia and dystonia could exacerbate disturbed behaviour. If an antipsychotic is to be used alone in people at high risk of dystonia, such as men under 35 years old, prophylactic anti-Parkinsonian drug treatment should be considered (Osser & Sigadel, 2001).

Benzodiazepines, although considerably safer, can cause cognitive impairment, behavioural disinhibition, oversedation and, most seriously, respiratory depression with the administration of high doses (Mendelson, 1992). The benzodiazepine partial antagonist flumazenil can counter these effects, but it is not easy to give in an emergency by those inexperienced in its use: flumazenil has a shorter half-life than the majority of benzodiazepines, meaning that repeated doses may be required. It can also induce seizures in people who have been receiving regular benzodiazepines.

5.5.2 Definition and aim of rapid tranquillisation

Rapid tranquillisation means the use of drug treatments to achieve rapid, short-term behavioural control of extreme agitation, aggression and potentially violent behaviour that places individuals or those around them at risk of physical harm (Broadstock, 2001). The aim of rapid tranquillisation is to achieve sedation sufficient to minimise the risk posed to the individual or to others. The individual should be able to respond to spoken messages throughout the period of sedation (Royal College of Psychiatrists, 1998).

5.5.3 Studies considered for review

The review team conducted a new review of drugs licensed for use in the UK that may be used for rapid tranquillisation. The team utilised a review of the effectiveness and safety of drug treatment for urgent sedation in psychiatric emergencies (Broadstock, 2001), as well as the Cochrane Review of zuclopenthixol acetate (Fenton *et al*, 2000a), when searching for RCTs. There are few well-conducted, comparative trials in this field, examining a small range of drugs and clinical settings (BATTAGLIA 1997; BRIER 2002; DOREVITCH 1999; GARZA-TREVINO 1989; TUASON 1986; WRIGHT 2001). They do not allow for confident generalisation of the findings to the various clinical situations in which urgent sedation might be warranted. As the drug regimens tested in the trials rarely reported side-effects, it was also not possible to comment with confidence on this area. The studies reviewed also included IM olanzapine, which is currently not available in the UK, but as the studies showed promise and olanzapine is licensed for use in the UK, the results are described below.

5.5.4 Results

The limited data on intramuscular antipsychotics that are available in the UK suggest that:

- there is limited evidence that the combination of IM haloperidol (5 mg) and IM lorazepam (4 mg) produces a faster clinical response than IM haloperidol (5 mg) alone (no clinical response at 30 min: $n=45$, RR=0.38, 95% CI 0.18 to 0.80; NNT=3, 95% CI 2 to 7; no clinical response at 60 min: $n=45$, RR=0.07, 95% CI 0.00 to 1.13) (Ib)

- there is insufficient evidence to determine if there is a clinically significant difference between IM flunitrazepam (1 mg) and IM haloperidol (5 mg) in terms of response to treatment ($n=28$, RR=2.60; 95% CI 0.31 to 22.05). (Ib)

The use of atypical antipsychotics, with a lower liability to cause extrapyramidal side-effects, shows promise for rapid tranquillisation. There is limited evidence suggesting that IM olanzapine (10 mg) is equivalent to IM haloperidol (7.5 mg) in reducing agitation at 2 h and 24 h after the first injection:

- PANSS Excited Sub-scale change score at 2 h ($n=343$; WMD=−0.56, 95% CI −1.74 to 0.61) (Ib)

- Agitated Behaviour Scale change score at 2 h ($n=342$; WMD=−0.11, 95% CI −0.26 to 0.04) (Ib)

- BPRS total change score at 2 h ($n=85$; WMD=−2.80, 95% CI −5.63 to −0.03) (Ib)

- PANSS Excited Sub-scale change score at 24 h ($n=343$; WMD=−0.25, 95% CI −1.28 to 0.78) (Ib)

- Agitated Behaviour Scale change score at 24 h ($n=342$; WMD=−0.44, 95% CI −1.63 to 0.74) (Ib)

- BPRS total change score at 24 h ($n=86$; WMD=−1.70, 95% CI −4.92 to −1.52). (Ib)

There is limited evidence suggesting IM olanzapine (10 mg) has an equivalent or better side-effect profile than IM haloperidol (7.5 mg). For example:

- need for benzodiazepines ($n=343$, RR=0.95, 95% CI 0.58 to 1.58) (Ib)

- dystonia ($n=257$, RR=0.05, 95% CI 0.00 to 0.86; NNT=15, 95% CI 12 to 100) (Ib)

- EPS ($n=257$, RR=0.14, 95% CI 0.02 to 1.10) (Ib)

- received anticholinergic drugs ($n=257$, RR=0.22, 95% CI 0.09 to 0.52; NNT=7, 95% CI 5 to 13) (Ib)

- QT_c interval change score ($n=343$, WMD=−3.02 ms, 95% CI −8.08 to 2.05). (Ib)

5.5.5 Clinical summary

A combination of IM haloperidol and IM lorazepam may produce a faster response than IM haloperidol alone. It was not possible to identify any clinical significant difference between a benzodiazepine and an antipsychotic when they were compared for use as rapid tranquillisers. There was limited evidence to suggest that IM olanzapine might be as effective at managing behavioural agitation and have a better side-effect profile than IM haloperidol.

5.5.6 Health economic evidence

It has been hypothesised that the different modes of rapid tranquillisation might also differ in their cost-effectiveness.

The economic review identified four eligible studies, two of which were conducted in the UK (Hyde & Harrower-Wilson, 1996; Hyde *et al*, 1998). One analysis was a modelling study (Laurier *et al*, 1997), one study was based on a controlled trial with historical controls (Hyde *et al*, 1998) and two studies used case series data. None of the studies used clinical data from an RCT, and two studies reported results with a high risk of bias. Two studies calculated the cost of an average rapid tranquillisation episode without attempting to compare two or more different interventions (Ricard *et al*, 1989; Hyde & Harrower-Wilson, 1996).

The studies by Hyde & Harrower-Wilson (1996) and Laurier *et al* (1997) demonstrated that the major cost components of rapid tranquillisation are hospital stay and nursing time. Drug costs accounted for only approximately 0.5% of the total cost within a psychiatric intensive care unit (Hyde & Harrower-Wilson, 1996). The authors of these studies concluded that drugs with higher sedative and violence-preventive effects should be more cost-effective.

Two studies compared zuclopenthixol acetate with haloperidol IM (Laurier *et al*, 1997; Hyde *et al*, 1998). The study by Hyde *et al* reported that the total costs of using zuclopenthixol acetate for rapid tranquillisation were less than for haloperidol, while the clinical effectiveness of the two drugs was equivalent. The study by Laurier *et al* showed zuclopenthixol acetate to be both more costly and more effective.

5.5.6.1 Health economic conclusions

The quantity of the available evidence is poor, and it is difficult to draw any firm conclusion from it about the cost-effectiveness of zuclopenthixol acetate compared with haloperidol IM. However, the available evidence suggests that drug acquisition cost is an inferior cost driver in rapid tranquillisation, and drugs with higher violence-preventive effects are expected to be more cost-effective.

5.5.7 Clinical practice recommendations

The recommendations below are drawn from a consideration of the evidence reviewed by the GDG and from the section of the Royal College of Psychiatrists guideline on the management of imminent violence that related to rapid tranquillisation (Royal College of Psychiatrists, 1998). These recommendations are given at length, in consideration of the serious potential for harm.

5.5.7.1 Health professionals should identify and take steps to minimise the environmental and social factors that might increase the likelihood of violence and aggression during an episode, particularly during periods of hospitalisation. Factors to be routinely identified, monitored and corrected include: overcrowding; lack of privacy; lack of activities; long waiting times to see staff; poor communication between patients and staff; and weak clinical leadership. (C)

5.5.7.2 Staff who use rapid tranquillisation should be trained in the assessment and management of service users specifically in this context: this should include assessing and managing the risks of drugs (benzodiazepines and antipsychotics), using and maintaining the techniques and equipment needed for cardiopulmonary resuscitation, prescribing within therapeutic limits, and using flumazenil (benzodiazepine antagonist). (C)

Training for behavioural control and rapid tranquillisation

5.5.7.3 Staff need to be trained to anticipate possible violence and to 'de-escalate' the situation at the earliest opportunity, and physical means of restraint or seclusion should be resorted to 'only after the failure of attempts to promote full participation in self-care'. (C)

5.5.7.4 Training in the use and the dangers of rapid tranquillisation is as essential as training for de-escalation and restraint. Doctors and nurses should be as familiar with the properties of benzodiazepines as they are with those of antipsychotics. (C)

5.5.7.5 Specifically, health professionals should:

- be able to assess the risks associated with rapid tranquillisation, particularly when the person is highly aroused and may have been misusing drugs or alcohol, be dehydrated or possibly be physically ill
- understand the cardiorespiratory effects of the acute administration of these drugs and the need to titrate dosage to effect
- recognise the importance of nursing, in the recovery position, people who have received these drugs and also of monitoring pulse, blood pressure and respiration
- be familiar with, and trained in, the use of resuscitation equipment; this is essential, as an anaesthetist or experienced 'crash team' may not be available
- undertake annual retraining in resuscitation techniques
- understand the importance of maintaining an unobstructed airway. (C)

Principles of rapid tranquillisation

5.5.7.6 The psychiatrist and the multi-disciplinary team should, at the earliest opportunity, undertake a full assessment, including consideration of the medical and psychiatric differential diagnoses. (C)

5.5.7.7 Drugs for rapid tranquillisation, particularly in the context of restraint, must be used with caution because of the following risks:

- loss of consciousness instead of sedation
- oversedation with loss of alertness
- possible damage to the therapeutic partnership between service user and clinician
- specific issues in relation to diagnosis. (C)

5.5.7.8   Resuscitation equipment and drugs, including flumazenil, must be available and easily accessible where rapid tranquillisation is used. (C)

5.5.7.9   Because of the serious risk to life, service users who are heavily sedated or using drugs or alcohol should not be secluded. (C)

5.5.7.10 If a service user is secluded, the potential complications of rapid tranquillisation should be taken particularly seriously. (C)

5.5.7.11 Violent behaviour can be managed without the prescription of unusually high doses or of 'drug cocktails'. The minimum effective dose should be used. The BNF recommendations for the maximum advisory dose should be adhered to unless exceptional circumstances arise. (C)

5.5.7.12 Because of growing awareness that involuntary procedures produce traumatic reactions in recipients, following the use of rapid tranquillisation service users should be offered the opportunity to discuss their experiences and should be provided with a clear explanation of the decision to use urgent sedation. This should be documented in their notes. (GPP)

5.5.7.13 Service users should be given the opportunity to write their own account of the experience of rapid tranquillisation in their notes. (GPP)

Route of drug administration for rapid tranquillisation

5.5.7.14 Oral medication should be offered before parenteral medication. (C)

5.5.7.15 If parenteral treatment proves necessary, the intramuscular route is preferred to the intravenous one from a safety point of view. Intravenous administration should be used only in exceptional circumstances. (C)

5.5.7.16 Vital signs must be monitored after parenteral treatment is administered. Blood pressure, pulse, temperature and respiratory rate should be recorded at regular intervals (agreed by the multi-disciplinary team), until the service user becomes active again. If the service user appears to be or is asleep, more intensive monitoring is required. (C)

Pharmacological agents used in rapid tranquillisation

5.5.7.17 The intramuscular preparations recommended for use in rapid tranquillisation are lorazepam, haloperidol and olanzapine. Wherever possible, a single agent is preferred to a combination. (C)

5.5.7.18 When rapid tranquillisation is urgently needed, a combination of IM haloperidol and IM lorazepam should be considered. (C)

5.5.7.19 Intramuscular diazepam is not recommended for the pharmacological control of behavioural disturbances in people with schizophrenia. (C)

5.5.7.20 Intramuscular chlorpromazine is not recommended for the pharmacological control of behavioural disturbances in people with schizophrenia. (C)

5.5.7.21 When using IM haloperidol (or any other IM conventional antipsychotic) as a means of behavioural control, an anticholinergic agent should be given to reduce the risk of dystonia and other extrapyramidal side-effects. (C)

5.5.8 Research recommendations

5.5.8.1   Quantitative and qualitative research is required to investigate the usefulness, acceptability and safety of available drugs for urgent sedation (including atypical antipsychotics), in studies with adequately large samples, in settings that reflect current clinical practice, and with systematic manipulations of dosage and frequency of drug administration.

5.5.8.2   Quantitative and qualitative research is required to evaluate the role of non-pharmacological methods in behavioural control.

5.6 Treatment-resistant schizophrenia

5.6.1 Introduction

Although the introduction of antipsychotic medication provided the first specific treatment proved to be efficacious, a sizeable number of individuals receiving these drugs failed to respond adequately. Initially, higher doses of antipsychotic drugs were given on the grounds that some individuals might have lower sensitivities to dopamine-blocking agents, perhaps as a result of dopamine receptor abnormalities, or that different people might metabolise antipsychotics at different rates. An alternative explanation for 'treatment-resistant schizophrenia' (TRS) is that schizophrenia is a heterogeneous group of similar conditions with different pharmacological responses, a view finding some confirmation in the differential response of some people to antipsychotics with a different mode of action, such as clozapine.

Treatment-resistant schizophrenia is relatively common, in that between a fifth and a third of service users show a disappointing response to adequate trials of conventional antipsychotic drugs (Brenner et al, 1990; Lieberman et al, 1992; Conley & Buchanan, 1997). Even a small proportion of people experiencing their first episode of schizophrenia will fail to improve to a degree that allows an early discharge from hospital (May, 1968; MacMillan et al, 1986; Lieberman et al, 1989, 1992).

The treatment options for TRS include increasing the dosage of the antipsychotic drug, or decreasing it if poor treatment adherence is the result of adverse drug effects. Clinicians may switch to another class of conventional antipsychotic drugs, although the research evidence on the possible value of such a strategy is not consistent (Kinon et al, 1993; Shalev et al, 1993). However, the advent of clozapine in the 1970s led to suggestions that its unusual mode of action might be of value to people with TRS. Since then, other atypical antipsychotics have also been suggested as possible alternatives in the treatment of TRS.

An alternative strategy has been to try to potentiate antipsychotics by combining them, either with each other (see section 5.7), or with other classes of drugs. Possible adjuncts to antipsychotic treatment include mood stabiliser and anticonvulsant drugs such as lithium, carbamazepine, sodium valproate, lamotrigine, antidepressants and benzodiazepines (Barnes et al, 1996; Chong & Remington, 2000; Durson & Deakin, 2001). The use of adjunctive treatments to augment the action of antipsychotics is beyond the scope of this guideline. The review undertaken for the GDG was, therefore, restricted to the use of atypical antipsychotic drugs in the treatment of TRS.

Chakos *et al* (2001) conducted a meta-analysis of seven RCTs comparing conventional and atypical antipsychotics. These authors concluded that clozapine was superior to conventional antipsychotics in both efficacy (as measured by improvement in overall psychopathology) and safety (in terms of extrapyramidal side-effects). They noted that the magnitude of the clozapine treatment effect was not consistently robust. The efficacy data for other atypical antipsychotics in the treatment of refractory schizophrenia were considered inconclusive.

There is growing evidence that monitoring plasma clozapine concentration may be helpful in establishing the optimum dose of clozapine in terms of risk–benefit ratio (Freeman & Oyewumi, 1997; Perry *et al*, 1998; Gaertner *et al*, 2001; Llorca *et al*, 2002), particularly for service users showing a poor therapeutic response or experiencing significant side-effects despite appropriate dosage. Several studies have examined the relationship between plasma clozapine concentrations and response. Some investigators have suggested that a threshold plasma level of 350–420 ng/ml is associated with an increased probability of a good clinical response to the drug (Hasegawa *et al*, 1993; Miller *et al*, 1994; Miller, 1996; Bell *et al*, 1998). However, other authorities (Task Force of the World Psychiatric Association, 2002) have referred to the work of Van der Zwaag *et al* (1996), who argue that the optimal plasma clozapine levels lie between 200 ng/ml and 250 ng/ml and that some service users have even responded to levels below this range.

With regard to risperidone, a meta-analysis by Gilbody *et al* (2002) included the examination of five studies comparing risperidone and clozapine, largely among people with TRS. The authors concluded that while clozapine and risperidone seemed to be equally acceptable in the short term, as measured by numbers leaving the study early, for most other outcomes the data did not permit any statement about whether the two drugs were equally effective or whether one was actually superior.

5.6.2 Definition

The essence of treatment resistance in schizophrenia is the presence of poor psychosocial and community functioning, which persists despite trials of medication that have been adequate in terms of dose, duration and adherence. While treatment resistance is sometimes conceptualised in terms of enduring positive psychotic symptoms, other features of schizophrenia can contribute to poor psychosocial and community functioning, including negative symptoms, affective symptoms, drug side-effects, cognitive deficits and disturbed behaviour.

The definition of the term 'treatment-resistant schizophrenia' varies considerably in the studies covered in this review. Kane *et al* (1988) introduced criteria involving aspects of the clinical history, cross-sectional measures and prospective assessments. One trend has been a move away from the rigorous criteria of Kane *et al* (1988), to a wider-ranging definition of treatment resistance that allows the inclusion of a significant number of individuals who might otherwise be characterised as partial responders to treatment. For example, Bondolfi *et al* (1998) defined treatment resistance as a failure to respond to or intolerance of more than two different classes of antipsychotics in appropriate doses, for more than 4 weeks. Further, NICE stated that 'TRS is suggested by a lack of a satisfactory clinical improvement despite the sequential use of the recommended doses for 6 to 8 weeks of at least two antipsychotics at least one of which should be an atypical' (NICE, 2002). This reflects a broadening of the group of individuals who were viewed as clinically eligible for treatment with clozapine.

5.6.2.1   The first step in the clinical management of TRS is to establish that the disorder has failed to respond to adequate trials of conventional antipsychotic drugs in terms of dosage, duration and adherence. Other causes of non-response should be considered in the clinical assessment, such as comorbid substance misuse, the concurrent use of other prescribed medication and physical illness. (GPP)

5.6.3 Studies considered for review

The review of atypical antipsychotics for the NICE Technology Appraisal (NICE, 2002) was used by the GDG to evaluate the place of atypical antipsychotics in the management of TRS. The GDG review included 19 RCTs of head-to-head comparisons of antipsychotics (available in the UK) in service users with TRS. An additional 27 RCTs were excluded from the analysis because they failed to meet the GDG eligibility criteria. The total number of participants included was 2186. The studies included varied in the following ways:

- method (allocation, masking)
- dose (e.g. clozapine range 150–1000 mg/day)
- duration of treatment (range 4 weeks to 1 year)
- participants (age, mean duration of illness, diagnostic criteria used)
- site of treatment (not reported in the majority of studies; hospital)
- outcomes recorded.

5.6.4 Results

Of all the atypical antipsychotic drugs introduced, clozapine has the most convincing evidence for efficacy in those who are unresponsive to conventional antipsychotics according to relatively strict criteria, as used by Kane *et al* (1988).

There is strong evidence suggesting that, at the end of treatment, clozapine is superior to conventional antipsychotics after short-term treatment in terms of:

- improving mental state (BPRS score: $n=408$, WMD=−7.70, 95% CI −9.92 to −5.49) (Ia)
- symptom reduction after short-term treatment (not clinically improved: $n=349$, RR=0.71, 95% CI 0.64 to 0.79; NNT=4, 95% CI 3 to 5) (Ia)
- improving negative symptoms ($n=143$, WMD=−3.28, 95% CI −5.29 to −1.26). (Ia)

There is insufficient evidence to determine if there is a clinically significant difference between clozapine and conventional antipsychotics in the short term with regard to:

- relapse rates (not clinically improved: $n=375$, RR=1.04, 95% CI 0.61 to 1.78) (Ia)
- leaving the study early ($n=415$, RR=1.11, 95% CI 0.67 to 1.84). (Ia)

There is limited evidence suggesting that, at the end of treatment, clozapine is superior to conventional antipsychotics after longer-term treatment in terms of:

- symptom reduction (not clinically improved: $n=225$, RR=0.71, 95% CI 0.60 to 0.84; NNT=5, 95% CI 3 to 8) (Ib)
- leaving the study early ($n=225$, RR=0.52, 95% CI 0.39 to 0.69; NNT=4, 95% CI 3 to 6). (Ib)

There is no or insufficient evidence to suggest that, at the end of treatment, clozapine is superior to olanzapine for treatment of TRS in terms of:

- relapse in the short term ($n=36$, RR=0.28, 95% CI 0.04 to 2.16) or the medium term ($n=180$, RR=0.79, 95% CI 0.49 to 1.26) (Ib)
- symptom reduction in the short term (not clinically improved: $n=36$, RR=0.93, 95% CI 0.60 to 1.46) or in the medium term (not clinically improved: $n=180$, RR=1.16, 95% CI 0.84 to 1.61) (Ib)
- leaving the study early in the medium term ($n=180$, RR=1.03, 95% CI 0.72 to 1.46). (Ib)

There is no or insufficient evidence to suggest that, at the end of treatment, clozapine is superior to risperidone for treating TRS in terms of:

- relapse in the short term ($n=379$, RR=1.13, 95% CI 0.79 to 1.62) (Ia)
- symptom reduction in the short term (not clinically improved: $n=135$, RR=1.03, 95% CI 0.71 to 1.49) (Ia) or in the medium term (not clinically improved: $n=60$, RR=0.60, 95% CI 0.25 to 1.44) (Ib)
- leaving the study early in the short term ($n=467$, RR=1.01, 95% CI 0.74 to 1.38) (Ia) or in the medium term ($n=60$, RR=0.75, 95% CI 0.30 to 1.90). (Ib)

5.6.5 Clinical summary

Although there is convincing evidence to support the use of clozapine in TRS, principally from studies comparing clozapine with conventional antipsychotics, the evidence that any other atypical is similarly effective for this condition is inconclusive. However, in head-to-head comparisons of clozapine with both olanzapine and risperidone, the superior efficacy of clozapine for TRS has not been consistently demonstrated. Clozapine is the only antipsychotic with a licensed indication for TRS.

5.6.6 Health economic evidence

This guideline used the NICE Technology Appraisal of atypical antipsychotics (NICE, 2002) for an evaluation of the economic evidence regarding the cost-effectiveness of atypical antipsychotics in the treatment of TRS. Further searching uncovered some additional papers that had not been identified by the appraisal. Seven new studies were found to be eligible, while 11 further papers were unavailable. The results of the new studies were analysed and compared with those of the Technology Appraisal's literature review (see also section 5.2.6). Here we present conclusions regarding the use of atypicals in the treatment of TRS and chronic schizophrenia.

5.6.6.1 Health economic conclusions

The following conclusions are based upon, and extracted from, all available published evidence on the cost-effectiveness of atypical antipsychotics.

There is evidence that clozapine is more cost-effective than haloperidol or chlorpromazine in treatment-resistant schizophrenia.

There is evidence that risperidone is more cost-effective than haloperidol or chlorpromazine in chronic schizophrenia.

There is evidence that olanzapine is more cost-effective than haloperidol in chronic schizophrenia.

5.6.7 Clinical practice recommendations

5.6.7.1   The first step in the clinical management of treatment-resistant schizophrenia is to establish that therapy with antipsychotic drugs has been adequately tried in terms of dosage, duration and adherence. Other causes of non-response should be considered in the clinical assessment, such as comorbid substance misuse, poor treatment adherence, the concurrent use of other prescribed medicines, and physical illness. (GPP)

5.6.7.2   If the symptoms of schizophrenia are unresponsive to conventional antipsychotics, the prescribing clinician and service user may wish to consider an atypical antipsychotic in advance of a diagnosis of treatment-resistant schizophrenia and a trial of clozapine. In such cases, olanzapine or risperidone may be worth considering. Service users should be informed that while these drugs may possibly be beneficial, the evidence for improvement in this situation is more limited than for clozapine. (C)

5.6.7.3   In individuals with evidence of TRS, clozapine should be introduced at the earliest opportunity. Treatment resistance is suggested by a lack of satisfactory clinical improvement, despite the sequential use of the recommended doses for 6–8 weeks of at least two antipsychotics, at least one of which should be an atypical. (NICE 2002)

5.6.8 Research recommendations

5.6.8.1   Head-to-head comparative trials of clozapine against other atypical antipsychotics and between other atypicals in TRS are required, including evaluation of their impact upon quality of life.

5.6.8.2   Further controlled studies are required to test claims that clozapine is particularly effective in reducing hostility and violence, and the inconsistent evidence for a reduction in suicide rates in people with schizophrenia.

5.7 Combining antipsychotic drugs

5.7.1 Introduction

In clinical practice, individuals may receive a combination of antipsychotic drugs for a variety of reasons. For example, during a gradual changeover from one antipsychotic drug to another, both drugs may be administered for a while. Further, individuals receiving depot treatment who experience an exacerbation of their illness may be prescribed an oral antipsychotic, as a short-term addition, to stabilise their illness. However, perhaps the most common reason for combining antipsychotics is the lack of a satisfactory response to a single antipsychotic.

The mechanisms underlying any increase in therapeutic effect with combined antipsychotics have not been systematically studied (McCarthy & Terkelsen, 1995). However, in relation to the strategy of adding a conventional antipsychotic to clozapine, Chong & Remington (2000) suggested that any pharmacodynamic synergy might be related to an increased level of D2 dopamine receptor occupancy, above a threshold level. However, such an increase might be expected to be associated with an increased risk of extrapyramidal side-effects. An alteration of the interaction between serotonin (5-hydroxytryptamine) and D2 activity has also been suggested as a relevant mechanism (Shiloh et al, 1997). Further, pharmacokinetic interactions might play a part, although there is no consistent evidence that adding a conventional antipsychotic leads to increased clozapine plasma levels (Shiloh et al, 1997; Procopio, 1998).

A multi-centre audit of the prescription of antipsychotic drugs for in-patients in 47 mental health services in the UK (Harrington et al, 2002), involving over 3000 in-patients, found that nearly half were receiving more than one antipsychotic drug. In the majority of cases the reason given for this polypharmacy was that a single antipsychotic had not been effective. Similarly, prescription surveys in the UK by Taylor et al (2000, 2002) found that conventional and atypical antipsychotics are commonly co-prescribed, usually to tackle persistent symptoms resistant to treatment with one agent alone. In the majority of cases an atypical antipsychotic was prescribed first and a conventional drug added later.

The addition of a conventional antipsychotic to clozapine treatment would seem to be a relatively common strategy. There have been reports that conventional antipsychotics are used in around a third of those receiving clozapine in some European countries (Leppig et al, 1989; Peacock & Gerlach, 1994; McCarthy & Terkelsen, 1995).

5.7.2 Definition

For the purposes of this guideline, combined therapy refers to the concurrent administration of more than one antipsychotic drug. More recent trials (e.g. Shiloh et al, 1997) have explicitly combined antipsychotics that are believed to differ in their receptor and side-effect profiles.

5.7.3 Studies considered for review

No systematic review was identified following extensive searching of the published literature. However, one RCT of the addition of sulpiride to clozapine (Shiloh et al, 1997) was located. The GDG therefore elected to pursue studies with lower levels of evidence.

Yuzda (2000) reviewed the evidence for efficacy with combined antipsychotics. This author identified two open prospective trials (Henderson & Goff, 1996; Mowerman & Siris, 1996), one retrospective review (Friedman et al, 1997), four anecdotal reports (McCarthy & Terkelsen, 1995; Gupta et al, 1998; Takhar, 1999; Waring et al, 1999) and one RCT of sulpiride added to clozapine (Shiloh et al, 1997).

The evidence for the efficacy of combining another antipsychotic with clozapine in individuals having only a partial response to clozapine monotherapy is limited to case reports, case series and small studies. Adjunctive antipsychotics tested include pimozide (Friedman *et al*, 1997), sulpiride (Stubbs *et al*, 2000), olanzapine (Gupta *et al*, 1998), loxapine (Mowerman & Siris, 1996) and risperidone (Koreen *et al*, 1995; McCarthy & Terkelsen, 1995; Tyson *et al*, 1995; Chong *et al*, 1996; Henderson & Goff, 1996; Morera *et al*, 1999; Raskin *et al*, 2000; Adesanya & Pantelis, 2001).

Chong & Remington (2000) specifically reviewed adjunctive antipsychotics with clozapine. They considered that a limitation common to all the published studies was the lack of information regarding the previous exposure of study participants to the adjunctive antipsychotic. They argued that without such data, it remained uncertain whether any benefit observed could be attributed to the combination or simply to the second antipsychotic alone. Some authors have raised the issue of the safety of such combinations, and reported the occurrence of side-effects (Koreen *et al*, 1995; Godlesky & Sernyak, 1996; Raskin *et al*, 2000; Mujica & Weiden, 2001).

5.7.4 Results

The efficacy of combining two or more conventional antipsychotics, or two or more atypical antipsychotics has not been established. (IV)

There is limited evidence that, at the end of treatment, adding a conventional antipsychotic to clozapine may produce benefits compared to clozapine alone in terms of:

- mental state (BPRS change score: $n=28$, WMD$=-6.40$, 95% CI -11.77 to -1.03) (Ib)
- symptom reduction (not clinically improved, as measured by a 20% reduction on the BPRS: $n=28$, RR$=0.55$, 95% CI 0.32 to 0.92; NNT$=3$, 95% CI 2 to 8). (Ib)

Combining one antipsychotic with another may increase the risk of adverse effects and pharmacokinetic interactions. (IV)

Combined antipsychotic therapy is a factor influencing the probability of receiving a high dose. (IV)

5.7.5 Summary

There is no convincing evidence to support the routine use of combined antipsychotics, and such use may increase the likelihood of adverse events and high doses of drugs. There is some limited evidence to support the use of combined antipsychotics for people with TRS.

5.7.6 Clinical practice recommendations

5.7.6.1 Antipsychotic drugs, whether atypical or conventional, should not be prescribed concurrently, except for short periods to cover changeover. (C)

5.7.6.2 The addition of a second antipsychotic drug to clozapine may, however, be considered for people with treatment-resistant schizophrenia for whom clozapine alone has proved insufficiently effective. (C)

5.7.7 Research recommendations

5.7.7.1   Adequately powered RCTs reporting all relevant outcomes, including quality of life, are required to test the clinical efficacy and acceptability of combined antipsychotic therapy (including clozapine) in service users for whom monotherapy has proved unsatisfactory.

6 Psychological interventions in the treatment and management of schizophrenia

6.1 Introduction

Although pharmacological interventions have been the mainstay of treatment since their introduction in the 1950s, the limited response of some people to antipsychotic treatments, the high incidence of side-effects and the poor adherence to treatment have necessitated a more broadly based approach combining different treatment options, tailored to the needs of individual service users and their families. Such options include psychological and psychosocial interventions. This chapter addresses the evidence base for the application of psychological and psychosocial treatments in combination with antipsychotic medication for individuals, groups and families.

6.1.1 Principles of psychological treatment

6.1.1.1 The stress-vulnerability model

Although the rationales for medical, psychological and psychosocial interventions are derived from a variety of different biological, psychological and social theories, the development of the stress-vulnerability model (Zubin & Spring, 1977; Nuechterlein, 1987) has facilitated the theoretical and practical integration of disparate treatment approaches (see Chapter 2). In this model, pharmacological treatments protect a vulnerable individual and reduce the likelihood of relapse, as well as reducing the severity and/or length of the episode. Psychological interventions may be used similarly, and in addition may have a longer-term effect upon an individual's vulnerability.

6.1.1.2 Engagement

A prerequisite for any psychological or other treatment is the effective engagement of the service user in a positive therapeutic or treatment alliance (Roth *et al*, 1996). Engaging people effectively during an acute schizophrenic illness is often difficult and demands considerable flexibility in the approach and pace of therapeutic working. Moreover, once engaged in a positive therapeutic alliance, it is equally necessary to maintain this relationship, often over long periods, with the added problem that such an alliance may wax and wane, especially in the event of service users becoming subject to compulsory treatment under the Mental Health Act. Special challenges in the treatment of schizophrenia include social withdrawal, cognitive and information-processing problems, developing a shared view with the service user about the nature of the illness, and the impact of stigma and social exclusion.

The use of psychological and psychosocial interventions in the treatment of a person with schizophrenia is intended to decrease the person's vulnerability, reduce the impact of stressful events and situations, improve the quality of life, enhance treatment adherence, decrease distress and disability, minimise symptoms, reduce risk and improve communication and coping skills. Research into psychological interventions needs to address this range of outcomes as far as possible.

6.1.2 Therapeutic approaches identified

Contemporary approaches to the psychological treatment of schizophrenia included for review in this guideline were identified by the Guideline Development Group (GDG) to include the following:

- cognitive–behavioural therapy
- cognitive remediation
- counselling and supportive psychotherapy
- family interventions
- psychoanalysis and psychoanalytic/psychodynamic psychotherapy
- psychoeducation
- social skills training.

6.1.3 Results presented

The following sections present data for the core outcomes of suicide, relapse, symptom reduction, and remaining in treatment, for all interventions evaluated (if available). If the evidence review suggested that an intervention had no clinically significant effect on the core outcomes, no other data are shown. If the evidence review suggested that an intervention had a clinically significant effect of value in the treatment of schizophrenia, additional data are given to allow a more complete evaluation of the treatment effects.

6.1.4 Clinical questions for psychological interventions

The primary objective in identifying clinical questions was to ascertain whether the psychological intervention under consideration had any positive impact upon the broad range of health outcomes in schizophrenia. The clinical questions developed by the GDG for psychological interventions are as follows.

(a) What treatments are most likely to achieve improvements in the identified outcomes?

(b) Does the specified treatment produce benefits over and above other psychological treatments?

(c) Are the identified treatments more acceptable (greater satisfaction, lower number of people leaving the study early) than comparator treatments?

(d) What are the effective service settings in which to provide treatment?

(e) What should the duration of the specified treatment be?

(f) Does the intervention reduce the risk of self-harm/suicide?

(g) What are the most effective formats for the treatment?

6.2 Cognitive–behavioural therapy

6.2.1 Introduction

Cognitive–behavioural therapy (CBT) was originally developed in the 1970s for the treatment of depression (Beck, 1976), and has since been applied to many other clinical conditions. Cognitive–behavioural therapy for psychotic disorders is a later development, informed by new cognitive psychological models of positive psychotic symptoms (Slade & Bentall, 1988; Frith, 1992; Garety & Hemsley, 1994). Its initial focus was accordingly on work with people with persistent delusions and hallucinations. During the 1990s its use was extended to therapeutic work with a wider range of service users and addressing outcomes other than symptom reduction (Garety *et al*, 2000).

In the treatment and management of schizophrenia, the wide variety of applications of CBT have all generally attempted to modify psychotic experiences and symptoms, or their effects upon a person's thoughts, feelings and behaviour. As with other psychological interventions, CBT depends upon the effective development of a positive therapeutic alliance (Roth *et al*, 1996).

6.2.2 Definition

The definition used by the GDG was drawn from a systematic review by Pilling *et al* (2002*a*), in which CBT was defined as a discrete psychological intervention that:

- encourages recipients to establish links between their thoughts, feelings or actions with respect to the current or past symptoms
- allows recipients to re-evaluate their perceptions, beliefs or reasoning related to the target symptoms
- involves at least *one* of the following: (a) monitoring of recipients' own thoughts, feelings or behaviour with respect to the symptom; (b) promotion of alternative ways of coping with the target symptom; (c) reduction of stress.

6.2.3 Studies considered for review

The systematic review selected for consideration by the GDG (Pilling *et al*, 2002*a*) included eight randomised controlled trials (RCTs), one of which (Carpenter, 1987) was excluded because it failed to meet the definition set by the GDG. In addition, a further six recent RCTs (LEVINE 1998; HADDOCK 1999; BRADSHAW 2000; TURKINGTON 2000, 2002; LEWIS 2002) that met the inclusion criteria were incorporated in the evidence review. Additional follow-up data for one of the original RCTs (DRURY 1996) were also incorporated. Thus, a total of 13 RCTs were included in the current review, providing data on 1297 participants. All participants in these trials were also receiving antipsychotic drugs, and most often CBT was targeted at individuals with long-standing or treatment-resistant psychosis. Control groups received 'standard care', recreational activities, befriending or supportive counselling. Ten studies were conducted in the UK, two in the USA, and one in Israel.

Variation between studies in the precise method or focus of CBT was inevitable as this approach is of necessity flexible, in order to fit the particular individual's needs and circumstances. Studies also varied in terms of:

- method (allocation, masking)
- duration and frequency of sessions
- duration of treatment programme
- participants (age, mean duration of illness, diagnostic criteria used)
- site of treatment (in-patient, out-patient, day patient settings)
- comparator treatment (standard care, other active treatments)
- outcomes recorded
- length of follow-up (up to 5 years).

It is important to note that the CBT studies included in the review employed trained therapists with regular supervision in which adherence to therapy manuals was monitored, with one exception (TURKINGTON 2002) in which community psychiatric nurses were given a brief 10-day training programme.

6.2.4 Results

6.2.4.1 Effect of CBT on suicide and relapse rates

Only three of the 13 RCTs in this review reported on suicide, and although two suicides were reported in the control groups and none in those undergoing CBT, the evidence is insufficient to draw conclusions.

There is insufficient evidence to determine whether CBT improves relapse rates:
- when compared with 'standard care' during treatment (n=121, RR=0.88, 95% CI 0.46 to 1.66) (Ib)
- when compared with 'standard care' at 12 months post-treatment follow-up (n=61, RR=1.51, 95% CI 0.79 to 2.87) (Ib)
- when compared with other psychological treatments at 1–2 years post-treatment follow-up (n=154, RR=0.82, 95% CI 0.60 to 1.13). (Ia)

However, there is stronger evidence that treatment programmes of longer duration (>3 months) reduce relapse rates compared with all other interventions (n=177, RR=0.72, 95% CI 0.52 to 0.99; NNT=7, 95% CI 4 to 100). (Ia)

6.2.4.2 Effects of CBT upon symptoms

Cognitive–behavioural therapy reduces symptoms, at the end of treatment and at 9–12 months' follow-up, when compared with 'standard care' or other interventions.

There is limited evidence that CBT reduces symptoms, when compared with standard care, at the end of treatment (no important improvement as measured by a 40% reduction in BPRS total score/50% reduction in BPRS positive symptoms: n=121, RR=0.78, 95% CI 0.66 to 0.92; NNT=5, 95% CI 4 to 13). (Ib)

There is strong evidence that CBT improves mental state, when compared with standard care, at the end of treatment (PANSS/BPRS/CPRS total end-point scores: n=580, SMD=–0.21, 95% CI –0.38 to –0.04). (Ia)

There is limited evidence that CBT reduces symptoms, when compared with other psychological interventions, at the end of treatment (no important improvement as measured by a 50% reduction in BPRS positive symptoms or 'clinical recovery': n=121, RR=0.76, 95% CI 0.62 to 0.93; NNT=5, 95% CI 3 to 15). (Ib)

There is limited evidence that CBT reduces symptoms, when compared with standard care, at 9–12 months post-treatment follow-up (no important improvement as measured by a 20% reduction in BPRS total score/20% reduction in BPRS positive symptoms: n=121, RR=0.68, 95% CI 0.52 to 0.88). (Ib)

There is limited evidence that CBT reduces symptoms, when compared with other interventions, at 9–12 months post-treatment follow-up (no improvement as measured by a 50% reduction in CPRS score/50% reduction in BPRS positive symptoms: n=149, RR=0.79, 95% CI 0.63 to 1.00). (Ib)

6.2.4.3 Other effects of CBT

There is limited evidence suggesting that CBT specifically focused on adherence to drug treatment does improve adherence. Cognitive–behavioural therapy also appears to improve insight compared with standard care and other treatments at the end of treatment. Improvements in insight were still significant in one study 5 years after treatment. This therapy added to a day-treatment programme may also improve social functioning, when compared with this 'non-standard care' alone.

There is limited evidence that CBT, when compared with all other comparator treatments, increases the likelihood of:

- adherence to drug treatment, compared with 'non-specific counselling', measured by the Drug Attitudes Inventory (at end of treatment: n=74, WMD=−6.30, 95% CI −9.67 to −2.93; at 12 months post-treatment follow-up: n=44, WMD=−4.90, 95% CI −9.38 to −0.42) (Ib)
- improvements in insight, compared with other treatments, at end of treatment (Expanded Schedule for Assessment of Insight: n=74, WMD= −22.40, 95% CI −35.12 to −9.68) (Ib)
- improvements in insight, compared with other treatments, at 12 months post-treatment follow-up (Expanded Schedule for Assessment of Insight: n=50, WMD= −20.80, 95% CI −39.22 to −2.38) (Ib)
- improvements in insight, compared with other treatments, at 5 years post-treatment follow-up (self-report Insight Scale: n=31, WMD=−1.18, 95% CI −3.21 to −0.39) (Ib)
- improvements in social functioning, compared with 'non-standard care,' at end of treatment (Role Functioning Scale: n=15, WMD=−4.85, 95% CI −7.31 to −2.39). (Ib)

There is strong evidence that CBT increases the likelihood of:

- improvements in insight, compared with standard care, at end of treatment (Insight Rating Scale: n=422, WMD=−1.33, 95% CI −1.95 to −0.71). (Ia)

6.2.4.4 Acceptability of treatment with CBT

Cognitive–behavioural therapy generally appears to be no more or less acceptable to service users than 'standard care', although there is some suggestion that CBT may be more acceptable than standard care when used in first episodes of psychosis.

Based on the number of people leaving the study early, there is little evidence to suggest that CBT is more acceptable to service users than standard care at end of treatment (n=543, random effects RR=0.93, 95% CI 0.32 to 2.71) (Ia) or at post-treatment follow-up (n=264, random effects RR=1.37, 95% CI 0.18 to 10.38). (Ia)

When CBT is used to treat a first episode of psychosis, there is limited evidence suggesting CBT is more acceptable than standard care (leaving the study early by 5 weeks follow-up: *n*=203, RR=0.55, 95% CI 0.36 to 0.85; NNT=7, 95% CI 4 to 25). (Ib)

6.2.4.5 Use of CBT in first episodes of psychosis

At present, evidence for the use of CBT of short duration in the acute phase of a first episode of psychosis is either limited or insufficient to come to any firm conclusion.

There is limited evidence, from two trials both using CBT of short duration in the acute phase, suggesting that there is no clinically significant difference between CBT and supportive counselling on continuous measures of mental state (BPRS/PANSS end-point scores at 2–5 weeks: *n*=134, SMD=0.11, 95% CI –0.23 to 0.45; PANSS end-point scores at 1–5 weeks follow-up: *n*=149, SMD=0.10, 95% CI –0.22 to 0.42). (Ib)

There is insufficient evidence from one small trial using CBT of short duration in the acute phase to determine if there is a clinically significant difference between CBT and supportive counselling on relapse rate (*n*=21, RR=0.69, 95% CI 0.34 to 1.41). (Ib)

There is insufficient evidence to determine whether CBT used in the acute phase is more acceptable than supportive counselling as measured by participants leaving the study early (end of treatment: *n*=21, RR=3.27, 95% CI 0.15 to 72.4; follow-up: *n*=207, RR=0.69, 95% CI 0.44 to 1.08). (Ib)

6.2.4.6 When and how to provide CBT

Within the systematic review and meta-analysis, data were extracted to examine when and how to provide CBT. The review found some evidence that CBT (compared with the other interventions, tested at post-treatment follow-up) produces a stronger and more consistent effect in service users with persisting symptoms than in those with acute symptoms, and appears to have greater efficacy when the duration of treatment is longer and/or the number of sessions is greater. This adds weight to the finding above that CBT given for longer than 3 months significantly decreases the likelihood of relapse.

In service users with persisting symptoms:
- there is limited evidence that CBT reduces symptoms at 9 months follow-up (no important improvement as measured by a 20% reduction in BPRS: *n*=60, RR=0.53, 95% CI 0.35 to 0.81; NNT=3, 95% CI 2 to 6) (Ib)
- there is strong evidence that CBT improves mental state at post-treatment follow-up (BPRS/CPRS: *n*=182, SMD=–0.56, 95% CI –0.85 to –0.26). (Ia)

In service users with acute symptoms:
- there is limited evidence that CBT reduces symptoms compared with other interventions (no clinical recovery by 6 months, BPRS: *n*=62, RR=0.74, 95% CI 0.56 to 0.97; NNT=5, 95% CI 3 to 25) (Ib)
- there is limited evidence to suggest that CBT does not improve mental state compared with other interventions (at end of treatment, BPRS/PANSS: *n*=129, SMD=–0.01, 95% CI –0.35 to 0.3; at post-treatment follow-up, PANSS: *n*=138, SMD=–0.14, 95% CI –0.48 to 0.19). (Ib)

There is some limited evidence suggesting that the duration and/or number of CBT sessions may influence treatment efficacy:

- there is limited evidence that CBT of more than 6 months' duration and including more than 10 sessions leads to improved mental state compared with the other interventions tested (BPRS/CPRS end-point score at post-treatment follow-up: $n=137$, SMD$=-0.59$, 95% CI -0.93 to -0.25) (Ib)

- there is insufficient evidence to suggest that CBT comprising fewer than 10 sessions or of less than 3 months' duration improves mental state compared with the other interventions tested (BPRS/PANSS end-point score: $n=195$, SMD$=-0.26$, 95% CI -0.55 to 0.03) (Ib)

- there is strong evidence to suggest that, in the treatment of people with schizophrenia, CBT comprising fewer than 10 sessions or of less than 3 months' duration produces a modest improvement in depressive symptoms compared with treatment as usual (Montgomery & Åsberg Depression Rating Scale: $n=422$, WMD$=-1.19$, 95% CI -1.89 to -0.49), but does not improve psychotic symptoms (Schizophrenia Change Scale: $n=422$, SMD$=0.12$, 95% CI -0.32 to 0.08). (Ia)

6.2.5 Clinical summary

Overall, there is good evidence that cognitive–behavioural therapy reduces symptoms in people with schizophrenia at up to 1 year of follow-up when compared with 'standard care' and other treatments. The evidence is stronger when CBT is used for the treatment of persisting psychotic symptoms rather than for acute symptoms. The evidence for the use of CBT in the acute phase of a first episode of schizophrenia is unclear. This therapy can also improve insight and adherence to drug treatment, and may have a positive effect upon social functioning. The benefits of CBT are most marked when treatment is continued for more than 6 months and involves more than ten treatment sessions. Shorter-term treatment with CBT may produce modest improvements in depressive symptoms but is unlikely to have an impact upon psychotic symptoms. Moreover, when CBT is continued for longer than 3 months, there is stronger evidence that relapse rates are reduced.

6.2.6 Health economic evidence

Proponents of CBT as a psychological intervention for the treatment of schizophrenia have argued that this therapeutic approach has the potential to improve adherence to drug treatment, and thereby reduce the probability of relapse and further hospitalisation. In this regard, it has been hypothesised that CBT might produce savings in health care costs, which could offset the direct intervention costs of the therapy. Moreover, improved social functioning could lead to broader economic benefits concerning lost productivity, housing or legal costs.

The economic review identified two eligible studies, both based on RCTs measuring the long-term effects of CBT in the UK. Both studies compared costs and outcomes in the form of cost–consequence analyses (Healey et al, 1998; Kuipers et al, 1998). Both studies reported results with a low risk of bias. However, the two studies suffer from low study power and a lack of sensitivity analyses. They adapted broader cost perspectives, with Healey et al including social care and legal costs, and Kuipers et al measuring accommodation costs.

The results of the two studies showed that CBT is likely to be more cost-effective than 'non-specific counselling' (Healey et al, 1998) or 'standard care' (Kuipers et al, 1998). Both concluded that CBT is not a costly intervention. When providing CBT weekly or fortnightly, its mean cost per month was estimated to be £123 (s.d. 71) in 1996 (Kuipers *et al*, 1998). However, this estimation does not include capital and overhead costs, or possible implementation costs.

The quantity of the available economic evidence is poor. Cognitive–behavioural therapy is estimated to be a relatively inexpensive intervention. The available evidence suggests that CBT may be more cost-effective than 'standard care' or 'non-directive counselling'.

6.2.7 Clinical practice recommendations

6.2.7.1   Cognitive–behavioural therapy should be available as a treatment option for people with schizophrenia. (A)

6.2.7.2   In particular, CBT should be offered to people with schizophrenia who are experiencing persisting psychotic symptoms. (A)

6.2.7.3   Cognitive–behavioural therapy should be considered as a treatment option to assist in the development of insight. (B)

6.2.7.4   Cognitive–behavioural therapy may be considered as a treatment option in the management of poor treatment adherence. (C)

6.2.7.5   Longer treatments with CBT are significantly more effective than shorter ones, which may improve depressive symptoms but are unlikely to improve psychotic symptoms. An adequate course of CBT to generate improvements in psychotic symptoms in these circumstances should be of more than 6 months' duration and include more than ten planned sessions. (B)

6.2.8 Research recommendations

6.2.8.1   Adequately powered RCTs reporting all relevant clinical outcomes, including quality of life, are needed to evaluate further the use of cognitive–behavioural therapy in people experiencing a first episode of schizophrenia and in people at risk of relapse.

6.2.8.2   Cognitive–behavioural therapy is a relatively newly developed treatment option in the management of schizophrenia. Further research into its use and effects in the treatment of people with schizophrenia is needed to clarify its different roles and potential value in this context. Future studies should include reports on quality of life, and any adverse outcomes, including self-harm and death.

6.3 Cognitive remediation

6.3.1 Introduction

The presence of cognitive deficits in a proportion of people with schizophrenia has been recognised since the term was first coined (Bleuler, 1911). The precise cause of these deficits (such as physical brain disorder, deficit in cognitive information processing abilities or cognitive impact of the illness) remains contentious, whereas progress on characterising the cognitive problems that arise in schizophrenia has been substantial. Specific deficits identified include memory problems (Brenner, 1986), attention deficits (Oltmanns & Neale, 1975) and problems in executive functions (Weinberger *et al*, 1988).

Despite the success of cognitive rehabilitation and remediation in people with neurological disorders, the use of comparable methods in the treatment of schizophrenia is relatively new, and there is still uncertainty as to which techniques should be used and whether the outcomes hold any promise (Wykes & van der Gaag, 2001). The major methods used to date concentrate on repeating laboratory-based cognitive tests (Bellack *et al*, 1994) or repeated practice of procedures specifically designed to address a particular cognitive deficit (Wykes *et al*, 1999). The theory behind this approach asserts that the cognitive deficits contribute to a person's vulnerability to schizophrenia (either directly or through increasing the person's susceptibility to stress), and therefore correcting these deficits should, at least in theory, render a person less vulnerable.

Early studies reported some success, at least in improving performance on specific cognitive tests (Hermanutz & Gestrich, 1987; Heim *et al*, 1989). However, whether the improvements would generalise to day-to-day tasks that use the same cognitive function has been questioned (Spring & Ravdin, 1992). Attempts to integrate cognitive remediation with other psychosocial interventions have been claimed to have had some success, but it is unclear whether these successes are attributable to specific cognitive remediation techniques (Brenner *et al*, 1990).

6.3.2 Definition

For this guideline, cognitive remediation was defined as a programme focused upon improving specified cognitive functions, using procedures implemented with the intention of bringing about an improvement in the level of the specified cognitive function.

6.3.3 Studies considered for review

The GDG used the review by Pilling *et al* (2002*b*) incorporating five studies (BENEDICT 1994; TOMPKINS 1995; MEDALIA 1998, 2000; WYKES 1999) consistent with the criteria established by the GDG. In addition, further follow-up data from one of these studies (Wykes, 1999), as well as data from two new RCTs on cognitive remediation (BELLACK 2001; HADAS-LIDOR 2001) were incorporated. The GDG therefore considered seven RCTs, providing data on 295 study participants.

The comparison group in all but two studies was matched with the experimental group and differed only in that the former group did not receive cognitive remediation. The exceptions to this were the studies by HADAS-LIDOR 2000 and WYKES 1999, who used occupational therapy as the comparison condition. All studies excluded patients with history or evidence of brain injury.

Studies included varied in the following ways:
- number of treatment sessions (1 to 150)
- duration of treatment sessions (20 min to 1 h)
- frequency of treatment sessions (up to 3 times per week)
- duration of treatment programme (up to 1 year)

- site of treatment (in-patient, out-patient, day patient, community clinic)
- precise type of cognitive remediation
- country in which the study was conducted (USA 5, UK 1, Israel 1)
- outcomes recorded.

6.3.4 Results

The review found no consistent evidence to suggest that cognitive remediation improves outcomes in the targeted cognitive functions in people with schizophrenia, or in a range of other outcomes, such as symptom reduction. Individual studies did show specific improvements on some tasks, while showing no improvements on a range of other tasks. No evidence was available for suicide or relapse rates, or for the review team to discern the effects of duration or format for cognitive remediation.

There is insufficient evidence to determine if, at the end of treatment, cognitive remediation improves mental state (BPRS: $n=84$, WMD=−0.99, 95% CI −2.96 to 0.98; Present State Examination: $n=30$, WMD=−8.93, 95% CI −18.28 to 0.42). (Ib)

There is limited evidence to suggest that, at the end of treatment, people with schizophrenia receiving cognitive remediation, when compared with controls, show improvements in visual memory ($n=82$, SMD=−0.82, 95% CI −1.28 to −0.37) (Ib), improvements in verbal memory ($n=151$, SMD=−0.47, 95% CI −0.79 to −0.14) (Ia) and are more likely to live independently ($n=72$, RR=0.74, 95% CI 0.56 to 0.98; NNT=5, 95% CI 3 to 34). (Ib)

There is limited evidence to suggest that, at the end of treatment, people with schizophrenia receiving cognitive remediation, when compared with controls, show improvements in non-verbal reasoning ($n=58$, WMD=−8.93, 95% CI −13.67 to −4.19). (Ib)

There is insufficient evidence to determine if cognitive remediation is more acceptable than the comparator treatment, at the end of treatment (leaving the study early: $n=229$, RR=1.14, 95% CI 0.58 to 2.28). (Ia)

6.3.5 Summary

The review found no consistent evidence that cognitive remediation is effective in improving outcomes for people with schizophrenia, either in terms of specially targeted cognitive functions, or in terms of core outcomes such as symptom reduction.

6.3.6 Clinical practice recommendation

6.3.6.1 There is insufficient evidence to recommend the use of cognitive remediation in the routine treatment of people with schizophrenia. (B)

6.4 Counselling and supportive psychotherapy

6.4.1 Introduction

The different types of psychotherapy in the treatment and management of schizophrenia include psychoanalytic and psychodynamic approaches, cognitive–behavioural and behavioural approaches, family interventions, and various forms of education and training, usually in the context of a supportive therapeutic environment. These various interventions are based on different theoretical models and different specific technical innovations, while sharing general factors such as the added time spent talking, the focus upon the individual, the supportive and caring nature of the relationship between therapist and patient, and the potentially enhanced engagement of the service user in the broader therapeutic treatment programme.

These common factors are necessary for the development of a positive treatment alliance and are a prerequisite for any specific psychological intervention to stand a chance of success (Roth *et al*, 1996). Many of these factors are also part of high-quality 'standard care', as well as forming the key elements of counselling and supportive psychotherapy, and may, in themselves, be therapeutic. We therefore undertook a search for RCTs evaluating the effectiveness of counselling/supportive psychotherapy in the treatment of schizophrenia.

6.4.2 Definition

For the purposes of this systematic review, the GDG defined counselling and supportive psychotherapy as a discrete psychological intervention in which:

- the intervention is facilitative, non-directive and/or relationship-focused, with the content of sessions largely determined by the service user
- the intervention does not fulfil the criteria for any other psychological intervention.

'Standard care' was defined as the normal level of psychiatric care provided in the area where the trial was carried out.

6.4.3 Studies considered for review

The review team found no existing systematic review or meta-analysis of counselling and supportive psychotherapy in the treatment of schizophrenia. However, a number of studies already reviewed for the guideline used counselling and supportive psychotherapy, in either individual or group formats, as comparators. The review team therefore undertook a fresh systematic review, pooling data from a wide range of studies in which counselling or supportive psychotherapy was used as a control condition for comparison with other active or structured forms of psychological intervention. The team also undertook a search for studies of supportive therapy or counselling as the experimental treatment: three RCTs were located that compared CBT, supportive therapy and 'standard care,' with supportive therapy as one of the experimental conditions.

In total, 14 RCTs were identified as eligible for inclusion. Eight studies were from reviews already used in this guideline (FALLOON 1981; STANTON 1984; KEMP 1996; MARDER 1996; HOGARTY 1997; HADDOCK 1999; TARRIER 1998; SENSKY 2000), three were new studies added to the existing CBT review (LEVINE 1998; TURKINGTON 2000; LEWIS 2002), and three were studies not used in any other review used by the GDG (DONLON 1973; ECKMAN 1992; HERZ 2000). Together, the included studies span the period 1973 to 2002, and include data for 1143 participants divided between experimental and comparator groups.

The studies included varied in the following ways:

- duration and frequency of sessions (10–90 min; one to four times per week)

- duration of treatment (3 weeks to 3 years)
- diagnostic classification system (DSM–III–R, PSE, DSM–IV, ICD–10, DSM–II, DSM–III)
- duration of illness before treatment (first episode, 5–14 years, 'chronic')
- site of treatment programme (in-patient, out-patient, day patient, community, home)
- comparator treatments ('standard care', other active treatments)
- outcomes recorded.

6.4.4 Results

The review undertaken for this guideline incorporated studies not primarily designed to evaluate the effectiveness of counselling and supportive psychotherapy in the treatment of schizophrenia. Rather, these studies used counselling and supportive psychotherapy as a control for comparison with other active treatments. It is likely that the participants allocated to psychotherapy were not selected on the basis of their suitability for that treatment.

The review found no evidence that counselling and supportive psychotherapy, as defined by the GDG, had a therapeutic advantage in the treatment and management of schizophrenia when compared with either 'standard care' or other active psychological treatments using the outcomes identified above. In particular, when compared with standard care, there is insufficient evidence to determine if counselling and supportive therapy reduced relapse rates, improved mental state or influenced the number of deaths. There is limited evidence that counselling and supportive therapy does not reduce symptoms, and it is unclear whether it is any more acceptable than standard care.

When compared with standard care:

- there is insufficient evidence to determine if counselling or supportive therapy leads to a clinically significant improvement in relapse rates at end of treatment ($n=54$, RR=0.86, 95% CI 0.26 to 2.86) or at post-treatment follow-up ($n=54$, RR=1.08, 95% CI 0.51 to 2.29) (Ib)

- there is insufficient evidence to determine if counselling or supportive therapy leads to a clinically significant improvement in mental state at end of treatment (PANSS: $n=123$, WMD=−2.90, 95% CI −10.01 to 4.21) or at post-treatment follow-up (PANSS: $n=131$, WMD=−4.42, 95% CI −10.13 to 1.29) (Ib)

- there is limited evidence suggesting that counselling or supportive therapy does not lead to a clinically significant reduction in symptoms at end of treatment or at post-treatment follow-up (no important improvement as measured by a 50% reduction in BPRS positive symptoms: $n=54$, RR=0.95, 95% CI 0.77 to 1.17) (Ib)

- there is insufficient evidence to determine if counselling or supportive therapy leads to a greater number of deaths by post-treatment follow-up ($n=208$, RR=2.89, 95% CI 0.12 to 70.09) (Ib)

- there is no consistent evidence to suggest that counselling or supportive therapy is more or less acceptable as measured by the numbers of participants leaving the study early (by end of treatment: $n=54$, RR=4.31, 95% CI 0.51 to 36.08; by post-treatment follow-up: $n=262$, RR=0.88, 95% CI 0.63 to 1.25). (Ib)

When comparing counselling and supportive therapy with other psychological interventions the evidence favours other treatments with regard to mental state and positive symptoms, but evidence regarding relapse rates, death and the acceptability of treatment was insufficient.

When compared with other active interventions:

- there is insufficient evidence to determine if counselling or supportive therapy leads to a clinically significant improvement in relapse rates at the end of treatment (n=361, random effects RR=1.33, 95% CI 0.80 to 2.21) or at post-treatment follow-up (n=154, RR=1.21, 95% CI 0.89 to 1.66) (Ia)
- there is strong evidence suggesting that counselling or supportive therapy does not lead to a clinically significant improvement in mental state at the end of treatment (BPRS/PANSS/CPRS: n=316, SMD=0.02, 95% CI –0.20 to 0.24) and at post-treatment follow-up (BPRS/PANSS/CPRS: n=284, SMD=0.20, 95% CI –0.03 to 0.44) (Ia)
- there is limited evidence suggesting that counselling or supportive therapy does not lead to a clinically significant reduction in positive symptoms at the end of treatment (no important improvement as measured by a 50% reduction in BPRS positive symptoms: n=59, RR=1.27, 95% CI 0.95 to 1.70) (Ib)
- there is limited evidence suggesting that counselling or supportive therapy does not lead to a clinically significant reduction in positive symptoms at post-treatment follow-up (no important improvement as measured by a 50% reduction in CPRS positive symptoms: n=90, RR=1.66, 95% CI 1.06 to 2.59). (Ib)

There is insufficient evidence to determine if there is a clinically significant difference between counselling or supportive therapy and other active treatments in terms of number of deaths by post-treatment follow-up (n=281, RR=2.86, 95% CI 0.12 to 69.40). (Ib)

There is no consistent evidence to suggest that there is a clinically significant difference between counselling or supportive therapy and other active treatments in terms of leaving the study early (by end of treatment: n=708, RR=0.85, 95% CI 0.65 to 1.10; by post-treatment follow-up: n=352, RR=1.30, 95% CI 0.93 to 1.82). (Ia)

6.4.5 Clinical summary

Although the systematic review and meta-analysis conducted for this guideline found no evidence to suggest that counselling or supportive psychotherapy was superior to 'standard care' or 'other active treatments' in the treatment of people with schizophrenia, the limited availability of other psychological interventions of proven efficacy and the preferences of service users have been taken into account in forming recommendations. Moreover, supportive, empathic relationships between people with schizophrenia and their professional carers, in which sympathetic listening plays a central part in developing the therapeutic alliance, are an essential part of good practice.

6.4.6 Clinical practice recommendations

6.4.6.1 Counselling and supportive psychotherapy are not recommended as discrete interventions in the routine care of people with schizophrenia where other psychological interventions of proven efficacy are indicated and available. However, service-user preferences should be taken into account, especially if other, more efficacious psychological treatments are not locally available. (C)

6.5 Family interventions

6.5.1 Introduction

Family interventions in the treatment of schizophrenia have evolved from studies of the family environment and its possible role in affecting the course of schizophrenia (Vaughn & Leff, 1976). Brown and others (Brown *et al*, 1962; Brown & Rutter, 1966) developed a measure for the level of 'expressed emotion' within families and were able to show that the emotional environment within a family was an effective predictor of relapse in schizophrenia (Bebbington & Kuipers, 1994). The importance of this work lay in the realisation that it was possible to design psychological methods (in this case family interventions) that could influence the course of schizophrenia.

Since that time a number of different methods have been developed to help families cope with their relatives' illness more effectively, provide support and education for the family, reduce levels of distress and improve the ways in which the family communicates. Studies of family interventions vary considerably in the precise nature of the intervention. It should be noted that in this context, 'family' includes people who have a significant emotional connection to the service user, such as parents, siblings and partners.

6.5.2 Definition

For this review, the GDG used the following definition of family interventions: family sessions with a specific supportive or treatment function based on systemic, cognitive–behavioural or psychoanalytic principles, which must contain at least one of the following:

- psychoeducational intervention
- problem-solving and crisis management work
- intervention with the identified service user.

Studies were only included for review if the intervention was of at least 6 weeks' duration. In all the studies included, family interventions were provided as an adjunct to antipsychotic drug treatment.

6.5.3 Studies considered for review

The GDG used the systematic review of RCTs of psychological interventions in schizophrenia by Pilling *et al* (2002a). Using the above criteria for study inclusion, Pilling *et al* analysed a selected range of RCTs of family interventions up to 1999. Inclusion criteria related to the type of study (RCTs only), the participants (only those with schizophrenia spectrum disorders or if such data could be extracted) and the type of interventions (family interventions had to meet the definition above and comparator treatments had to be clearly defined). The review contained 16 trials (BLOCH 1995; BUCHKREMER 1995; FALLOON 1981; GLYNN 1992; GOLDSTEIN 1978; HOGARTY 1997; LEFF 1982, 1989; MCFARLANE 1995a,b; POSNER 1992; SCHOOLER 1997; TARRIER 1988; VAUGHAN 1992; XIONG 1994; ZHANG 1994).

Additional RCTs of family interventions have emerged since 1999. Further searches found two new RCTs (BARROWCLOUGH 1999; DYCK 2000) that fulfilled the criteria set by the

GDG. These have been incorporated into the current review, giving a total of 18 RCTs examining family interventions, with data for 1458 study participants and their families.

Comparator interventions included 'standard care' (11 studies) or 'non-standard care' (standard care plus supportive psychotherapy, family management, general family support, psychoeducation; 5 studies) for studies of single family interventions. Two studies of group family interventions used single family interventions as a comparator.

Studies included varied in the following ways:
- single family or multiple family group intervention
- whether the service user was included in the family intervention
- duration and frequency of intervention sessions and length of the treatment programme
- type of comparator intervention
- period and timing of follow-up
- outcome measures.

6.5.4 Results

6.5.4.1 The effect of family interventions on relapse and readmission rates

Family interventions for people with schizophrenia and their families effectively reduce relapse rates during treatment and after treatment at follow-up, and reduce hospital admissions during the treatment programmes, when compared with all other interventions (including standard care).

There is strong evidence that family interventions, when compared with all other interventions, decrease the likelihood of:
- relapse during treatment ($n=383$, random effects RR=0.57, 95% CI 0.37 to 0.88; NNT=5, 95% CI 3 to 15) (Ia)
- relapse at 4–15 months post-treatment follow-up ($n=305$, RR=0.67, 95% CI 0.52 to 0.88) (Ia)
- hospital admission 13–24 months into treatment ($n=185$, RR=0.44, 95% CI 0.28 to 0.67). (Ia)

However, there is strong evidence that family interventions do not reduce the likelihood of admission (up to 2 years) after treatment has ended ($n=330$, RR=1.01, 95% CI 0.79 to 1.28). (Ia)

Family interventions appear to be particularly effective for people who have persisting symptoms, and for those who have recently relapsed, both during treatment and at post-treatment follow-up.

There is limited evidence that family interventions, when compared with all other treatments (including standard care), reduce the likelihood of:
- relapse in people with persisting symptoms, after 12 months of treatment ($n=63$, RR=0.57, 95% CI 0.33 to 0.97; NNT=4, 95% CI 2 to 34) (Ib)
- relapse in people with persisting symptoms by 6 months post-treatment follow-up ($n=77$, RR=0.51, 95% CI 0.26 to 1.0; NNT=5, 95% CI 3 to 50). (Ib)

There is strong evidence that family interventions, when compared with all other comparator treatments (including standard care), reduce the likelihood of:

- relapse in people who have relapsed within the previous 3 months, after 12 months of treatment ($n=320$, random effects RR=0.55, 95% CI 0.31 to 0.97; NNT=5, 95% CI 3 to 25) (Ia)
- relapse in people who have relapsed within the previous 3 months, at 4–15 months post-treatment follow-up ($n=228$, RR=0.72, 95% CI 0.54 to 0.96). (Ia)

6.5.4.2 Effects of family intervention on the service user and carer

When compared with all other interventions (standard care and non-standard care combined), family interventions improve global adjustment scores and treatment adherence in service users, and reduce the burden upon carers. However, the review found that there was insufficient evidence to determine whether family interventions were superior to all other comparator treatments in their effects on the risk of self-harm or suicide among service users, symptom reduction or social functioning. Whether family interventions are more or less acceptable than other interventions, including standard care, was also uncertain.

There is limited evidence that family interventions, when compared with all other comparator treatments, increase the likelihood of improving global adjustment after 12 months of treatment (Global Assessment Scale: $n=74$, WMD=−6.51, 95% CI −10.97 to −2.05). (Ib)

There is strong evidence that, at the end of treatment, family interventions, when compared with all other comparator treatments, increase the likelihood of:
- treatment adherence among service users (non-adherence to drug treatment: $n=146$, RR=0.61, 95% CI 0.40 to 0.94; NNT=6, 95% CI 4 to 34) (Ia)
- reduction in the 'burden of care' upon carers ($n=146$, WMD=−0.35, 95% CI −0.65 to −0.05). (Ia)

However:
- there is insufficient evidence to determine whether family interventions increase the risk of suicide in service users ($n=341$, RR=0.94, 95% CI 0.39 to 2.23) (Ia)
- there is insufficient evidence to determine whether family interventions reduce the level of negative symptoms for service users (MSANS: $n=41$, WMD=−1.20, 95% CI −2.78 to 0.38) (Ib) or improve social functioning (Social Functioning Scale: $n=69$, WMD=−1.60, 95% CI −7.07 to 3.87) (Ib)
- based on the number of people leaving the study early, there is insufficient evidence to determine whether family intervention is either more or less acceptable to service users than other interventions (including standard care) ($n=655$, RR=1.19, 95% CI 0.82 to 1.73). (Ia)

6.5.4.3 How to provide family interventions

Within the systematic review and meta-analysis, data were extracted to examine the different methods of delivery of family interventions. There was stronger evidence for relapse prevention for programmes of longer duration and comprising a greater number of sessions, and when the service user was included in the family sessions.

When the treatment programme is provided over a period of 6 months or longer or for more than 10 planned sessions, there is strong evidence that family intervention reduces relapse (at 4–15 months post-treatment follow-up: $n=165$, RR=0.65, 95% CI 0.47 to 0.90). (Ia)

When the treatment programme is provided for a period of 3 months or less or comprises 10 or fewer sessions, there is insufficient evidence to determine whether family intervention improves relapse (at up to 15 months post-treatment follow-up: $n=140$, RR=0.71, 95% CI 0.45 to 1.12). (Ib)

When the service user is included in the family sessions, there is strong evidence that family intervention reduces relapse rates (at post-treatment follow-up: $n=269$, RR=0.68, 95% CI 0.50 to 0.91). (Ia)

When the service user is excluded from the family sessions, there is insufficient evidence to determine whether family intervention reduces relapse rates (at post-treatment follow-up: $n=36$, RR=0.67, 95% CI 0.36 to 1.23). (Ib)

Group family interventions and single family interventions are equally efficacious, although families undertaking single family interventions are significantly less likely to leave the study early. When families are selected on the basis of assessment of high expressed emotion, relapse rates are also reduced.

There is strong evidence to suggest that there is no difference in efficacy between single family and group family interventions (e.g. relapse at 13–24 months post-treatment follow-up: $n=508$, RR=0.97, 95% CI 0.76 to 1.25). (Ia)

When family interventions are provided for groups of families there is strong evidence that there is a greater likelihood that families will leave the study early compared with the application of family interventions to single families ($n=554$, RR=1.19, 95% CI 1.01 to 1.40; NNH=13, 95% CI 7 [harm] to 1755 [benefit]). (Ia)

When families are selected for family interventions on the basis of high expressed emotion, relapse rates are effectively reduced at 4–15 months post-treatment follow-up ($n=228$, RR=0.72, 95% CI 0.54 to 0.96). (Ia)

6.5.5 Clinical summary

There is strong evidence that family interventions improve the outcomes for people with schizophrenia living with (or having close contact with) their family, most notably in reducing the relapse rate both during treatment and for up to 15 months after treatment has ended. Family interventions are also effective in reducing relapse rates in those who have recently relapsed, and in those who remain symptomatic after resolution of an acute episode. The benefits are most marked if treatment is provided over a period of more than 6 months or for more than ten planned sessions, and if the service user is included in the family sessions. Treatment with family interventions may be less acceptable when delivered as a multi-family group intervention. There is insufficient evidence to know if suicide rates are altered by family interventions.

6.5.6 Health economic evidence

Given the large direct medical costs associated with relapse in schizophrenia, primarily resulting from the need for expensive in-patient treatment, it has been hypothesised that the relapse-reducing effect of family interventions could result in significant savings in health care costs and offset the extra costs of the interventions. Family interventions were designed to improve the relationship between service users and their family members, and to ease acceptance of schizophrenic illness within the family. These effects could lead to a reduction in the productivity loss of the family members, and a subsequent reduction in the indirect costs of schizophrenia. Family interventions may be delivered in several different ways (e.g. single family intervention or multi-family group intervention), which might impose different health care costs.

The economic review identified five eligible studies, and a further two studies were not available. The five studies included were based on RCTs. Three of them adapted simple costing methods (Tarrier *et al*, 1991; Goldstein, 1996; Leff *et al*, 2001), while two were economic evaluations (Liberman *et al*, 1987; McFarlane *et al*, 1995*a*). Two analyses were conducted in the UK (Tarrier *et al*, 1991; Leff *et al*, 2001); two others were based on clinical data from the UK, but the economic analyses were conducted within a US context (Liberman *et al*, 1987; Goldstein, 1996). Most of these studies are methodologically weak, with the potential for a high risk of bias in their results. Another common problem was the low statistical power of the studies to show cost differences between the comparators. All studies focused narrowly on direct medical costs, so that economic evaluation of family interventions from a broader perspective is impossible.

One study (Tarrier *et al*, 1991) compared family intervention with standard care and concluded that family intervention was significantly less costly. Two analyses compared family intervention with individual supportive therapy (Liberman *et al*, 1987; Goldstein, 1996). Both studies used clinical data from the same RCT, but their evaluation methodology differed. They concluded that the treatment costs of family intervention were higher than those of individual supportive therapy, but were offset by savings relating to other health care costs. One study (Leff *et al*, 2001) showed economic benefits of family intervention combined with two psychoeducational sessions, over psychoeducation alone; however, the difference was not significant. One study (McFarlane *et al*, 1995*a*) demonstrated that multi-family group intervention is more cost-effective than single family intervention.

6.5.6.1 Health economic conclusions

The quality of the available economic evidence is generally poor. Such as it is, the evidence suggests that providing family interventions may represent good 'value for money'.

There is limited evidence that group family interventions require fewer resources and are less costly than single family interventions.

6.5.7 Clinical practice recommendations

6.5.7.1   Family interventions should be available to the families of people with schizophrenia who are living with or who are in close contact with the service user. (A)

6.5.7.2   Family interventions should be offered to the families of people with schizophrenia who have recently relapsed or who are considered at risk of relapse. (A)

6.5.7.3   Family interventions should be offered to the families of people with schizophrenia who have persisting symptoms. (A)

6.5.7.4   The duration of the family intervention programme should normally be longer than 6 months and it should include more than ten sessions of treatment. (B)

6.5.7.5   The service user should normally be included in the family intervention sessions, as doing so significantly improves the outcome. Sometimes, however, it is not practicable. (B)

6.5.7.6   Service users and their carers may prefer single family interventions rather than multi-family group interventions. (A)

6.5.8 Research recommendations

6.5.8.1   Adequately powered RCTs reporting all relevant clinical outcomes, including quality of life, are needed to evaluate the use of family interventions for the families of people with schizophrenia presenting for the first time.

6.5.8.2   Research into methods of identifying the individuals who would most benefit from family interventions and methods of promoting the effective implementation of such interventions should be undertaken.

6.5.8.3   Further research is needed to evaluate the impact of family interventions upon the symptoms experienced by service users.

6.6 Psychodynamic psychotherapy and psychoanalysis

6.6.1 Introduction

Psychoanalysis and its derivatives, often termed psychoanalytic and psychodynamic psychotherapies, were originally regarded as unsuitable for the treatment of the psychoses (Freud, 1914, 1933). However, a number of psychoanalysts made attempts to treat people with schizophrenia and other psychoses, using more or less modified versions of psychoanalysis (Fromm-Reichmann, 1950; Stack-Sullivan, 1974).

Randomised controlled trials were undertaken in the 1970s and 1980s to investigate the use of psychoanalytically oriented psychotherapy. Research into the effects of psychoanalytic approaches in the treatment of schizophrenia has been repeated more recently, with mixed results (Fenton & McGlashan, 1995; Jones *et al*, 1999; Mari & Streiner, 1999), leading to the publication of a Cochrane Review of the subject (Malmberg & Fenton, 2001).

6.6.2 Definition

The GDG adopted the criteria of the recent Cochrane Review (Malmberg & Fenton, 2001), which defined psychodynamic psychotherapy as:

> "Regular individual therapy sessions with a trained psychotherapist, or a therapist under supervision. Therapy sessions had to be based upon a psychodynamic or psychoanalytic model, using a variety of strategies, including exploratory insight-oriented, supportive or directive activity, applied flexibly, working with the transference, but with the therapists using a less strict technique than that used in psychoanalysis" (Malmberg & Fenton, 2001).

Psychoanalysis was defined as:

> "Regular individual sessions, planned to last a minimum of 30 minutes, with trained psychoanalysts 3 to 5 times per week, and planned to continue for at least one year. To be considered well-defined psychoanalysis, the analysts were required to conform to a strict definition of psychoanalytic technique, explicitly working within the transference and focusing upon infantile sexual relations and their contemporary manifestations" (Malmberg & Fenton, 2001).

Comparator treatments included 'standard care' (the treatment patients would receive had they not been included in a research trial, including 'waiting-list control groups' where people received drug or other interventions), other psychosocial therapies (non-directive counselling, supportive therapy, CBT and other 'talking therapies') or 'no care' (people were randomised to no treatment or to a waiting list without receiving any care).

6.6.3 Studies considered for review

The review by Malmberg & Fenton (2001) synthesised and analysed data from three RCTs, incorporating data for 492 participants (O'BRIEN 1972; MAY 1976; GUNDERSON 1984). A search for more recent RCTs was unproductive. The studies included varied in the following ways:

- duration of treatment (6 months to 20 months)
- duration of follow-up (up to 3 years of usable data)
- phase of illness (first episode or subsequent episode)
- type of comparator treatments (individual *v.* group; therapy *v.* drugs; therapy and drugs *v.* therapy, electroconvulsive therapy, milieu therapy and drugs; psychodynamic *v.* reality-adaptive supportive psychotherapy)
- outcomes recorded.

It was unclear to what extent the trials included used psychoanalysis or psychodynamic psychotherapy, and no attempt was made to ascertain the degree of the therapists' fidelity to the model of therapy in the studies reviewed. Moreover, one of the studies (MAY 1976) included data comparing psychoanalytic/psychodynamic psychotherapy without drug treatment against drug treatment for people with schizophrenia. The results from this part of the study are not reported here.

6.6.4 Results

6.6.4.1 Psychodynamic psychotherapy with drug treatment

No evidence was available to determine whether psychodynamic psychotherapy combined with drugs, when compared with drug treatment alone, improved the core outcomes of reduced relapse rates, symptom reduction or the acceptability of treatment.

There was insufficient evidence to determine whether individual psychodynamic psychotherapy compared with 'standard care' affected:

- inability to be discharged at the end of treatment (*n*=92, RR=1.09, 95% CI 0.16 to 7.42) (Ib)
- treatment not being considered successful by the treatment team at the end of treatment (*n*=92, RR=2.18, 95% CI 0.20 to 23.23) (Ib)

- being given drug treatment during 12 months and 36 months post-treatment follow-up (by 12 months: $n=92$, RR=0.95, 95% CI 0.85 to 1.06; by 36 months: $n=92$, RR=0.95, 95% CI 0.89 to 1.02). (Ib)

There was insufficient evidence to suggest that, at the end of treatment, individual psychodynamic psychotherapy affected overall health compared with standard treatment (Menninger Health Sickness scale: $n=90$, WMD=−0.80, 95% CI −5.35 to 3.75). (Ib)

There was insufficient evidence to determine if, at the end of treatment, psychodynamic psychotherapies reduce the risk of self-harm or suicide compared with drug treatment alone ($n=92$, RR=0.16, 95% CI 0.01 to 2.93). (Ib)

However, service users receiving insight-oriented individual psychodynamic psychotherapy, compared with those receiving reality-adaptive psychotherapy, had an increased likelihood of remaining in the study at 6 months, 12 months and 24 months post-treatment follow-up (e.g. leaving the study early at 24 months post-treatment follow-up: $n=164$, RR=0.54, 95% CI 0.44 to 0.67; NNT=3, 95% CI 2 to 4). (Ib)

6.6.5 Summary

No consistent evidence was found to suggest that psychoanalytic or psychodynamic therapy combined with drugs, when compared with drug treatment alone, improves the outcome for people with schizophrenia.

6.6.6 Clinical practice recommendations

6.6.6.1 There is insufficient evidence to recommend the use of psychoanalytic or psychodynamic psychotherapy in the routine treatment of people with schizophrenia. (B)

6.6.6.2 Psychoanalytic and psychodynamic principles may be considered to help health professionals understand the experience of individual service users and their interpersonal relationships. (GPP)

6.7 Psychoeducation

6.7.1 Introduction

In a study of healthy people asked about their information requirements in the event of being diagnosed with a serious and life-threatening illness such as a cancer, 90% stated that they wanted access to the maximum information available (Kemp et al, 1984). However, given the volume and variation in the information available about illness and treatment, precisely what and how much information a person requires, and the degree to which the information provided is comprehensible, will vary from person to person.

According to the *Drug and Therapeutics Bulletin* (1993), published by the Consumers' Association, people have a right to know as much as possible about their treatment and care, and the Patients' Bill of Rights adopted by the American Hospital Association (1975) asserts that people should have access to accurate and complete knowledge about their illness, treatment and care.

Over and above legal and ethical reasons for providing reliable and accurate information for service users and their carers, it is also necessary for them to be able to participate meaningfully in the clinical decision-making process (Brody, 1980), a practice now enshrined in health policy in England and Wales (Department of Health, 1998). Formally teaching service users and their families has also been used to improve treatment adherence (Antai-Otong, 1989), to reduce the likelihood of side-effects or toxicity resulting from treatment (Peet & Harvey, 1991), and in an attempt to improve outcomes (Leff *et al*, 1982).

For people with schizophrenia and their carers, the provision of good and accurate information is arguably even more important than for people with serious physical illness, for the following reasons:

- the prolonged time course of many schizophrenic illnesses
- the many side-effects of the pharmacological treatment of schizophrenia, some of which are severe and/or irreversible
- the high recurrence rate of schizophrenic illness
- the special needs of a proportion of people with schizophrenia who have information-processing problems
- the lack of acceptance by many people with schizophrenia that they have a mental health problem
- the wide-ranging effects of schizophrenic illness, resulting in psychological, social, financial, medical and occupational difficulties
- the more frequent diagnosis of mental illness in members of ethnic minority groups
- the stigma, and the myriad misunderstandings, that surround the diagnosis of schizophrenia among service users, carers, the public and many professionals
- the unique ethical and legal position occupied by psychiatry and its patients, in that many of the latter are subject to the Mental Health Act 1983.

The considered and careful provision and use of information, either as a method of treatment or for reasons of ethics and good practice, is all the more important for this group of service users and carers, a view endorsed by the European Expert Panel on the Contemporary Treatment of Schizophrenia (Altamura *et al*, 2000).

In mental health, the use of education and information to serve the goals of treatment, and to help service users or their carers change their behaviour, skills and attitudes (Falvo, 1994) with consequent likely alteration of their cognitive, affective and psychomotor processes (Rankin & Stallings, 1996), has often been termed 'psychoeducation'. Psychoeducation has been developed as an aspect of treatment in schizophrenia with a variety of goals over and above the provision of accurate information. Desired outcomes in studies have included improvements in insight, treatment adherence, symptoms, relapse rates, and family knowledge and understanding (Pekkala & Merinder, 2001). There is thus considerable variability in the goals of the intervention.

6.7.2 Definition

For this review, the GDG used the following definitions of 'psychoeducation' (or 'patient teaching,' 'patient instruction' or 'patient education') to identify studies for inclusion:

- any group or individual programme involving an explicitly described educational interaction between the information provider and the service user or carer as the prime focus of the study

- a programme that addresses the illness from a multi-dimensional viewpoint, including familial, social, biological and pharmacological perspectives
- the provision to service users and carers of information, support and different management strategies (characteristic of most programmes).

Programmes of 10 or fewer sessions were classified as 'brief', and those of 11 or more as 'standard', for this review.

Interventions including elements of behavioural training, such as social skills or life skills training, were excluded. Educational programmes performed by service user peers, and staff education studies, were also excluded.

6.7.3 Studies considered for review

The GDG used the Cochrane Review of psychoeducation for schizophrenia (Pekkala & Merinder, 2001), which included data from ten RCTs. However, five of the RCTs were excluded, either because they did not meet the GDG's definition of psychoeducation, or because of serious methodological flaws. The five remaining studies were by ATKINSON 1996, BAUML 1996, HORNUNG 1995, MACPHERSON 1996 and MERINDER 1999.

New and additional RCTs that met the GDG inclusion criteria were those by HAYASHI 2001, CUNNINGHAM OWENS 2001, JONES 2001, LECOMPTE 1996 and SMITH 1987. The GDG therefore included ten RCTs for review and meta-analysis, with data for 1070 participants. Studies included varied in the following ways:
- duration of intervention programme (1 week to 5 months)
- duration of follow-up (up to 5 years)
- treatment setting (in-patient, out-patient, day patient, community-based institution)
- country in which study took place (UK, Japan, Denmark, Germany)
- diagnostic classification system (ICD–9, ICD–10, DSM–III–R, SADS)
- mode of educational materials used (oral-didactic, audiovisual, video, written, homework exercises)
- outcomes recorded.

There was considerable variation in the nature of what was described as psychoeducation in the studies included in terms of content, format, complexity and aims. Moreover, very few of the outcomes assessed in each trial were common to other trials, making comparisons and pooling of data difficult.

6.7.4 Results

In reviewing studies of psychoeducation in the treatment of schizophrenia, the GDG found it difficult to distinguish psychoeducation from the provision of good-quality information as required in standard care, and from good-quality family engagement, where information is provided with family members also present. There is clearly an overlap between good standard care and psychoeducation, and between psychoeducation and family interventions. It is noteworthy that most of the studies reviewed here did not take place in the UK, and the nature and quality of the information provision in standard care may differ from services in the UK setting.

The evidence concerning the efficacy of psychoeducation in the treatment and management of schizophrenia is generally inconclusive. The review found strong evidence that psychoeducation, when compared with standard care, had no effect upon relapse rates. However, there was some limited evidence that psychoeducation, when compared with standard care, may improve mental state and treatment adherence, but there was no consistent evidence that insight is improved on a range of measures.

There is strong evidence that psychoeducation, when compared with standard care, did not produce a clinically important decrease in the likelihood of relapse at 12 months post-treatment follow-up ($n=520$, RR=0.90, 95% CI 0.78 to 1.04). (Ia)

There is limited evidence suggesting that psychoeducation, compared with standard care, increased the likelihood of improved mental state at 1 year post-treatment follow-up (BPRS: $n=159$, WMD=−6.00, 95% CI −9.15 to −2.85). (Ib)

There is also limited evidence suggesting that psychoeducation, compared with standard care, increased the likelihood of improved drug treatment adherence ($n=163$, WMD= −0.40, 95% CI −0.62 to −0.18). (Ib)

There is strong evidence suggesting there is no clinically significant difference between psychoeducation and standard care in terms of treatment acceptability (leaving the study early: $n=797$, RR=1.08, 95% CI 0.84 to 1.37). (Ia)

There is no consistent evidence of a clinically significant difference between psychoeducation and standard care on a range of measures of insight.

6.7.5 Summary

The review found limited evidence to suggest that psychoeducation can produce benefits on the basis of individual studies; however, the evidence at present is mixed and inconclusive. There is no evidence to suggest that psychoeducation reduces relapse rates.

6.7.6 Clinical practice recommendations

6.7.6.1   The use of psychoeducation as a discrete intervention aimed at reducing relapse rates or for symptom reduction is not recommended in the routine treatment of people with schizophrenia. (B)

6.7.6.2   Health professionals should provide accessible information about schizophrenia and its treatment to service users and carers; this should be considered an essential part of the routine treatment and management of schizophrenia. (GPP)

6.7.6.3   In addition to the provision of good-quality information, families and carers should be offered the opportunity to participate in family or carer support programmes, where these exist. (GPP)

6.8 Social skills training

6.8.1 Introduction

An early psychological approach to the treatment of schizophrenia involved the application of behavioural theory and methods with the aim of normalising behaviour

(Ayllon & Azrin, 1965), improving communication or modifying vocalisation (Lindsley, 1963). Given the complex and often debilitating behavioural and social effects of schizophrenia, social skills training was developed as a more sophisticated treatment strategy derived from behavioural and social learning traditions (see Wallace *et al*, 1980, for a review), and designed to help people with schizophrenia regain their social skills and confidence, improve their ability to cope in social situations, reduce social distress, improve their quality of life, and aid symptom reduction and relapse prevention.

Social skills training programmes begin with a detailed assessment and behavioural analysis of individual social skills, followed by individual and group interventions using positive reinforcement, goal setting, modelling and shaping. Initially, smaller social tasks (such as responses to non-verbal social cues) are worked on, and gradually new behaviours are built up into more complex social skills such as conducting a meaningful conversation. There is a strong emphasis on homework assignments to help generalise newly learned behaviour away from the treatment setting.

Although this psychosocial treatment approach became very popular in the USA, it gained much less support in the UK, at least in part as a result of doubts in the UK about the capacity of social skills training to generalise from the treatment situation to real social settings (Hersen & Bellack, 1976; Shepherd, 1978).

6.8.2 Definition

For this guideline, the GDG defined social skills training programmes as any structured psychosocial intervention, group or individual or both, aimed at enhancing social performance and reducing distress and difficulty in social situations. The key components are:

- careful, behaviourally based assessment of a range of social and interpersonal skills
- an emphasis on both verbal and non-verbal communication
- training focused upon (a) an individual's perception and processing of relevant social cues, and (b) an individual's ability to provide appropriate social reinforcement
- homework tasks as well as clinic-based interventions.

Programmes in which social skills training was a component of a more complex rehabilitation intervention such as token economies, life skills training or other milieu-based approaches were excluded. Studies including people diagnosed as having schizophrenia with comorbid substance misuse were also excluded.

6.8.3 Studies considered for review

The review of psychological interventions in schizophrenia by Pilling *et al* (2002*b*) was used by the GDG to evaluate the place of social skills training in the management of schizophrenia. This review included nine RCTs, of which eight satisfied the criteria developed by the GDG (Bellack, 1984; Dobson, 1995; Finch & Wallace, 1977; Hayes, 1995; Liberman, 1998; Lukoff, 1986; Marder, 1996; Peniston, 1988). One new RCT (Daniels, 1998) was also located.

All controls were defined as 'standard care' or 'discussion groups' and lacked any of the components defined above. Data were therefore available for 436 service users.

The studies included varied in the following ways:

- duration of treatment (4 weeks to 2 years)
- follow-up (6 months to 2 years)
- treatment setting (out-patient, in-patient, day patient and mixed settings)
- participants' gender (mixed, all male)
- country of study (USA 7, Australia 1, Canada 1)
- outcomes recorded.

6.8.4 Results

The systematic review used for this guideline found insufficient evidence to determine whether social skills training, compared with all other interventions including 'standard care', improved relapse or readmission rates, length of stay in hospital or quality of life, although the included studies are small. However, there was limited evidence that social skills training, compared with standard care, improved mental state and social functioning. The review found no information on suicide rates.

Although one study set in the USA (Peniston & Kulkosky, 1988) found that social skills training increased the number of patients who could be discharged, and significantly decreased harm to others when compared with standard care, this was an unusual study in a secure in-patient setting, where success on the treatment programme was linked to possible discharge, and was primarily focused upon coping with a range of threatening interpersonal situations.

It is also important to note that all but two trials (Finch & Wallace, 1977; Peniston & Kulkosky, 1988) compared social skills training with other group or social interventions, which themselves might have had a therapeutic effect.

The review found insufficient evidence as to whether social skills training, when compared with other interventions and/or standard care, altered the likelihood of:

- reduced relapse or readmission rates by 1 year into treatment (*v.* standard care: $n=64$, RR=1.14, 95% CI 0.52 to 2.49; *v.* other treatments: $n=80$, RR=0.94, 95% CI 0.63 to 1.40) (Ib)
- improved mental state, compared with other interventions (BPRS: $n=64$, WMD= −1.80, 95% CI −7.85 to 4.25) **(Ib)**
- improved quality of life (*v.* standard care: $n=40$, WMD=−9.67, 95% CI −22.56 to 3.22; *v.* other interventions: $n=80$, WMD=−0.09, 95% CI −0.42 to 0.24) (Ib)
- shorter length of stay in hospital (*v.* other interventions: $n=33$, WMD=−11.95, 95% CI −24.43 to 0.53). (Ib)

There was, however, limited evidence that social skills training, when compared with standard care alone, increased the likelihood of:

- improved mental state (BPRS: $n=40$, WMD=−7.18, 95% CI −13.62 to −0.74; SANS: $n=40$, WMD=−8.03, 95% CI −15.27 to −0.79). (Ib)
- improved social functioning (Behavioural Assessment Task: $n=40$, WMD= −2.61, 95% CI −4.56 to −0.66). (Ib)

6.8.5 Summary

There is no clear evidence that social skills training is effective as a discrete intervention in improving outcomes in schizophrenia when compared with generic social and group activities, and it shows little if any consistent advantage over standard care.

6.8.6 Clinical practice recommendations

6.8.6.1 Social skills training as a discrete intervention is not recommended in the routine treatment of people with schizophrenia. (B)

6.8.6.2 Social, group and physical activities are an important aspect of comprehensive service provision for people with schizophrenia as the acute phase recedes, and afterwards. All care plans should record the arrangements for social, group and physical activities. (GPP)

7 Service-level interventions in the treatment and management of schizophrenia

7.1 Introduction

Up to the 1950s most people with a diagnosis of schizophrenia were treated in large mental hospitals, where they resided for much of their lives. It was not until most Western governments began to implement a policy of de-institutionalisation that other types of services began to develop, such as out-patient clinics, day hospitals, community mental health teams and community mental health centres. However, by the 1970s, the new community services developed as a response to long-stay hospital closures failed to meet the needs of those most needing care (Audit Commission, 1986; Melzer et al, 1991), evidenced by sharply rising readmission rates (Rossler et al, 1992; Ellison et al, 1995).

In recognition of the limitations of community-based service provision, a second generation of teams and services were developed. These aimed: to prevent or reduce readmission, by providing more home and community-based treatment; to improve engagement with service users; and to improve clinical, social and occupational outcomes.

The services included for review in this guideline are community mental health teams, assertive outreach (assertive community treatment), acute day hospital care, vocational rehabilitation, non-acute day hospital care, crisis resolution and home treatment teams, early intervention services, and case management.

In reviewing the evidence for the effectiveness of these different services, the Guideline Development Group (GDG) decided to focus on randomised controlled trials. Specific problems of this type of study design in the evaluation of service-level interventions relate to the difficulty in precisely defining such interventions; the fact that the 'intervention' and 'standard care' may vary between studies, between countries and over time; and the tendency for experimental interventions to overlap with standard care. However, service-level interventions that claim superiority over other methods of delivering care must be able to characterise clearly what they do, how they do it, and how they differ from alternative types of service and from the standard care they hope to replace. For these reasons, it is essential for new services to be subjected to the rigour of evaluation through randomised controlled trials (RCTs). Although other types of study might help to differentiate, evaluate and refine services and the ways in which they operate, services must be able to demonstrate their overall value in comparison with other interventions, in order to remain a supportable component of care within the National Health Service.

Thus, the GDG asked the review team to focus upon systematic reviews, meta-analyses and RCTs dealing with service-level interventions. This was possible for all the forms of care reviewed here, with the exception of early intervention services, for which no RCT evidence was available (see below).

7.2 Community mental health teams

7.2.1 Introduction

One of the earliest service developments in community-based care was that of the community mental health team (CMHT) (Merson *et al*, 1992). Community mental health teams are multi-disciplinary teams, comprising all the main professions involved in mental health, including nursing, occupational therapy, psychiatry, psychology and social work. Having developed in a relatively pragmatic way, CMHTs have become the mainstay of community-based mental health work in developed countries (Bouras *et al*, 1986; Bennett & Freeman, 1991), as well as in many other nations (Pierides, 1994; Slade *et al*, 1995; Isaac, 1996). Nevertheless, concerns about CMHTs have been raised, particularly regarding the incidence of violence (Coid, 1994), the quality of day-to-day life for people with serious mental health problems and their carers, and the impact upon society (Dowell & Ciarlo, 1983).

7.2.2 Definition

The GDG used the Cochrane Review (Tyrer *et al*, 2002) of the effects of CMHT management when compared with non-team community management for people with serious mental health problems. The definitions used in this review for CMHTs and the comparator 'standard care' or 'usual care' were as follows:

- CMHT care was 'management of care from a multi-disciplinary, community-based team (that is, more than a single person designated to work within a team)'
- 'standard care' or 'usual care' must be stated to be the normal care in the area concerned, non-team community care, out-patient care, admission to hospital (where acutely ill people were diverted from admission and allocated to CMHT or in-patient care) or day hospital care.

The review specifically focused upon CMHT management, and therefore excluded studies that involved any additional method of management in the CMHT.

7.2.3 Studies considered for review

The review by Tyrer *et al* (2002) included five studies of CMHTs, three undertaken in London (MERSON 1992 (London); BURNS 1993 (London); TYRER 1998 (London)), one from Australia (HOULT 1981 (Sydney)) and one from Canada (FENTON 1979 (Montreal)). For the purposes of the GDG review, however, BURNS 1993 was excluded on the grounds of inadequate allocation concealment, and the Canadian and Australian studies were excluded because the GDG regarded them to be primarily studies of crisis intervention teams rather than CMHTs. An additional search by the review team for recent RCTs evaluating CMHTs identified one suitable study, set in Manchester (GATER 1997).

The review team conducted a new analysis using the three studies selected (MERSON 1992 (London); GATER 1997 (Manchester); TYRER 1998 (London)), with data for 334 participants. All studies were undertaken in urban or inner-city settings. Only published data were used for analysis, except in the case of the London 1992 study, for which unpublished data were available for further analysis. In all three studies the most common diagnosis was schizophrenia, but each study also included a significant minority of participants with non-psychotic disorders.

Studies included varied in the following ways:

- follow-up period (3 months to 2 years)
- proportion of individuals with schizophrenia (38% to 55%)
- type of interventions used by the CMHT.

7.2.4 Results

The studies considered in this review included people with a variety of diagnoses, making recommendations specifically for people with schizophrenia tentative. With this caveat in mind, the review found the evidence insufficient to determine whether CMHTs, when compared with 'standard care', reduced admission rates or death rates, improved the mental state of service users, improved contact with services, or improved social functioning. The review did not combine data from the studies by MERSON 1992 (London) and TYRER 1998 (London), because in the latter study the service was dealing with discharged psychiatric patients, who presumably are more likely to be readmitted to hospital and to be more severely ill than those seen in the other two trials. This would appear to be confirmed by the enormously high admission rates in the Tyrer study.

Based on two studies (which could not be combined in a meta-analysis), there is insufficient evidence to determine if CMHTs reduce admission rates to hospital, compared with standard care (MERSON 1992 (London): $n=100$, RR=0.71, 95% CI 0.42 to 1.19; TYRER 1998 (London): $n=155$, RR=0.88, 95% CI 0.76 to 1.01). (Ib)

There is insufficient evidence to determine if CMHTs are associated with increased death rates (MERSON 1992 (London): $n=100$, RR=0.54, 95% CI 0.05 to 5.78; TYRER 1998 (London): $n=155$, RR=0.89, 95% CI 0.06 to 13.98). (Ib)

There is insufficient evidence to determine if CMHTs are associated with a loss of contact with services (MERSON 1992 (London): $n=100$, RR=1.24, 95% CI 0.49 to 3.16; TYRER 1998 (London): $n=155$, RR=1.04, 95% CI 0.60 to 1.79). (Ib)

There is insufficient evidence to determine if CMHTs are associated with improvements in mental state (CPRS: $n=100$, WMD=−0.80, 95% CI −5.74 to 4.14). (Ib)

There is insufficient evidence to determine if CMHTs are associated with improvements in social functioning (Social Functioning Questionnaire: $n=100$, WMD=0.70, 95% CI −1.18 to 2.58). (Ib)

7.2.5 Clinical summary

Despite the fact that CMHTs remain the mainstay of community mental health care, there is surprisingly little evidence to show that they are an effective way of organising services. As such, evidence for or against the effectiveness of CMHTs in the management of schizophrenia is insufficient to make any evidence-based recommendations.

7.2.6 Health economic evidence

It has been hypothesised that the provision of services by community mental health teams has the potential for cost saving, resulting from better organisation of the delivery of care and the low establishment costs of community teams.

The economic review identified five eligible studies, all of which were conducted in the UK. Four studies were based on RCTs (Burns & Raftery, 1993; Merson *et al*, 1996; Gater *et al*, 1997; Tyrer *et al*, 1998), while another reported data from a controlled study with concurrent controls (McCrone *et al*, 1998). Four studies evaluated only costs, and one was a cost-minimisation analysis estimating the cost difference between interventions (Burns & Raftery, 1993). All studies contained a low risk of bias, with the exception of the study by Tyrer *et al* (1998).

Four studies compared CMHTs with 'standard care'. The study by Gater *et al* (1997) found standard care to be less costly both for the health care system and for families, although none of the cost differences was significant. Three studies showed that CMHTs are cheaper than standard care. However, Merson *et al* (1996) did not calculate the significance of the difference, and the other two savings were not statistically significant (Burns & Raftery, 1993; Tyrer *et al*, 1998). One study compared CMHTs with intensive case management (McCrone *et al*, 1998), and found that none of the interventions resulted in significant cost savings compared with the costs in the period before the introduction of the new services. The result of the between-intervention comparison was not reliable, owing to differences in the disability status of the comparison populations.

7.2.6.1 Health economic conclusions

The available evidence on health economics is unclear. The non-significant differences between standard care and CMHTs, and between pre-intervention period and intervention period, suggest that CMHTs provide no real cost savings or extra costs.

7.2.7 Clinical practice recommendations

7.2.7.1   There is insufficient evidence to make any recommendation for the use of community mental health teams in the treatment and management of schizophrenia. (B)

7.2.7.2   Community mental health teams are an acceptable way of organising community care and may have the potential for effectively coordinating and integrating other community-based teams providing services for people with schizophrenia. However, there is insufficient evidence of their advantages to support a recommendation that precludes or inhibits the development of alternative service configurations. (C)

7.2.8 Research recommendations

7.2.8.1   High-quality research, including health economic outcomes, should be conducted to establish the clinical and economic effectiveness, including the impact upon quality of life, of community mental health teams compared with other ways of delivering care for people with schizophrenia.

7.2.8.2   Studies are needed to establish the relative effectiveness of specialist teams (e.g. crisis resolution and home treatment, and early intervention) compared with community mental health teams augmented or enhanced to deliver these functions.

7.3 Assertive outreach (assertive community treatment)

7.3.1 Introduction

Assertive outreach, usually known outside the UK as assertive community treatment, is a method of delivering treatment and care for people with serious mental health problems in the community (Thompson *et al*, 1990). First developed in the 1970s as a means of preventing or reducing admission to hospital, the model of care has since been defined and validated, based upon the consensus of an international panel of experts (McGrew *et al*, 1994; McGrew & Bond, 1995). Assertive outreach is now a well-defined model of service delivery, with the following aims:

- to keep people with serious mental health problems in contact with services
- to reduce the extent (and cost) of hospital admissions
- to improve outcomes (particularly quality of life and social functioning).

7.3.2 Definition

The GDG adopted the definition used in a systematic review of assertive community treatment (ACT) by Marshall & Lockwood (2002), which identified the following key elements:

- care is provided by a multi-disciplinary team (usually involving a psychiatrist with dedicated sessions)
- care is exclusively provided for a defined group of people (those with serious mental illness)
- team members share responsibility for clients, so that several members may work with the same client, and members do not have individual case-loads (unlike case management)
- the team attempts to provide all the psychiatric and social care for each service user, rather than making referrals to other agencies
- care is provided at home or in the workplace, as far as possible
- treatment and care are offered assertively to uncooperative or reluctant service users ('assertive outreach')
- medication concordance is emphasised.

For a study intervention to be accepted as ACT, Marshall & Lockwood required that the trial report described the experimental intervention as 'Assertive Community Treatment, Assertive Case Management or PACT; or as being based on the Madison, Treatment in Community Living, Assertive Community Treatment or Stein and Test models.' Assertive community treatment and similar models of care are long-term interventions for those with severe and enduring mental illnesses, and so the review did not consider ACT as an alternative to acute hospital admission. The review also excluded studies of 'home-based care', as this was regarded as a form of crisis intervention; these studies are reviewed in the section on crisis resolution and home treatment teams (section 7.7).

7.3.3 Studies considered for review

The review team undertook a search for recent RCTs, locating two further studies (CHANDLER (California; 2); FEKETE (Indiana)) for inclusion and reanalysis with the Marshall & Lockwood (2002) review. Studies included had to conform to the definition of ACT given above, and comparator treatments were standard community care, hospital-based rehabilitation, and case management. A total of 22 trials were incorporated for review, including data on 3722 participants.

Studies included varied in the following ways:

- follow-up period (up to 2.4 years)
- country of study (Sweden 1, UK 1, USA 18, Canada 2)
- gender of participants (mixed, male)
- setting (urban, rural, inner city)
- comparator treatment (standard community care, hospital-based rehabilitation, case management).

Trials were only included if the participants were described as having a 'severe mental disorder', defined as a schizophrenia-like disorder, bipolar disorder or depression with psychotic features.

7.3.4 Results

7.3.4.1 Effect of ACT on use of services

Most of the studies reviewed here were undertaken in the USA, and although the ACT model is well defined, comparisons with standard care must limit our confidence in generalising findings to the UK. Nevertheless, the evidence is persuasive in the American context, and shows that for people with severe mental disorders, ACT improves contact with services, reduces bed usage and hospital admission, and increases satisfaction with services, when compared with standard community care.

There is strong evidence suggesting that those receiving ACT were more likely to remain in contact with services than people receiving standard community care (number lost to follow-up: $n=1757$, RR=0.62, 95% CI 0.52 to 0.74). (Ia)

There is strong evidence suggesting that ACT teams decrease the likelihood of hospital admission, compared with standard care ($n=1047$, random effects RR=0.71, 95% CI 0.52 to 0.97; NNT=7, 95% CI 4 to 100). (Ia)

There is limited evidence suggesting that ACT teams decrease the likelihood of hospital admission, compared with hospital-based rehabilitation ($n=185$, RR=0.47, 95% CI 0.33 to 0.66; NNT=3, 95% CI 3 to 5). (Ib)

Assertive community treatment is associated with an average 40% reduction in bed usage. (Ia)

There is limited evidence suggesting that ACT is associated with increased satisfaction with services, compared with standard care (Client Satisfaction Scale: $n=120$, WMD= −0.56, 95% CI −0.77 to −0.36). (Ib)

Service users receiving ACT are less likely to be homeless, are more likely to be living independently and are less likely to be unemployed than those receiving standard care. However, these data include a study that specifically targeted homeless people and people at risk of being homeless.

There is strong evidence that ACT decreases the likelihood that service users would be homeless, compared with standard care (n=374, RR=0.22, 95% CI 0.09 to 0.56; NNT=10, 95% CI 7 to 20). (Ia)

There is strong evidence suggesting that those receiving ACT were more likely to live independently than people receiving standard community care (not living independently at end of study: n=362, RR=0.70, 95% CI 0.57 to 0.87; NNT=7, 95% CI 5 to 17). (Ia)

There is strong evidence suggesting that people receiving ACT were less likely to be unemployed at the end of the study than people receiving standard community care (n=604, RR=0.86, 95% CI 0.80 to 0.91; NNT=8, 95% CI 6 to 13). (Ia)

7.3.4.3 Effect of ACT on symptoms and quality of life

Service users receiving ACT are more likely to experience modest improvements in both mental state and quality of life than those receiving standard care.

There is strong evidence suggesting a statistically significant difference in mental state between those receiving ACT and those receiving standard care, but this difference is small in terms of clinical significance (BPRS/Brief Symptom Inventory/Colorado Symptom Index: n=255, SMD=−0.16, 95% CI −0.41 to −0.08). (Ia)

There is limited evidence suggesting that homeless people receiving ACT are more likely to experience a clinically significant improvement in quality of life, compared with standard care (General Wellbeing in Quality of Life Scale: n=125, WMD=−0.52, 95% CI −0.99 to −0.05). (Ib)

7.3.5 Clinical summary

Caution is necessary in the interpretation and translation of these findings for application in a UK context. Also, when assertive outreach is targeted at people who tend not to receive services and have little social support or help, such as the homeless, improvements in areas such as quality of life will be measured from a very low baseline. Generalising such findings to people with better access to services and/or better social support is problematic. With these caveats in mind, this review found evidence that for people with severe mental disorders, ACT compared with standard care is more likely to improve contact and satisfaction with services, decrease the use of hospital services, improve quality of life, and improve work and accommodation status.

7.3.6 Health economic evidence

It has been hypothesised that assertive outreach achieves significant cost reduction by shifting the focus of care into the community, reducing hospital admissions and improving concordance with the provided services. The cost-effectiveness of assertive outreach compared with other forms of service provision, such as case management and CMHTs, was also of interest.

The economic review identified 11 eligible studies, none of which originated in the UK. All studies were based on RCTs, with the exception of one study by Preston & Fazio (2000), which used data from a study with concurrent controls. Five studies adapted simple costing methods (Bond et al, 1988; Quinlivan et al, 1995; Hu & Jerrell, 1998; Salkever et al, 1999; Preston & Fazio, 2000) and six studies were economic evaluations (De Cangas, 1994; Wolff et al, 1997; Essock et al, 1998; Rosenheck & Neale, 1998; Chandler et al, 1999; Lehman et al, 1999). Six studies demonstrated a high risk of bias, and none of the studies used sensitivity analyses to investigate the robustness of their findings. Although the international results are unambiguous, interpretation of them within a UK context should be treated with caution.

Six studies compared ACT with 'standard care'. Bond et al (1988) found discrepancies in the cost-saving characteristics of ACT between the three participating study sites. All the remaining studies demonstrated that ACT was a cost-saving form of service provision (Quinlivan et al, 1995) or that ACT was more cost-effective than standard care (De Cangas, 1994; Rosenheck & Neale, 1998; Chandler et al, 1999; Lehman et al, 1999).

Six studies compared ACT with different approaches to case management. The study by Preston & Fazio (2000) demonstrated intensive care management to be more cost-saving than ACT, relative to the costs measured in the period before the introduction of these new forms of service provision. However, baseline data suggest a difference between the two comparison groups, and the analysis focused only on narrow cost components. Salkever et al (1999) found no significant cost difference between standard case management and ACT, but the study suffered from flaws similar to those of the analysis by Preston et al (2000). A more reliable result by Essock et al (1998) showed equal cost-effectiveness of the two forms of service provision. Hu & Jerrell (1998) demonstrated that ACT was more cost-saving in the long term, while Quinlivan et al (1995) also found ACT to be less costly, although the difference was not significant. Another study showed that ACT is equally as costly but more effective than case management (Wolff et al, 1997). None of the studies compared ACT with CMHTs.

Two studies investigated the cost-effectiveness of ACT specifically for homeless people with severe mental illness, and found that ACT was more cost-effective than standard care (Lehman et al, 1999) and more cost-effective than case management (Wolff et al, 1997).

7.3.6.1 Health economic conclusions

There is evidence that assertive community treatment is more cost-effective than standard care, representing a good 'value for money' form of service provision.

Comparing ACT with case management, the evidence suggests that there is no significant cost difference between the two forms of service provision.

There is evidence that ACT is a cost-effective form of service provision for homeless people with severe mental illness.

7.3.7 Clinical practice recommendations

7.3.7.1   Assertive outreach teams should be provided for people with serious mental disorders, including schizophrenia. (B)

7.3.7.2   Assertive outreach teams should be provided for people with serious mental disorders (including schizophrenia) who make much use of in-patient services and who have a history of poor engagement with services, leading to frequent relapse and/or social breakdown (manifested by homelessness or seriously inadequate accommodation). (B)

7.3.7.3   Assertive outreach teams should be provided for people with schizophrenia who are homeless. (B)

7.3.7.4   Where the needs of the service user or carer exceed the capacity of the assertive outreach team, referral to crisis resolution and home treatment teams, acute day hospitals or in-patient services should be considered. (GPP)

7.3.8 Research recommendations

7.3.8.1   Adequately powered RCTs reporting all relevant outcomes, including quality of life, are needed to establish the efficacy of assertive outreach teams for people with schizophrenia (and other serious mental disorders) in the UK. Studies should evaluate the suitability and efficacy of assertive outreach for different service user subgroups, and include economic analyses applicable to the UK setting.

7.4 Acute day hospital care

7.4.1 Introduction

Given the substantial costs and high level of use of in-patient care, the possibility of day hospital treatment programmes acting as an alternative to acute admission gained credence in the early 1960s, initially in the USA (Kris, 1965; Herz *et al*, 1971), and later in Europe (Wierma *et al*, 1989) and the UK (Dick *et al*, 1985; Creed *et al*, 1990).

7.4.2 Definition

Acute psychiatric day hospitals were defined by the GDG as units that provided 'diagnostic and treatment services for acutely ill individuals who would otherwise be treated in traditional psychiatric in-patient units'. Thus, trials would only be eligible for inclusion if they compared admission to an acute day hospital with admission to an in-patient unit. Participants were people with acute psychiatric disorders (all diagnoses) who would have been admitted to in-patient care had the acute day hospital not been available. Studies were excluded if they were largely restricted to people who were under 16 years or over 65 years old, or to those with a primary diagnosis of substance misuse or organic brain disorder.

7.4.3 Studies considered for review

The GDG selected a Health Technology Assessment (Marshall *et al*, 2001) as the basis for a fresh systematic review and meta-analysis. This assessment reviewed nine trials of acute day hospital treatment published between 1966 and 2000, including data for

1568 participants. A search for recent RCTs did not uncover any suitable new studies of acute day hospital treatment. Some difficulties were encountered in synthesising the outcome data, as a number of similar outcomes were presented in slightly different formats.

Studies included varied in the following ways:

- country of study (UK 3, The Netherlands 2, USA 4)
- follow-up (2 months to 2 years)
- patient mix by diagnosis (schizophrenia 23.5% to 39%; in one RCT all patients had been treated for a psychosis previously; in two trials the exact diagnostic composition of the samples was unknown)
- additional services (none, out-of-hours back-up, 'back-up bed')
- point of randomisation (unsuitable patients excluded prior to randomisation or randomisation at referral)
- outcomes recorded.

7.4.4 Results

The studies included in this review examined the use of acute day hospitals as an alternative to acute admission to an in-patient unit. The individuals involved in the studies were a diagnostically mixed group, including between a quarter and just over a third of people with a diagnosis of schizophrenia. Moreover, acute day hospitals are not suitable for people subject to compulsory treatment, and some studies explicitly excluded people with families unable to provide effective support at home. Clearly, the findings from this review, and the recommendations based upon them, cannot be generalised to all people with schizophrenia who present for acute admission.

The review found strong evidence that people attending acute day hospitals, when compared with in-patient care, spend fewer days in hospital and do not recover more slowly. The review also found that the burden on families was no greater than for in-patient care, and that social functioning of service users is much the same in either treatment setting. Insufficient evidence was found to ascertain whether treatment in an acute day hospital led to a reduction in readmission, compared with in-patient care.

There is insufficient evidence to determine whether there was a significant difference in readmission rates between acute day hospital patients and in-patients ($n=667$, RR=0.91, 95% CI 0.72 to 1.15). (Ia)

There is strong evidence suggesting that people attending acute day hospitals are more likely to spend fewer days in in-patient care than those admitted directly to in-patient units (in-patient days per month: $n=465$, WMD=−2.75, 95% CI −3.63 to −1.87). (Ia)

There is strong evidence suggesting that acute day hospitals do not lead to slower rates of recovery than in-patient care (all hospital days per month: $n=465$, WMD=−0.38, 95% CI −1.32 to 0.55). (Ia)

There is limited evidence suggesting that there is no clinically significant difference between acute day hospitals and in-patient care on a measure of family burden (e.g. Social Behaviour Assessment Scale Burden Score at 3 months: $n=160$, WMD=−0.59, 95% CI −1.62 to 0.44). (Ib)

There is limited evidence suggesting that there is no clinically significant difference between acute day hospital patients and in-patients on a measure of social functioning at 12 months and 24 months (Groningen Social Disabilities Schedule overall role score at 24 months: $n=95$, WMD$=-0.19$, 95% CI -0.58 to 0.20). (Ib)

7.4.5 Clinical summary

For a mixed population of service users, including those with a diagnosis of schizophrenia, acute day hospital care is a viable alternative to in-patient care, reducing hospital bed use without adversely affecting the family, the rate of recovery or social functioning.

7.4.6 Health economic evidence

Given the large direct medical costs associated with relapse in schizophrenia, primarily resulting from expensive in-patient treatment, it has been suggested that the lower operational cost of acute day hospitals could result in substantial savings for the health service. On the other hand, there have been fears that these savings would be achieved by shifting the cost burden to families and carers, offering no real reduction in the overall cost to society.

The economic review identified three eligible studies. Two economic analyses were based on RCTs (Sledge *et al*, 1996; Creed *et al*, 1997); the third used data from a controlled study with concurrent controls (Francois *et al*, 1993). The UK-based study (Creed *et al*, 1997) adapted a cost–consequences method with a broad societal perspective; the other two studies were simple cost analyses focusing on direct medical care costs. All three studies reported results with a low risk of bias.

Each of the studies compared acute day hospitals with routine in-patient treatment, and concluded that acute day hospitals are less costly than in-patient care. In the UK study, the significant median cost saving for the health trust using acute day hospitals was £1923 per patient (95% CI 750 to 3174). The savings originated mainly from reduced operational costs (Creed *et al*, 1997). Moreover, Creed *et al* demonstrated that acute day hospitals are both cheaper and more effective than in-patient treatment. Those caring for day hospital patients may bear additional costs, but other sources of caregiver burden are reduced. Accordingly, for society as a whole, acute day hospitals remain a more cost-effective alternative than routine in-patient services, with significant cost savings of £1994 per patient at 1994–1995 prices (Creed *et al*, 1997). Although some cost savings for acute day hospitals were reported in the US study by Sledge *et al* (1996), this was not of statistical significance for the subgroup of service users with psychosis.

7.4.6.1 Health economic conclusions

There are few economic studies of acute day hospitals. There is evidence that acute day hospital care is more cost-effective than routine in-patient care, saving nearly £2000 per patient per year for the NHS.

Carers of day hospital patients may bear additional costs, although other caregiver burden is significantly less.

7.4.7 Clinical practice recommendations

7.4.7.1   Acute day hospitals should be considered as a clinical and cost-effective option for the provision of acute care, both as an alternative to acute admission to in-patient care and to facilitate early discharge from in-patient care. (A)

7.4.8 Research recommendations

7.4.8.1   More high-quality, direct economic evaluations are necessary to establish the cost-effectiveness of acute day hospitals compared with other acute service provisions, such as crisis resolution and home treatment teams.

7.5 Vocational rehabilitation

7.5.1 Introduction

Most people with mental health problems want to work (Hatfield *et al*, 1992; Shepherd *et al*, 1994), yet unemployment rates among mental health service users are extremely high, both in the UK (61–73%; McCreadie, 1992; Meltzer *et al*, 1995) and in the USA (75–85%; Lehman *et al*, 1995; Ridgeway & Rapp, 1998). These high rates of unemployment are only in part a reflection of the disability experienced by people with schizophrenia, as suggested by evidence that other disabled groups experience lower unemployment than people with severe mental health problems (Office of National Statistics, 1998). Other factors contributing to high unemployment include discrimination by employers and the low priority given to employment status by mental health services (Lehman *et al*, 1998). Nevertheless, work and employment schemes (vocational rehabilitation) have an established place in the history of contemporary psychiatry. The development of these schemes has been motivated partly by a belief that work itself can be therapeutic, and partly to help service users develop the skills and gain the confidence to re-enter competitive employment (for a brief review, see Marshall *et al*, 2001).

Two models of vocational rehabilitation have emerged over recent years, using different methods and principles, both aiming to improve employment outcomes. In prevocational training programmes, service users undergo a preparation phase, and sometimes a transitional employment phase, intended to help them become re-accustomed to working, and to develop the skills necessary for later competitive employment. There are both traditional (sheltered workshop) and 'clubhouse' versions of this approach. In supported employment programmes, on the other hand, service users are placed as quickly as possible in competitive employment, with training and support provided by 'job coaches' (Anthony & Blanch, 1987) in the real work setting, without a lengthy, prevocational preparation phase. Ordinary service provision is tailored to meet the needs and work situation of the individual.

In the UK, it is estimated that there are about 135 organisations offering prevocational training schemes and 77 offering supported employment programmes (ERMIS European Economic Interest Grouping database, 1998, cited by Marshall *et al*, 2001). Proponents of each model (or variants thereof) have claimed superiority with varying degrees of evidential support. The GDG therefore elected to review the evidence base for each form of vocational rehabilitation compared with standard community care and with each other, and to examine specific modifications (such as payment or psychological interventions) designed to enhance motivation and improve outcomes.

7.5.2 Definitions

For this review, the GDG used the following definitions:

- Prevocational training is defined as any approach to vocational rehabilitation in which participants are expected to undergo a period of preparation before being encouraged to seek competitive employment. This preparation phase could involve either work in a sheltered environment (such as a workshop or work unit), or some form of pre-employment training or transitional employment. This included both traditional (sheltered workshop) and 'clubhouse' approaches.

- Supported employment is any approach to vocational rehabilitation that attempts to place service users immediately in competitive employment. It was acceptable for supported employment to begin with a short period of preparation, but this had to be of less than 1 month's duration and not involve work placement in a sheltered setting, training, or transitional employment.

- Modifications of vocational rehabilitation programmes are defined as either prevocational training or supported employment that has been enhanced by some technique to increase participants' motivation. Typical techniques consist of payment for participation in the programme, or some form of psychological intervention.

- Standard care is defined as the usual psychiatric care for participants in the trial, without any specific vocational component. In all trials where an intervention was compared with standard care, unless otherwise stated participants would have received the intervention in addition to standard care. Thus, for example, in a trial comparing prevocational training and standard community care, participants in the prevocational training group would also have been in receipt of standard community services such as out-patient appointments.

7.5.3 Studies considered for review

The GDG selected a Cochrane Review (Crowther *et al*, 2001) of 18 RCTs, updated with two new RCTs (MUESER (Hartford); LEHMAN (Baltimore)), for further systematic review and meta-analysis. All included trials fulfilled the GDG definitions for the different types of vocational rehabilitation. Trials primarily evaluating case management or assertive outreach were excluded.

Specific inclusion criteria were age 16–65 years and a diagnosis of severe mental disorder, including schizophrenia and schizophrenia-like disorders, bipolar disorder and depression with psychotic features. Trials were excluded if the majority of participants had a learning disability, or substance misuse as their primary or sole diagnosis. Trials involving people with substance misuse as a secondary diagnosis to a mental disorder were included.

Studies included varied in the following ways:

- follow-up period (5 months to 4 years)
- numbers lost to follow-up (0% to 37%, some unclear)
- rater independence (independent, not independent, unclear)
- diagnostic mix of clients (27% to 100% for schizophrenia and schizophrenia-like disorders; not clearly specified in three studies)
- mean age (19–46 years)

- history of employment (variable or unknown)
- country of study (USA 19, UK 1)
- outcomes recorded.

7.5.4 Results

All except one of the studies considered in this review were conducted in the USA, where employment practices, employment law, social structures and health and social care services are substantially different from those of the UK. Nevertheless, cautious translation of the findings of this review into a UK context is defensible.

7.5.4.1 Supported employment *v.* prevocational training

There is strong evidence that supported employment is superior to prevocational training, improving employment prospects and hours per week spent in competitive employment significantly more when the two are compared.

In studies from the USA, supported employment, when compared with prevocational training, strongly increases the likelihood that people with serious mental health problems will gain competitive employment at 4, 6, 9, 12, 15, 18 and 24 months (e.g. numbers not in competitive employment at 18 months: $n=718$, RR=0.82, 95% CI 0.77 to 0.88; NNT=7, 95% CI 5 to 9; at 24 months: $n=290$, RR=0.81, 95% CI 0.73 to 0.89; NNT=6, 95% CI 4 to 10). (Ia)

Supported employment increases the likelihood of people with serious mental health problems spending more time in competitive employment; for example, in three trial reports (DRAKE (New Hampshire; 1); DRAKE (Washington); GERVEY (New York)) service users in supported employment spent on average significantly more hours per month in competitive employment than those receiving prevocational training (e.g. DRAKE (New Hampshire; 1): supported employment group mean 33.7 h, prevocational training group mean 11.4 h; $t=3.7$, $P<0.001$). (Ib)

7.5.4.2 Prevocational training *v.* standard care; modified prevocational training *v.* standard prevocational training

There is insufficient evidence to determine whether prevocational training confers any additional benefit on employment prospects for people with serious mental health problems, when compared with standard care. However, the addition of either payment or psychological interventions to prevocational training results in a limited but clinically significant improvement in outcomes.

In one study from the USA there is limited evidence to suggest that prevocational training does not increase the likelihood that people with serious mental health problems will enter competitive employment, compared with standard care (not in competitive employment at 18–24 months: $n=243$, RR=0.99, 95% CI 0.82 to 1.18). (Ib)

In US studies there is insufficient evidence to determine if there is a clinically significant difference between prevocational training and standard care in admission rates (by 1 year: $n=887$, random effects RR=0.71, 95% CI 0.48 to 1.04). (Ia)

There is limited evidence that combining prevocational training with a psychological intervention improves the chances of entering competitive employment, compared with prevocational training alone at 9 months (not in competitive employment: $n=122$,

RR=0.90, 95% CI 0.83 to 0.98; NNT=10, 95% CI 6 to 50). Another very small study failed to detect this difference at 6 months, although the confidence intervals are wide (n=20, RR=0.56, 95% CI 0.29 to 1.07). (Ib)

There is limited evidence that combining prevocational training with payment improves the chances of gaining any form of employment, compared with prevocational training alone, at 6 months (not in competitive employment: n=150, RR=0.40, 95% CI 0.28 to 0.57; NNT=3, 95% CI 2 to 4). (Ib)

7.5.4.3 Supported employment v. standard care

The evidence from this review suggests that supported employment has a significant additional effect on employment prospects for people with serious mental health problems, compared with standard care.

There is limited evidence that supported employment significantly increases the likelihood that people with serious mental health problems will return to employment of any kind, compared with standard care alone (n=256, RR=0.79, 95% CI 0.70 to 0.90; NNT=6, 95% CI 4 to 12). (Ib)

Supported employment increases the likelihood that people with serious mental health problems will enter competitive employment, compared with standard care, at 24 months follow-up (n=256, RR=0.92, 95% CI 0.85 to 0.99; NNT=13, 95% CI 7 to 100) and at 36 months follow-up (n=256, RR=0.88, 95% CI 0.82 to 0.96; NNT=10, 95% CI 6 to 25), but not at 12 months follow-up (not in competitive employment: n=256; RR=1.01, 95% CI 0.93 to 1.09). (Ib)

7.5.5 Clinical summary

There is evidence from studies in the USA to suggest that supported employment is superior to prevocational training programmes in helping people with serious mental health problems gain competitive employment.

7.5.6 Health economic evidence

One way in which schizophrenia imposes a heavy burden on families and broader society is in the form of additional unemployment resulting from the illness. Interventions aiming to improve employment outcomes, such as vocational rehabilitation programmes, have been hypothesised to provide cost savings to society through reduced productivity losses, as well as additional economic benefits associated with improved social functioning (e.g. housing costs, legal costs, social benefit costs). Improved employment status might also have indirect effects on health service use. Vocational rehabilitation programmes may be delivered in several different ways, which may differ in their cost-effectiveness.

The economic review identified seven eligible studies, while a further study was not available. Three studies were based on RCTs (Bell & Lysaker, 1995; Bond et al, 1995; Clark et al, 1998), one was a controlled study with concurrent controls (Warner et al, 2000), two were mirror-image studies based on before-and-after data (Rogers et al, 1995; Clark et al, 1996) and one was an observational study (Hallam & Schneider, 1999). Three studies adapted simple costing methods, while four could be considered as economic evaluations. Only the study by Hallam & Schneider was conducted in the UK. One study was prone to a high risk of bias due to its validity (Warner *et al*, 2000), but the studies generally were not without methodological flaws. Common problems were small study samples, known biasing effects, and the lack of sensitivity analyses to confirm the robustness of the results. Results should be treated with caution when interpreted within a UK context.

One study compared the 'clubhouse' approach to prevocational training with standard care (Warner *et al*, 2000), and another compared supported employment with standard care (Rogers *et al*, 1995). Warner *et al* showed prevocational training to be less costly, but the result was not adjusted to the difference in disease severity between the two groups. Rogers *et al* found standard care to be more efficient. When supported employment was compared with historical rehabilitative day treatment, the former seemed to improve vocational outcomes without increasing costs (Clark *et al*, 1996).

When different forms of vocational rehabilitation were compared, two studies found supported employment to be more cost-saving than prevocational training, although the differences were not significant, and the direct programme cost was estimated to be greater for supported employment (Bond *et al*, 1995; Clark *et al*, 1998). One study compared the sheltered workshop form of prevocational training with the 'clubhouse' approach in the UK, and showed that the sheltered workshop form is cheaper. Its net cost per placement was £3449, compared with £6172 per placement for the 'clubhouse' approach, in the year 1994–1995 (Hallam & Schneider, 1999). Bell & Lysaker (1995) compared the cost-effectiveness of prevocational training with payment to the participants against prevocational training without payment, and found that the paid form of prevocational training was more cost-effective.

7.5.6.1 Health economic conclusions

It is impossible to draw any firm conclusion about the cost-effectiveness of vocational rehabilitation programmes compared with standard forms of service provision on the basis of the available evidence.

It seems that supported employment is equally cost-saving or more cost-saving than prevocational training.

There is limited evidence that the paid form of prevocational training is more cost-effective than unpaid prevocational training.

The available evidence suggests that the 'clubhouse' approach is more costly than the sheltered workshop form.

7.5.7 Clinical practice recommendations

7.5.7.1   Supported employment programmes should be provided for people with schizophrenia who wish to return to work or gain employment. However, it should not be the only work-related activity offered when individuals are unable to work or are unsuccessful in their attempts to find employment. (C)

7.5.7.2   Mental health services, in partnership with social care providers and other local stakeholders, should enable people to use local employment opportunities, including a range of employment schemes to suit the different needs and levels of skill of people with severe mental health problems, including schizophrenia. (GPP)

7.5.8 Research recommendations

7.5.8.1   Randomised controlled trials, recording all relevant outcomes, including quality of life and self-esteem, should be conducted to establish the clinical, economic and occupational effectiveness of supported employment in the UK.

7.5.8.2   Research should be conducted, recording all relevant outcomes, including quality of life and self-esteem, to identify the most beneficial types of work-related daytime activity for people with schizophrenia and other serious mental health problems.

7.6 Non-acute day hospital care

7.6.1 Introduction

Although the earliest use of day hospitals in mental health care was to provide an alternative to in-patient care (Cameron, 1947), non-acute day hospitals have also been used for people with refractory mental health problems unresponsive to treatment in out-patient clinics. Two broad groups of people have been referred for non-acute day hospital care: those with anxiety and depressive disorders who have residual or persistent symptoms, and those with more severe and enduring mental disorders such as schizophrenia. For the latter group, day hospital care has been used to improve outcomes, reduce admission rates and enhance engagement (Marshall *et al*, 2001). The evidence for the effectiveness of non-acute day hospital care in improving clinical outcomes for people with severe mental illness has been challenged (Hoge *et al*, 1992), and indeed some think such centres may even be doing harm (Tantam & McGrath, 1989).

Given the need for services for people with severe and enduring mental health problems who are refractory to other forms of treatment, the GDG undertook a review of the evidence comparing the efficacy of non-acute day hospitals with that of traditional out-patient treatment programmes.

7.6.2 Definition

For this review, and following the Cochrane Review by Marshall *et al* (2001), the GDG agreed the following definition for non-acute day hospitals, in so far as they apply to people with serious mental health problems, including schizophrenia:

* psychiatric day hospitals offering continuing care to people with severe mental disorders

Studies were excluded if the participants were predominantly either over 65 years or under 18 years of age.

7.6.3 Studies considered for review

A systematic (Cochrane) review of non-acute day hospitals and out-patient clinics, recently published as a Health Technology Assessment (Marshall *et al*, 2001), was selected for reanalysis. Of the eight original trials, four were excluded because more than 80% of the participants in each study had been given diagnoses other than schizophrenia. The excluded studies were those by Bateman & Fonaghy (1999) in London, Dick *et al* (1991) in Dundee, Piper *et al* (1993) in Alberta, and Tyrer & Remington (1979) in Southampton. No additional trial was found suitable for inclusion for further analysis. Three of the four studies included were set in New York (MELTZOFF 1966; WELDON 1979; GLICK 1986), and one (LINN 1979) was conducted elsewhere in the USA.

Studies included varied in the following ways:

- follow-up period (3–24 months)
- diagnosis of participants (schizophrenia: 47% up to 100%)
- gender of participants (male 2, mixed 2)
- comparator treatments (standard out-patient care, out-patient care plus additional psychotherapy input).

7.6.4 Results

As all the studies in this review were conducted in the USA, application of their findings to the UK should be tentative. Also, it should be borne in mind that the people referred to psychiatric day hospitals, both in the USA and the UK, are those who have responded less than optimally to standard treatment. The review found no evidence to suggest that non-acute day hospitals increased the likelihood of improving outcomes when compared with standard out-patient care.

There is insufficient evidence to determine if there is a clinically significant difference between non-acute day hospital care and out-patient care for people with severe mental disorders on numbers lost to follow-up (at 18 months: n=80, RR=1.75, 95% CI 0.56 to 5.51). (Ib)

There is insufficient evidence to determine if there is a clinically significant difference between day care centres and out-patient care on admission rates (at 12 months: n=162, RR=0.86, 95% CI 0.61 to 1.23; at 24 months: n=162, RR=0.82, 95% CI 0.64 to 1.05). (Ib)

There is insufficient evidence to determine whether there is a clinically significant difference between day care centres and out-patient care on a measure of mental state (Symptom Check List–90: n=30, WMD=0.31, 95% CI –0.20 to 0.82). (Ib)

There is insufficient evidence to determine if there is a clinically significant difference between day care centres and out-patient care on social functioning (Community Adaptation Scale: n=30, WMD=–0.03, 95% CI –0.30 to 0.24). (Ib)

7.6.5 Clinical summary

The limited evidence found at review suggests that non-acute day hospital care offers no discernible advantage over standard out-patient care for people with serious mental health problems who have responded less than optimally to standard care.

7.6.6 Clinical practice recommendations

There was insufficient evidence to make any recommendation about day care activities in a day hospital setting. (C)

7.7 Crisis resolution and home treatment teams

7.7.1 Introduction

Traditionally, a first episode or acute exacerbation of schizophrenia is managed by admission to an acute in-patient unit. However, in recent years there has been growing interest in attempting to manage such episodes in the community. If this could be done safely, it might avoid the stigma and costs associated with hospital admission, thus providing benefits to both service users and service providers. Crisis resolution and home treatment teams (CRHTTs) are a form of service that aims to avoid admitting acutely ill people to hospital by providing intensive home-based support. A Cochrane Review of crisis intervention for people with serious mental health problems (Joy *et al*, 2002) was selected by the GDG for review and further analysis.

7.7.2 Definition

The GDG adopted the inclusion criteria developed by the Cochrane Review team for studies of CRHTTs in the management of people with schizophrenia. Crisis intervention and the comparator treatment were defined as follows:

- crisis resolution is any type of crisis-oriented treatment of an acute psychiatric episode by staff with a specific remit to deal with such situations, in and beyond 'office hours'
- 'standard care' is the normal care given to those suffering from acute psychiatric episodes in the area concerned; this involved hospital-based treatment for all studies included.

The focus of the review was to examine the effects of CRHTT care for people with serious mental illness experiencing an acute episode, compared with the standard care they would normally receive.

7.7.3 Studies considered for review

The Cochrane Review of CRHTTs (Joy *et al*, 2002) included five RCTs (PASAMANICK 1964 (Ohio), FENTON 1979 (Montreal), HOULT 1981 (Sydney), MUIJEN (UK; 2), STEIN 1975 (Madison, Wisconsin)). A further search identified one new RCT (FENTON 1998 (Maryland)) not included in the Cochrane Review and suitable for inclusion for this guideline. Data from these six studies, including 883 participants, were pooled and reanalysed. All studies selected participants on the basis of their referral for acute admission and treatment.

Studies included varied in the following ways:
- follow-up (6 months to 2 years)
- diagnosis of participants (schizophrenia: 41.9% to 100%)
- participants excluded (three studies excluded people with organic brain syndrome, three excluded alcoholism or dual diagnosis, one made no exclusion on the basis of psychopathology, and one study excluded participants who were suicidal, homicidal or whose family were unable to provide support at home)
- setting (inner city, urban, suburban, mixed)
- outcomes recorded.

Evidence from this review suggests that CRHTTs, when compared with standard care, decrease the likelihood of people with serious mental health problems being admitted while being treated by the CRHTT, and increase the likelihood of shorter admissions.

Compared with standard care:

- there is strong evidence that CRHTTs substantially decrease the likelihood of admission (admission rates at 12 months: $n=400$, RR=0.39, 95% CI 0.33 to 0.47; NNT=2, 95% CI 2 to 2) (Ia)

- there is limited evidence that for service users cared for by CRHTTs there is a clinically significant reduction in the duration of acute in-patient care (all admissions) after 3–4 months ($n=122$, WMD=−19.61, 95% CI −24.99 to −14.23), 8 months ($n=122$, WMD=−10.25, 95% CI −16.12 to −4.38) and 12 months ($n=121$, WMD=−8.42, 95% CI −16.36 to −0.48). (Ib)

It appears that CRHTTs do not change the likelihood of people with serious mental health problems being readmitted, or reduce the duration of in-patient treatment (for non-index admissions), when compared with standard care.

Compared with standard care:

- there is insufficient evidence to determine whether CRHTTs alter the likelihood of people being readmitted to acute care by 12 months ($n=601$, random effects RR=0.51, 95% CI 0.21 to 1.20) and by 24 months ($n=306$, random effects RR=0.76, 95% CI 0.36 to 1.63) (Ia)

- there is insufficient evidence to determine whether CRHTTs affect the duration of acute in-patient care (non-index admissions only) by 6 months ($n=108$, WMD= −0.74, 95% CI −18.15 to 16.67). (Ib)

People found treatment by CRHTTs to be more acceptable (participant more satisfied, less likely to leave the study early) than standard care. The review found insufficient evidence to determine the effect of CRHTTs on death rates, and evidence for CRHTTs improving mental state and global functioning was either limited or insufficient to determine, compared with standard care.

There is limited evidence that people cared for by CRHTTs are more satisfied with services at 6 months, 12 months and 20 months (e.g. Satisfaction Scale at 20 months: $n=137$, WMD=−5.40, 95% CI −6.89 to −3.91). (Ib)

There is strong evidence that people cared for by CRHTTs are less likely to leave treatment early (leaving the study early at 12 months: $n=600$, RR=0.72, 95% CI 0.55 to 0.95; NNT=13, 95% CI 7 to 100). (Ia)

There is insufficient evidence to determine if CRHTTs are associated with an increase in the rate of attempted suicide ($n=250$, RR=1.33, 95% CI 0.87 to 2.03). (Ib)

There is insufficient evidence to determine if the mental state of people cared for by CRHTTs is improved at 6 months and 12 months. However, at 20 months there is limited evidence of significant improvement in mental state (BPRS at 6 months: $n=129$, WMD= -2.10, 95% CI -6.40 to 2.20; at 12 months: $n=131$, WMD=-2.00, 95% CI -6.03 to 2.03; at 20 months: $n=142$, WMD=-4.50, 95% CI -8.68 to -0.32). (Ib)

There is limited evidence suggesting that CRHTTs lead to a small improvement in global functioning at 6 months, but the evidence is insufficient at 12 months and 20 months (PEF/GAS end-point scores at 6 months: $n=226$, SMD=-0.32, 95% CI -0.59 to -0.06; at 12 months: $n=231$, SMD=-0.07, 95% CI -0.33 to -0.19; at 20 months: $n=142$, SMD= -0.31, 95% CI -0.64 to -0.02). (Ib)

7.7.5 Clinical summary

For people with schizophrenia and other serious mental health problems in an acute crisis, CRHTT care is superior to standard hospital-based care in reducing admissions and shortening stay in hospital, and appears to be more acceptable than hospital-based care for acute crises. Crisis resolution and home treatment teams are less likely to lose contact with service users, and may also have a marginally better effect on some clinical outcomes.

7.7.6 Health economic evidence

It has been hypothesised that community treatment of acutely ill people with schizophrenia might reduce admissions and shorten hospital stays, enabling savings in expensive in-patient treatment that might offset the extra costs of running the CRHTT service. On the other hand, there have been fears that these savings would be achieved by shifting the cost burden to families and carers, offering no real reduction in the cost to society.

The economic review identified four eligible studies, three based on RCTs (Weisbrod *et al*, 1980; Fenton *et al*, 1984; Knapp *et al*, 1998) and one based on a controlled study with concurrent controls (Ford *et al*, 2001). One study was a simple cost analysis (Fenton *et al*, 1984), while the others were in the form of economic evaluations. All studies reported results with a low risk of bias, except the study by Weisbrod *et al* (1980).

The study by Fenton *et al* (1984) showed that CRHTTs are cost-saving from a narrow health-care provider perspective. This result is in agreement with the conclusions of studies employing broader costing perspectives, which demonstrated that CRHTTs are significantly more cost-effective than standard care (Weisbrod *et al*, 1980; Knapp *et al*, 1998) or hospital-based acute psychiatric treatment (Ford *et al*, 2001). Ford *et al* estimated that the annual cost of providing the service was £481 000. Knapp *et al* estimated the cost difference to be £236 per week during the first year (fiscal year 1996– 1997). The UK-based studies by Ford *et al* (2001) and Knapp *et al* (1998) also confirmed the cost-effectiveness of CRHTTs by sensitivity analysis and by the analysis of biasing effects. Two studies investigated the long-term outcomes of CRHTT care (Fenton *et al*, 1984; Knapp *et al*, 1998) and found that the difference in cost between CRHTTs and standard care decreased continuously after 12 months. Family burden costs were not measured systematically in any of the studies, but analyses showed no difference between subsamples for which data were available (Weisbrod *et al*, 1980; Knapp *et al*, 1998).

There is evidence that CRHTTs are cost-saving for at least 1 year compared with standard care, and for at least 6 months compared with hospital-based acute psychiatric treatment.

There is evidence that CRHTTs lose their cost-effectiveness in the long term.

7.7.7 Clinical practice recommendations

7.7.7.1   Crisis resolution and home treatment teams should be used as a means to manage crises for service users, and as a means of delivering high-quality acute care. In this context, teams must pay particular attention to risk monitoring as a high-priority routine activity. (B)

7.7.7.2   Crisis resolution and home treatment team care should be considered for people with schizophrenia who are in crisis, to augment the services provided by early intervention services and assertive outreach teams. (C)

7.7.7.3   Crisis resolution and home treatment team care should be considered for people with schizophrenia who might benefit from early discharge from hospital following a period of in-patient care. (C)

7.7.8 Research recommendations

7.7.8.1   Adequately powered RCTs recording all relevant clinical, social and economic outcomes, including quality of life and the methods and effects of risk monitoring, are needed to compare the effectiveness of treatment by acute day hospitals, in-patient units, and crisis resolution and home treatment teams.

7.8 Early interventions

7.8.1 Introduction

The National Health Service Plan has set out a clear requirement for mental health services to establish the first elements of an early intervention service by April 2004. Early intervention services are expected to provide care for people aged between 14 years and 35 years with a first presentation of psychotic symptoms during the first 3 years of their illness. Early intervention is a relatively new idea and therefore there are only a few models available to guide service development: in England, for example, services have been pioneered in Birmingham (Initiative to Reduce the Impact of Schizophrenia; IRIS, 2002) and in London (Lambeth Early Onset Service; Garety & Jolley, 2000); examples in other countries are the early intervention services in Stavanger (Johannessen *et al*, 2001) and Melbourne (National Early Psychosis Project; NEPP, 2002).

Early intervention is primarily concerned with identification and initial treatment. Identification may be directed either at people in the prodromal phase of the illness ('earlier early intervention') or at those who have already developed psychosis ('early intervention'). Intervention with prodromal 'patients' is an interesting but potentially controversial area, which at present is outside the scope of this guideline. The GDG is, however, aware of recent developments in the field, which may be reviewed in future versions of the guidelines (e.g. McGorry *et al*, 2002).

Early identification of people with psychotic disorders does not, however, fall within the scope of the guidelines. Central to the rationale for this type of early identification is the concept of duration of untreated psychosis (DUP). A number of researchers have reported that the longer the psychosis goes untreated, the poorer the prognosis becomes (e.g. Loebel *et al*, 1992; McGorry *et al*, 1996). This finding has led them to argue that new services are required to reduce the length of time people with psychosis remain undiagnosed and untreated. Moreover, these researchers have argued that such services should offer specialised, phase-specific treatment to their users, to maximise their chances of recovery.

7.8.2 Review of early intervention services

To date, no formal high-quality evaluation of the impact of early intervention services on the initial treatment of psychosis is available. A descriptive study from Australia (Power *et al*, 1998) suggested that some benefit might be derived from the introduction of specialist early intervention services over standard care, but a number of factors (including other service changes) limit the conclusions that can be drawn from this study.

To reduce the DUP, a Scandinavian study compared a sector with a specialist early detection system against two other sectors that relied on the existing detection and referral system. The enhanced detection system managed to reduce DUP from 1.5 years (mean) to 0.5 years (Johannessen *et al*, 2001).

There is increasing interest in investigating the possible connections between DUP and prognosis, but this is complicated by issues such as severity of symptoms and duration thresholds. Also, there is increasing interest in developing and evaluating means of shortening DUP through early identification and intervention, but the evidence base is slight as yet.

The rationale for an early intervention service is powerful, both ethically (helping people with serious mental health problems at an early stage to reduce distress and possibly disability) and in terms of choice (service users and carers want help sooner than is usually available). The GDG agreed that the government's investment into new services, including (and especially) the development of early intervention services, was to be supported. Moreover, the nature of such an intervention means that it is difficult to evaluate unless there is substantial investment in setting up suitable services. We therefore welcome the Department of Health's decision to provide new funding, but must emphasise the overriding importance of high-quality evaluation to answer important questions that the GDG could not answer with the current evidence base. For example, will reducing DUP alter the prognosis for people with schizophrenia? What will the impact of early intervention be on key measures such as suicide rates, relapse rates, admission rates and mental state? How will it fit in with existing services? Will it be cost-effective? Will it manage to make any impact on the current stigma associated with psychosis, or will a specialist, early detection service inadvertently achieve exactly the opposite?

7.8.3 Health economic evidence

Early intervention services have been hypothesised to reduce long-term health care resource use and improved social functioning, leading to savings that might offset the cost of providing early intervention. This supposition is based on the evidence for a potential link between shorter duration of untreated psychosis and better outcome in schizophrenia.

The economic review identified one eligible study (Mihalopoulos *et al*, 1999), which is a cost-effectiveness analysis from Australia based on a controlled study with historical controls. No RCT addressing the cost-effectiveness question was identified. The results of the study by Mihalopoulos *et al* have a low risk of bias, and the robustness of the findings was confirmed by sensitivity analysis. However, the authors costed only direct health care services, so it is impossible to estimate any broader economic effects of early intervention.

The results showed that the Early Psychosis Prevention and Intervention Centre had a clear advantage over standard care in economic terms, being more effective and cost-saving (Mihalopoulos *et al*, 1999). Nevertheless, an interpretation of this result in the context of UK or other types of early intervention services should be treated with caution.

7.8.3.1 Health economic conclusions

The quantity of the available evidence is very poor. Early interventions on the Australian model can represent cost-effective service provision.

7.8.4   Clinical practice recommendations

7.8.4.1   Because many people with actual or possible schizophrenia have difficulty in getting help, treatment and care at an early stage, it is recommended that early intervention services are developed to provide the correct mix of specialist pharmacological, psychological, social, occupational and educational interventions at the earliest opportunity. (GPP)

7.8.4.2   Where the needs of the service user or carer exceed the capacity of early intervention services, referral to crisis resolution and home treatment teams, acute day hospitals or in-patient services should be considered. (GPP)

7.8.5 Research recommendations

7.8.5.1   It is recommended that early intervention services be evaluated using adequately powered RCTs reporting all relevant clinical, social, occupational and economic outcomes, including quality of life and longer-term outcomes.

7.9 Intensive case management

7.9.1 Introduction

Many people who develop schizophrenia have a wide range of needs for health and social care. For most people this will be provided by family and carers, primary care health workers, secondary mental health services, social services, legal and forensic services, and work and education organisations. Each individual service user will have a unique combination of needs. Moreover, each service user's health and social care needs will vary, often considerably, over time. For the delivery of variable and often complex treatment and care arrangements in a flexible and well-integrated way, especially when service users live in the community outside psychiatric institutions, services need systematic methods of coordinating care reliably. Case management (CM) was introduced as a means of ensuring that people with serious mental health problems remain in contact with services, and of improving the coordination of the provision of treatment across services and between agencies.

Although CM always involves allocating each service user a named and known professional to act as a case manager, whose role is to maintain contact with the service user and to individually arrange and coordinate care across all agencies, numerous models of this approach exist. These include 'brokerage', intensive case management (ICM) and the care programme approach (CPA). Also, studies of case management often use the same term for rather different approaches, sometimes describing assertive outreach or 'home-based' care as case management. Nevertheless, case management, in the form of the CPA, has been formally endorsed as the preferred method of coordinating care by the Department of Health (2002), and all service users with more than one service involved in the delivery of their treatment and care (as is usually the case for people with schizophrenia) are subject to a more intensive version known as 'enhanced CPA' (eCPA).

7.9.2 Definition

The GDG identified a Cochrane Review of case management (Marshall *et al*, 2002) for updating and reanalysis. Given the variation in the models studied, the GDG followed the Cochrane Review team's approach: an intervention was considered to be 'case management' if it was described as such in the trial report. In the original review no distinction, for eligibility purposes, was made between 'brokerage', 'intensive', 'clinical' or 'strengths' models. For the purposes of the current review, ICM was defined as a case-load of 15 or fewer. The UK terms 'care management' and 'care programme approach' were also treated as synonyms for case management. However, the review excluded studies of two types of intervention often loosely classed as case management: assertive community treatment and 'home-based care'.

7.9.3 Studies considered for review

The Cochrane Review (Marshall *et al*, 2002) incorporated ten trials of case management published between 1966 and 1997 (CURTIS (New York); FRANKLIN (Houston); JERRELL (Carolina); MACIAS (Utah); QUINLIVAN (California); SOLOMON (Philadelphia); MUIJEN (London; 2); FORD (London); TYRER (London); MARSHALL (Oxford). The GDG undertook a further search for additional trials published since the review and found three trials of case management that fulfilled the definition and passed quality criteria. The additional studies were: BURNS (UK700); HOLLOWAY (London); ISSAKIDIS (Sydney). This gave a total of 13 trials, with data for 2546 participants, for review and meta-analysis.

Studies included varied in the following ways:
- country of study (UK 6, USA 6, Australia 1)
- follow-up period (6–52 months)

- participants with diagnosis of schizophrenia (38% to 89%; two studies unknown/ unclear)
- gender of participants (mixed 12, all male 1)
- mean age for trial (36–49 years)
- experimental group (ICM, CM)
- comparator treatments (standard care, CM, ACT)
- case-loads for case managers (1:4 to 1:40)
- setting (inner city, urban, suburban, men discharged from prison to urban centre)
- inclusion criteria (however, most services included people with serious mental health problems and excluded people presenting with organic brain disorder, learning disabilities or drug misuse problems).

7.9.4 Results

There is strong evidence suggesting that intensive case management is associated with increased contact with services, compared with that provided by standard case management (number lost to follow-up after 2 years: $n=1060$, RR=0.54, 95% CI 0.39 to 0.74). (Ia)

There is insufficient evidence to determine whether there is a clinically significant difference between ICM and standard CM in terms of numbers of participants who lost contact with their case manager ($n=780$, RR=1.27, 95% CI 0.85 to 1.90). (Ia)

We found insufficient evidence to be able to differentiate ICM and standard CM with regard to admission rates or adherence to medication, but there was strong evidence that there was no difference between ICM and standard CM in their effects upon the mental state and social function of those in either service. There was insufficient evidence to determine any difference between ICM and CM with regard to suicide (of 780 participants only, there was one suicide in each group).

There is insufficient evidence to determine whether there is a clinically significant difference between ICM and standard CM in terms of admission rates ($n=747$, RR=0.95, 95% CI 0.85 to 1.05). (Ia)

There is insufficient evidence to determine if there is a clinically significant difference in adherence to medication regimens between ICM and standard CM (non-adherence: $n=68$, RR=1.32, 95% CI 0.46 to 3.75). (Ib)

There is strong evidence that there is no clinically significant difference between ICM and standard CM in terms of mental state (BPRS/CPRS end-point score: $n=823$, SMD=0.02, 95% CI –0.12 to 0.16). (Ia)

There is strong evidence that there is no clinically significant difference between ICM and standard CM in terms of social functioning (Disability Assessment Schedule/Life Skills Profile: $n=641$, SMD=–0.08, 95% CI –0.24 to 0.07). (Ia)

The review found inconsistent evidence when comparing ICM with standard CM with regard to contact with services. Compared with standard CM, there was strong evidence that ICM reduced the likelihood that service users would be lost to follow-up, but it was unclear whether people in ICM services were any less likely to lose contact with their case manager.

7.9.5 Clinical summary

The review found insufficient evidence to make an adequate comparison between the impact of ICM and that of standard CM. Where sufficient evidence was available, the review found little to differentiate ICM from standard CM.

7.9.6 Health economic evidence

It has been suggested that case management might reduce costs by providing an efficient way of coordinating treatment and care, and by ensuring that people with schizophrenia remain in contact with services, thereby reducing the likelihood of hospital admission. The cost-effectiveness of CM compared with other forms of service provision, such as assertive outreach and community mental health teams, was also of interest.

The economic review identified 12 eligible studies, of which nine were based on RCTs and three used data from controlled studies with concurrent controls (Galster *et al*, 1995; McCrone *et al*, 1998; Preston & Fazio, 2000). Four studies were conducted in the UK (McCrone *et al*, 1994; Ford *et al*, 1997; McCrone *et al*, 1998; Byford *et al*, 2000). Six of the studies used simple costing methods, while the others were economic evaluations (McCrone *et al*, 1994; Wolff *et al*, 1997; Essock *et al*, 1998; Ford *et al*, 1997; Johnston *et al*, 1998; Byford *et al*, 2000). The results of four studies were prone to a high risk of bias. In addition, only three of the studies carried out sensitivity analyses (Ford *et al*, 1997; Johnston *et al*, 1998; Byford *et al*, 2000).

Three of the eligible studies compared case management with standard care. Two studies showed no significant differences in costs (McCrone *et al*, 1994; Quinlivan *et al*, 1995), although both studies demonstrated some cost savings in the case of CM, and McCrone found CM to be more cost-effective during the first 6 months. Both studies had small sample sizes. Ford *et al* (1997) showed that ICM is more costly than standard care, with only limited extra benefits.

Six studies compared different approaches to CM with assertive outreach (assertive community treatment). The study by Preston & Fazio demonstrated ICM to be more cost-saving than ACT, in relation to the costs measured in the period prior to the introduction of these new forms of service provision. However, baseline data suggest a difference between the two comparison groups, and the analysis focused only on narrow cost components. Salkever *et al* (1999) found no significant cost difference between standard CM and ACT, but the study suffered from flaws similar to those of the analysis by Preston *et al*. A more reliable result by Essock *et al* (1998) showed the two forms of service provision to be equally cost-effective. Hu & Jerrell (1998) demonstrated that CM was less cost-saving in the long term, while Quinlivan *et al* (1995) also found that CM was more costly than ACT, although the difference was not significant. One study showed that CM was as costly as ACT but less effective (Wolff *et al*, 1997). One study compared ICM with community mental health teams (McCrone *et al*, 1998), and found that none of the interventions resulted in significant savings relative to the costs in the period before the introduction of the new services.

Three studies compared standard CM with ICM. One study found that standard CM was significantly cheaper than ICM (Galster *et al*, 1995); another found standard CM to be not only cheaper but also more effective (Johnston *et al*, 1998). A large-scale RCT from the UK showed the two approaches to be equally cost-effective, and sensitivity analysis confirmed this conclusion (Byford *et al*, 2000).

It is difficult to draw any firm conclusion about the cost-saving characteristics of case management compared with standard care on the basis of the available evidence.

Comparing CM with assertive community treatment or care by community mental health teams, the evidence suggests that there is no significant cost difference between these forms of service provision. There is evidence that reduced case-loads have no clear beneficial effect on the cost-effectiveness of CM.

7.9.7 Clinical practice recommendations

7.9.7.1   There is insufficient evidence to make any recommendation about intensive case management for routine use in the NHS in England and Wales. (B)

7.9.7.2   Integrating the care of people with schizophrenia who receive services from community mental health teams, assertive outreach teams, early intervention services and crisis resolution and home treatment teams should be carefully considered. The care programme approach should be the main mechanism by which the care of individuals across services is properly managed and integrated. (GPP)

7.10 Interface between primary and secondary care

The following good practice points and recommendations relate to the treatment and management of people with schizophrenia in primary care and across the interface between primary and secondary care. The list is not comprehensive and should be complemented by recommendations made in other parts of the guideline. This section is focused particularly on the management of people with schizophrenia presenting to primary care with no past history of the disorder (first episode schizophrenia) and those with an established diagnosis managed either partially or wholly in primary care, including those with a history of schizophrenia who have recently moved into a new primary care catchment area.

7.10.1 First episode schizophrenia

People at the outset of a psychotic illness are frequently seen by their general practitioner. Schizophrenia is often characterised by a long prodromal phase with a range of ill-defined, insidious and non-specific symptoms, and a gradual change in psychosocial functioning. The symptoms could include changes in affect (such as anxiety, irritability and depression), cognition (such as difficulty in concentration or memory), thought content (such as preoccupation with new ideas), physical state (such as sleep disturbance, loss of energy), social withdrawal and impairment of role functioning. The majority of such presentations, however, do not develop into schizophrenia. It is beyond the scope of this guideline to deal with the identification of people with schizophrenia. Nevertheless, people presenting with these types of symptoms to primary care should be monitored in primary care, although requests for referral to secondary care should be supported.

A minority of people with what appear to be possible prodromal symptoms of schizophrenia will develop 'attenuated' positive symptoms such as mild thought disorder, ideas of reference, suspiciousness, odd beliefs and perceptual distortion of a milder variety than that observed in established schizophrenia. Referral in these instances to a mental health professional is advisable. Some will develop more florid symptoms including delusions, hallucinations, disturbed behaviour and disrupted family and social relationships, suggestive of an acute episode of schizophrenia. For these people urgent referral to secondary mental health services should be arranged at the earliest opportunity. This might involve the local crisis resolution or home treatment team, community mental health team or other similar community-based service.

Sometimes people will present to primary care at a stage when they are already experiencing an acute episode of schizophrenia, and informed discussion is not possible. In these circumstances it is essential for primary care workers to contact relatives or arrange for an advocate to help, in the hope of persuading the person to accept anti-psychotic medication. An atypical antipsychotic drug should be offered, as the incidence of extrapyramidal side-effects is lower. Urgent referral for people at this stage of the illness may involve use of the Mental Health Act, arranged in conjunction with secondary services.

After the first episode, some people refuse to accept the diagnosis and sometimes also reject the treatment offered. Bearing in mind the consequences of a diagnosis of schizophrenia, many people in this position, perhaps unsurprisingly, want a second opinion from another consultant psychiatrist.

7.10.2 Clinical practice recommendations

7.10.2.1 In primary care, all people with suspected or newly diagnosed schizophrenia should be referred urgently to secondary mental health services for assessment and development of a care plan. If there is a presumed diagnosis of schizophrenia, then part of the urgent assessment should include early assessment by a consultant psychiatrist. (GPP)

7.10.2.2 The choice of antipsychotic drug should be made jointly by the individual and the clinician responsible for treatment, based on an informed discussion of the relative benefits of the drugs and their side-effect profiles. The individual's advocate or carer should be consulted where appropriate. (NICE 2002)

7.10.2.3 Where there are acute symptoms of schizophrenia, the general practitioner should consider prescribing an atypical antipsychotic drug at the earliest opportunity – before the individual is seen by a psychiatrist, if necessary. Wherever possible, this should be following discussion with a psychiatrist, and referral should be a matter of urgency. (GPP)

7.10.2.4 When full discussion between the clinician responsible for treatment and the individual concerned is not possible, in particular in the management of an acute schizophrenic episode, the oral atypical drugs should be considered as the treatment option of choice because of the lower potential risk of extrapyramidal side-effects. The individual's carer or advocate should be consulted where possible and appropriate. Although there are limitations with advance directives regarding the choice of treatment for individuals with schizophrenia, it is recommended that they are developed and documented in individuals' care programmes whenever possible. (NICE 2002)

7.10.3 People with an established diagnosis of schizophrenia in primary care

People with an established diagnosis of schizophrenia who are managed in primary care require regular assessment of their health and social needs. This should include monitoring of mental state, medication use, medication adherence, side-effects, social isolation, access to services, and occupational status. All such people should have a care plan developed jointly between primary care and secondary mental health services. Regular monitoring of physical health is also essential. Non-professional carers should also be seen at regular intervals for assessment of their health and social care needs. Carers should also be offered an assessment of their needs.

Advance directives about the choice of medication should be documented in the service user's notes. These should be copied from secondary services to the responsible general practitioner. If service users have no secondary service involved in their care (because they have recently moved to the area, for example), the general practitioner should ensure that any existing advance directives are copied to the secondary services to whom referral is made.

Individuals managed solely in primary care who experience a relapse in their schizophrenic illness should be considered for referral to secondary care. Increasing drug dosage should be done following discussion with the service user and carer or advocate where possible, and should be within the recommended dosage range found in the *British National Formulary*. Polypharmacy with more than one antipsychotic medication is to be avoided.

When referring a service user to secondary mental health services, primary care professionals should take the following into account:

- Previous history: if a person has previously responded effectively to a particular treatment without experiencing unwanted side-effects, and is considered safe to manage in primary care, referral may not be necessary.

- Views about referral: the views of the mental health service user should be fully taken into account before making a referral. If the service user wants to be managed in primary care, it is often necessary to work with the family and carers. Sharing confidential information about the service user with carers raises many ethical issues, which should be dealt with through full discussion with the service user.

- Non-adherence to treatment: this may be the cause of the relapse, possibly as a result of lack of concordance between the views of the service user and of the health professionals, with the former not recognising the need for medication. Alternatively, non-adherence might be the consequence of side-effects. Finding the right antipsychotic medicine specifically suited to the service user is an important aim in the effective management of schizophrenia.

- Side-effects of medication and poor response to treatment: the side-effects of antipsychotic drugs are personally and socially disabling, and must be routinely monitored. Side-effects are also a cause of poor response to treatment. About 40% of people given antipsychotics do not effectively respond.

- Concerns about comorbid drug and alcohol misuse: substance misuse by people with schizophrenia is increasingly recognised as a major problem, both in terms of its prevalence and its clinical and social effects (Banerjee *et al*, 2002). Monitoring drug and alcohol use is an essential aspect of the management of people with schizophrenia in primary and secondary care.

- Level of risk to self and others: people with schizophrenia, especially when relapse is impending or apparent, are at risk of suicide and are often vulnerable to exploitation or abuse. During an acute episode of illness, conflicts and difficulties may manifest themselves through social disturbances or even violence.

People presenting to primary care services who are new to the area (not known to local services) with previously diagnosed psychosis should be referred to secondary care mental health services for assessment, subject to their agreement. The general practitioner should attempt to establish details of any previous treatment, and pass on any relevant information about this to the community mental health team.

Finally, people with schizophrenia have a higher rate of physical illness than many others. Just as with other groups at high risk, regular physical checks and health advice are an essential contribution of primary care to the treatment and management of people with schizophrenia. Increased mortality and morbidity from cardiovascular disease and endocrine disorders in people with schizophrenia suggest that it is good practice to screen for diabetes (by routine testing for urinary glucose and random testing for blood glucose) and cardiovascular risk factors (particularly smoking history, blood pressure and measures of serum cholesterol and high-density and low-density lipid levels). It would be good practice also to screen for side-effects of drug therapy. The effectiveness of any of these screening procedures has yet to be tested in an RCT.

The identification of patients suffering from schizophrenia in a well-organised computerised practice is feasible (Kendrick *et al*, 1991; Nazareth *et al*, 1993). The organisation and development of practice case registers is to be encouraged, as it is often the first step in monitoring people with schizophrenia in general practice.

7.10.4 Clinical practice recommendations

7.10.4.1 The organisation and development of practice case registers for people with schizophrenia is recommended as an essential step in monitoring the physical and mental health of people with schizophrenia in primary care. (GPP)

7.10.4.2 Although there are limitations with advance directives regarding the choice of treatment for individuals with schizophrenia, it is recommended that they are developed and documented in individuals' care programmes whenever possible. (NICE 2002)

7.10.4.3 Copies of advance directives should be placed in both the primary care and secondary care case notes and care plans, and copies given to the service user and the user's care coordinator. If appropriate, and subject to agreement with the service user, a copy should also be given to the carer. (GPP)

7.10.4.4 The decision to refer a service user from primary care back to mental health services is a complex clinical judgement that should take account of the views of the service user and (where appropriate) the carers. Issues of confidentiality should be respected when involving carers. Referral may be considered in a number of circumstances:
- if treatment adherence is a problem, referral is usually indicated
- a poor response to treatment makes referral a higher priority
- if comorbid substance misuse is suspected, referral is indicated
- if the level of risk to self or others is increased, referral to secondary services is indicated

- when a person with schizophrenia first joins a general practice list, referral to secondary services for assessment and care programming is indicated, subject to the full agreement of the service user. (GPP)

7.10.4.5 General practitioners and other primary health care workers should regularly monitor the physical health of people with schizophrenia registered with their practice. The frequency of checks should be agreed between the service user and the clinician, and recorded in the case notes. (GPP)

7.10.4.6 Physical health checks should pay particular attention to endocrine disorders such as diabetes and hyperprolactinaemia, cardiovascular risk factors such as blood pressure and lipid levels, side-effects of medication, and lifestyle factors such as smoking. These must be recorded in the notes. (GPP)

7.10.5 Research recommendations

7.10.5.1 An evaluation of a coordinated approach of primary and secondary care in the early diagnosis and management of people with schizophrenia is recommended.

7.10.5.2 It is recommended that the role of the general practice team in crisis management of people with schizophrenia be evaluated.

7.10.5.3 It is recommended that a randomised controlled trial on the role of case registers in the long-term management of people with schizophrenia in general practice be conducted.

7.10.5.4 More research into the development and evaluation of effective interventions for managing the physical health of people with schizophrenia in general practice is required.

8 Criteria for auditing the management of schizophrenia

8.1 Objectives for the audit

Audits can be carried out in different care settings to ensure that:
- individuals with schizophrenia are involved in their own care
- treatment options are appropriately offered for individuals with schizophrenia.

8.2 Individuals to be included in an audit

A single audit could include all people with schizophrenia. Alternatively, individual audits could be undertaken on specific groups, such as:
- people newly diagnosed with schizophrenia
- people previously diagnosed with schizophrenia
- people with treatment-resistant schizophrenia/persisting symptoms.

The audits described can be carried out on a suitable sample of individuals and can be done jointly by mental health and primary care teams.

8.3 Measures that could be used as a basis for an audit

See Table 8.1.

Table 8.1 Measures that could be used as the basis for an audit

Criterion	Standard	Exception	Definition of terms
1 Family interventions			
Family interventions are offered to any family who lives with or is in close contact with a family member with schizophrenia, and especially where any of the following circumstances apply. The individual: • has experienced a recent relapse • is considered at risk of relapse • has persisting symptoms	Family interventions to be offered to 100% of families of individuals with schizophrenia who have experienced a recent relapse, are considered to be 'at risk' of relapsing, or who have persisting symptoms, and are living with or in close contact with their family	The individual with schizophrenia who is not able to participate in an informed discussion with the clinician responsible for treatment at the time and an advocate or carer is not available The individual with schizophrenia who refuses to allow discussion of family interventions with his or her family The family who refuses to participate in family interventions	The notes should indicate that the clinician responsible for treatment has discussed the process and benefits of family intervention with the individual and (subject to the individual's agreement) with the family, or that the individual was incapable of making a choice at the time. The notes should refer to the involvement of the individual's advocate or carer, where applicable
The course of family intervention should be for longer than 6 months with more than 10 planned sessions	All individuals who receive family interventions should be offered more than 10 sessions, the course of treatment lasting for more than 6 months		Individuals are 'at risk' following an acute episode, or if the person has had two or more episodes in the past year The term 'persisting symptoms' refers to positive or negative symptoms, which continue with limited or no response to antipsychotic medication

Table 8.1 *contd*

Criterion	Standard	Exception	Definition of terms
2 Cognitive–behavioural therapy			
Cognitive–behavioural therapy (CBT) is offered to any individual with schizophrenia, and especially to the individual who is experiencing persistent psychotic symptoms	100% of individuals with schizophrenia who are experiencing persisting psychotic symptoms should be offered CBT	The individual with schizophrenia who is not able to participate in an informed discussion with the clinician responsible for treatment at the time and for whom an advocate or carer is not available	The notes should indicate that the clinician responsible for treatment has discussed the process and benefits of CBT, or that the individual was incapable of making a choice at the time
The course of CBT offered should normally be of more than 6 months' duration and include more than 10 planned sessions	All individuals who receive CBT should be offered treatment lasting for over 6 months and including more than 10 planned sessions		The term 'persisting symptoms' refers to positive or negative symptoms, which continue with limited or no response to antipsychotic medication
3 Assertive outreach (assertive community treatment)			
Assertive outreach services are provided for people with schizophrenia who: • are at risk of repeated relapse • make high use of in-patient services • have a poor history of engagement with services • are homeless	100% of individuals with schizophrenia who are at risk of repeated relapse, have made high use of in-patient services, have a poor history of engagement with services, or are homeless are offered treatment by an assertive outreach team	The individual with schizophrenia has been accepted for treatment by an assertive outreach team but refuses all attempts to engage with the team	The notes should indicate that the clinician responsible for treatment has discussed the process and benefits of assertive outreach, or that the individual was not capable of making a choice at the time. The notes should refer to the involvement of the individual's advocate or carer, where applicable

Table 8.1 *contd*

Criterion	Standard	Exception	Definition of terms
3 Assertive outreach (assertive community treatment) *contd*			
		Individuals are 'at risk of repeated relapse' following an acute episode or if they have relapsed two or more times in the past year	Service users should report that this choice was offered The term 'high use' refers to the level of use of the top 100 patients in terms of frequency of in-patient admission and/or length of stay
4 Parenteral medication			
An individual who has received parenteral medication during rapid parenteral medication during rapid tranquillisation has baseline recordings, repeated at regular intervals, for blood pressure, pulse, temperature and respiratory rate	100% of individuals receiving parenteral medication during rapid tranquillisation have baseline and follow-up recordings of blood pressure, pulse, temperature and respiratory rate	Where such procedures would cause further agitation and increase the possible risk either to the individual with schizophrenia or to others	The notes contain a record of the individual's blood pressure, pulse, temperature and respiratory rate, monitored at the specified time intervals, which depends upon a full clinical assessment, which is recorded in the notes. Where baseline observations are absent the reasons for this are recorded in the clinical notes

Table 8.1 *contd*

Criterion	Standard	Exception	Definition of terms
5 Rapid tranquillisation			
Individuals who are subjected to rapid tranquillisation are debriefed and offered the opportunity to write their own account of the experience in the notes	100% of individuals who are subjected to rapid tranquillisation have recorded in their notes that they have been debriefed, with a record of the individual's entry in the notes	Individuals who refuse to be debriefed or to write in their own notes. This must be recorded in the notes	
6 Polypharmacy			
Individuals receive only one antipsychotic at a time	100% of individuals with schizophrenia	Individuals with schizophrenia who are receiving clozapine but have not responded sufficiently; individuals who are changing from one antipsychotic to another	The audit should include a discussion of the treatment choice with the individual with schizophrenia, relevant outcomes including the incidence of side-effects, and the reasons for prescribing antipsychotics, the reasons for prescribing additional antipsychotics, dose/dose range and total dose equivalents, and the prescribing of other drugs in combination with antipsychotics (such as anticholinergics, antidepressants and laxatives)

Table 8.1 *contd*

Criterion	Standard	Exception	Definition of terms
7 Advance directives (1)			
Care plans contain advance directives detailing the individual's treatment choices in the event of an acute episode of illness which might require rapid tranquillisation	100% of individuals with schizophrenia	The individual with schizophrenia who is not able to participate in an informed discussion with the clinician responsible for treatment at the time, and for whom an advocate or carer is not available	The Care Programme Approach (CPA) documentation contains an advance directive that describes preferred treatment choices in the event of the individual experiencing an acute episode of illness The term 'treatment choices' refers to the choice of oral antipsychotic, lorazepam or other treatments that might be used without the service user's consent
8 Advance directives (2)			
In the event of an acute episode of illness, the CPA coordinator ensures that the individual's advance directive is notified to the clinicians responsible for their care during the acute phase. The receipt of the advance directive is recorded in the individual's notes	100% of individuals with schizophrenia experiencing an acute episode of illness have advance directives in their notes where appropriate	No advance directive has been made	The notes indicate that the advance directive was received by the clinician responsible for the care of the individual during the acute episode of illness

Table 8.1 *contd*

Criterion	Standard	Exception	Definition of terms
9 Information			
Individuals and their families receive written material about their illness and treatment from the health care professionals who care for them, including a copy of the NICE schizophrenia guideline produced for people with schizophrenia, their advocates and carers, and the public	100% of individuals with schizophrenia and their families	None	Local services should agree what information is to be made available, by whom, and when Service users and their carers should report satisfaction with the accessibility and quality of information
10 Occupational needs			
Individuals have a comprehensive assessment of occupational status and potential, and vocational aspirations	100% of individuals with schizophrenia 100% of individuals on enhanced CPA to receive an assessment not less than once a year	Individuals who are employed, or who do not want an occupational assessment	Local CPA documentation should include review of occupational status and potential, and vocational aspirations. The CPA documentation should indicate that this is reviewed, or that the person is employed, or does not want to be assessed
11 Case registers in primary care			
Individuals are identified and recorded on a case register in primary care	100% of individuals with schizophrenia within primary care are recorded on a case register	Individuals who refuse to be included in a case register	The case register is used as the basis of monitoring the physical health needs and routine screening of people with schizophrenia, and for auditing the implementation of this guideline in primary care

Table 8.1 *contd*

Criterion	Standard	Exception	Definition of terms
12 Physical health in primary care			
Individuals have a physical health check at regular intervals. The frequency of health checks will be agreed between the general practitioner (GP) and the service user and documented in the notes	100% of individuals with schizophrenia who are registered with a GP are offered physical health screens within primary care	Those individuals who refuse physical health care in primary care or who wish to receive it from secondary services	The notes document the agreed frequency of health checks, and that checks are actually being made at this frequency
			(1) Health checks should include blood pressure monitoring, screening for diabetes, blood lipids testing in people with raised blood pressure, screening for smoking, alcohol and drug use
			(2) Health promotion advice is offered, e.g. advice on smoking, alcohol and drug use, and exercise
			(3) Screening for side-effects of drug treatments, including sexual dysfunction, lethargy, weight gain and extrapyramidal side-effects (including tardive dyskinesia)

Table 8.1 *contd*

Criterion	Standard	Exception	Definition of terms
13 Second opinion			
The individual with an initial diagnosis of schizophrenia who requests a second opinion should be supported in doing so	100% of individuals with an initial diagnosis of schizophrenia	None	The notes document that following a first episode where a diagnosis has been given, the GP or psychiatrist has offered a referral for a second opinion if requested by the service user
			Service users should report satisfaction with the support that they received when asking for a second opinion

Glossary

Acute day hospital   A unit that provides assessment and treatment services during daytime hours for acutely ill individuals who would otherwise be treated in traditional psychiatric in-patient units.

Adherence   The behaviour of taking medicine according to treatment dosage and schedule as intended by the prescriber. In this guideline, the term 'adherence' is used in preference to 'compliance', but is not synonymous with 'concordance', which has a number of meanings.

Advance directive   Written instructions agreed between a service user and health care professional in advance of treatment. Service users specify their preferred treatments and identify treatments they do not wish to receive; these preferences are used to guide clinicians in the event of the service user becoming incapable of making such decisions. For example, a service user might ask not to receive electroconvulsive therapy, or a drug found to have bad side-effects (such as haloperidol), and might specify the use of lorazepam rather than haloperidol in the event of needing rapid tranquillisation. The service user should understand the nature of the condition for which treatment might be required (e.g. an acute episode of schizophrenia), the need for treatment (antipsychotics during an acute episode, lorazepam to induce calm), the expected benefits of the proposed treatment, and the possible adverse consequences. Advance directives cannot be used to refuse treatment altogether when subject to the Mental Health Act (e.g. if a person does not want to take any antipsychotic drug during an acute episode of schizophrenia).

Agranulocytosis   A marked decrease in the number of granulocytes (a type of white blood cell) which usually leads to a number of characteristic symptoms and signs including lesions of the throat, other mucous membranes of the gastrointestinal tract and of the skin. It reduces the immune response and may cause death. Agranulocytosis is a potential side-effect of clozapine (although there are other causes).

Akathisia   A motor condition characterised by a feeling of restlessness, an urge to move about constantly and an inability to sit still; a common extrapyramidal side-effect of antipsychotic drugs.

Assertive community treatment   An alternative term for 'assertive outreach'.

Assertive outreach   Intensive treatment and care in a community setting for people with serious mental health problems. Care is provided by a multi-disciplinary team, and usually involves dedicated sessions with a psychiatrist; care is exclusively devoted to a defined group of people (those with serious mental illness). Team members share responsibility for clients, so that several members may work with the same client and members do not have individual case-loads; the team attempts to provide *all* psychiatric and social care, rather than referring to other agencies; care is provided at home or workplace as far as possible; treatment and care are offered assertively to uncooperative or reluctant service users; and team adherence to treatment regimens is emphasised.

Atypical antipsychotic   One of a class of newer antipsychotic drugs, including amisulpride, olanzapine, quetiapine, risperidone, sertindole and zotepine, which may be better tolerated than other antipsychotic agents, with a lower risk of extrapyramidal side-effects and hyperprolactinaemia. Clozapine is also listed in the *British National Formulary* as an atypical antipsychotic, but its use is restricted to individuals with schizophrenia who are unresponsive or intolerant to conventional antipsychotic therapy.

Care programme approach   A model of case management that was introduced in 1991 to provide a framework for effective mental health care. Its four main elements include systematic arrangements for assessing the health and social needs of people accepted into specialist mental health services, the formation of a care plan that identifies the health and social care required from a variety of providers, the appointment of a keyworker to keep in close touch with the service user and to monitor and coordinate care, and regular review and, where necessary, agreed changes to the care plan.

Cognitive–behavioural therapy   A psychological intervention designed to enable people to establish links between their thoughts, feelings or actions and their current or past symptoms, and to re-evaluate their perceptions, beliefs or reasoning about the target symptoms. The intervention should involve at least one of the following: (1) monitoring thoughts, feelings or behaviour with respect to the symptom; (2) being helped to use alternative ways of coping with the target symptom; (3) reducing stress.

Cognitive remediation therapy   A programme of therapy focused upon improving specified cognitive functions using procedures implemented with the intention of improving the level of the specified cognitive function. The same procedures can be used to test that cognitive function.

Cohort study   Also known as a follow-up, incidence, longitudinal or prospective study. An observational study in which a defined group of people (the cohort) is followed over time; outcomes are compared in subsets of the cohort who were exposed or not exposed (or exposed at different levels) to an intervention or other factor of interest. Cohorts can be assembled in the present and followed into the future (concurrent cohort study), or identified from past records and followed forward from that time up to the present (historical cohort study). Because random allocation is not used, matching or statistical adjustment is required to ensure that the comparison groups are as similar as possible.

Community mental health team   A multi-disciplinary, community-based team that offers assessment, treatment and care to adults with mental health problems. Many such teams operate using a case management model in which team members have their own individual case-loads.

Concordance   An agreement between a service user and a health care professional about when and how medicines are taken. The agreement is reached after negotiation that respects the beliefs and wishes of the user. Although the alliance is reciprocal, the health care professional recognises the primacy of the service user's decisions about taking the recommended medicine. The term is also used to describe agreement regarding the presence and nature of illness (lack of concordance between a service user and a health care professional is also sometimes described as a lack of insight on the part of the service user).

Confidence interval   The range within which the 'true' values (e.g. size of effect of an intervention) are expected to lie with a given degree of certainty (e.g. 95% or 99%). Confidence intervals represent the probability of random errors, but not systematic errors – or bias.

Conventional antipsychotic   One of the class of older antipsychotic drugs whose efficacy correlates with their D2 dopamine receptor blocking activity (e.g. chlorpromazine, haloperidol). Most of these drugs were developed before clozapine; in this guideline, the term 'conventional antipsychotic' refers to a 'typical antipsychotic' in contrast to an 'atypical antipsychotic' drug. It should be noted, however, that some drugs (e.g. sulpiride) now regarded as 'typical' or 'conventional' have pharmacological properties similar to the atypicals.

Cost analysis   The simplest economic study, measuring only the costs of a given intervention. It is inappropriate for direct comparison of two alternative treatments or policy options.

Cost–benefit analysis   An economic evaluation in which both costs and benefits are measured in the same monetary units. If benefits exceed costs, the evaluation would be a basis for recommending the treatment. It can address the question of whether a treatment or policy is socially worthwhile, in the broadest sense.

Cost–consequence analysis   A variant of cost-effectiveness analysis that compares alternative treatment or policy options to a specific patient group. Multiple outcomes are measured in non-monetary units and retained together with costs. This analysis does not attempt to reduce everything to a single ratio, but the different outcomes should be weighed up and compared with costs.

Cost-effectiveness analysis   An economic evaluation that compares alternative options for a specific patient group, looking at a single effectiveness dimension measured in a non-monetary (natural) unit. It expresses the result in the form of an incremental (or average or marginal) cost-effectiveness ratio.

Cost-minimisation analysis   An economic study concerned only with the comparative costs of different treatments or policies. It assumes (based on previous research) that the outcomes of the compared treatment or policy alternatives are identical. The aim is to look for the lowest cost alternative.

Cost-offset analysis   An analysis that measures only costs, and compares costs incurred with costs saved. If costs saved exceed costs incurred, the treatment or policy would be recommended.

Cost-of-illness studies   An economic analysis of the total costs to society incurred by a specific disease.

Costs (direct)   The costs of all the goods, services and other resources that are consumed in the provision of a health intervention. They can be medical or non-medical.

Costs (indirect)   The lost productivity suffered by the national economy as a result of an employee's absence from the workplace through illness, decreased efficiency or premature death.

Cost–utility analysis   A form of cost-effectiveness analysis that measures and values the impact of a treatment or policy alternative in terms of changes in health-related quality of life in utility units (see QALY). The result is expressed in the form of a cost–utility ratio. It gives a more generalisable result than a single-outcome cost-effectiveness study.

Counselling and support psychotherapy   For the purposes of this guideline, 'counselling and supportive psychotherapy' is defined as a discrete psychological intervention (regular planned meetings, usually 50 min or 1 h in length, which are facilitative, non-directive and/or relationship focused, with the content of sessions largely determined by the service user) that does not fulfil the criteria for any other psychological intervention.

Crisis resolution and home treatment A service that provides intensive home-based, crisis-oriented treatment of an acute psychiatric episode by staff with a special remit to deal with such situations during and beyond office hours. The objective is to manage acute episodes in the community rather than in hospital.

Data-mining study A study that uses techniques for finding patterns and trends in large data-sets.

Decision analytic modelling Decision analysis provides help in decision-making by using different modelling methods. It is used to calculate data that have not been measured, or to extrapolate existing data.

Depot antipsychotic A preparation of an ester of an antipsychotic compound in an oily solution, which is injected intramuscularly. Following injection, the drug is slowly released from the injection site. This results in relatively stable plasma drug levels over long periods, allowing the injections to be given every few weeks.

Detection bias Systematic differences between comparison groups in how outcomes are ascertained, diagnosed or verified. Also termed 'ascertainment bias'.

Double masking (double blind) A form of study design in which neither the participants nor the investigators (outcome assessors) are aware of which intervention the participants are given. The purpose of masking the participants (recipients and providers of care) is to prevent **performance bias**. The purpose of masking the investigators (outcome assessors) is to protect against **detection bias**.

Drop out A term no longer used to indicate leaving a study before its completion (the term 'leaving the study early' is now preferred).

Dystonia A state of disordered tonicity of muscles; an extrapyramidal side-effect of antipsychotic drugs.

Early intervention service Service that provides early identification and initial treatment to people aged 14–35 years with a first presentation of psychotic symptoms, during the first 3 years of their illness; a requirement set out by the National Health Service Plan.

Effectiveness The extent to which a specific intervention, when used under ordinary circumstances, does what it is intended to do. Clinical trials that assess effectiveness are sometimes called management trials.

Efficacy The extent to which an intervention produces a beneficial result under ideal conditions. Clinical trials that assess efficacy are sometimes called explanatory trials and are restricted to participants who fully cooperate. The randomised controlled trial is the accepted 'gold standard' for evaluating the efficacy of an intervention.

Extrapyramidal side-effect Movement disorder such as parkinsonism, akathisia and dystonia, commonly caused by antipsychotic pharmacotherapy, due to dopamine receptor blockade in the non-pyramidal tract neuronal pathways that influence or control movements.

Family intervention Family sessions with a specific supportive or treatment function based on systemic, cognitive–behavioural or psychoanalytic principles, which must contain at least one of the following: (1) psychoeducational intervention; (2) problem-solving and crisis management work; (3) interventions with the identified service user.

Forest plot   A graphical display of results from individual studies on a common scale, allowing visual comparison of trial results and examination of the degree of heterogeneity between studies.

Good practice point   Recommended good practice based on the clinical experience of the Guideline Development Group.

Guideline recommendation   A systematically developed statement that is derived from the best available research evidence, using predetermined and systematic methods to identify and evaluate evidence relating to the specific condition in question.

Loading dose   A very high initial dose of a drug, administered in an attempt to increase the rate of response.

Meta-analysis   The use of statistical techniques in a systematic review to integrate the results of the included studies. Also used to refer to systematic reviews that use meta-analysis.

Mirror-image studies   Known as before–after studies in epidemiology. These studies measure the costs and outcomes in a given population before and after the implementation of a new treatment or policy. The study population plays the part of the control group as well. These studies are prone to bias.

NICE 2002   In this guideline, 'NICE 2002' is used to indicate recommendations from the NICE Technology Appraisal 43 on the use of newer (atypical) antipsychotic drugs for the treatment of schizophrenia (see reference list).

Non-acute day hospital   Psychiatric day hospital that offers continuing care to people with severe mental disorders.

Number needed to harm   The number of people (calculated statistically) who need to be treated to cause one bad outcome. The lower the number needed to harm, the higher the likelihood of harm.

Number needed to treat   The number of people who need to be treated to prevent one bad outcome (i.e. a good outcome). It is the inverse of the risk difference.

Parkinsonism   A group of neurological disorders characterised by decreased muscular activity, tremor and muscular rigidity.

Patient   The terms 'service user' or 'person with schizophrenia' are preferred in this guideline. The term 'patient' is used under the following conditions: (1) a person under the care of a doctor in reports of research or recommendations in which care by doctors is a crucial element (e.g. 'Recent surveys suggest that about 10–15% of patients are managed solely in primary care …'); (2) generic and typical usages, such as 'NICE programmes for patients' and 'Patient Bill of Rights'; (3) NICE recommendations that are required to be quoted verbatim; (4) frequently used noun compounds (e.g. 'drug-naïve patients', 'patient sample').

Performance bias   Systematic differences in care provided apart from the intervention being evaluated. For example, if study participants know they are in the control group, they might be more likely to use other forms of care; people who know they are in the experimental (intervention) group might experience placebo effects, and care providers might treat patients differently according to which group they are in. Masking of study participants (both the recipients and the providers of care) is used to protect against performance bias.

Prevocational training   Any approach to vocational rehabilitation in which participants are expected to undergo a period of preparation, such as work in a sheltered environment or other form of assistance, before being encouraged to seek competitive employment.

Psychodynamic psychotherapy   Regular individual therapy sessions with a trained psychotherapist, or a therapist under supervision, based on a psychodynamic or psychoanalytic model, which use a variety of strategies, including exploratory insight-oriented, supportive or directive activity, applied flexibly, working with transference, but with the therapist using a less strict technique than that used in psychoanalysis.

Quality-adjusted life year (QALY)   A form of utility measure, calculated by estimating the total life-years gained from a treatment and weighting each year with a quality-of-life score in that year.

Randomisation   Method used to generate a random allocation sequence, such as using tables of random numbers or computer-generated random sequences. The method of randomisation should be distinguished from concealment of allocation, because if the latter is inadequate selection bias may occur despite the use of randomisation. For instance, a list of random numbers might be used to randomise participants, but if the list were open to the individuals responsible for recruiting and allocating participants, those individuals could influence the allocation process, either knowingly or unknowingly.

Randomised controlled trial   Also termed 'randomised clinical trial'. An experiment in which investigators randomly allocate eligible people into groups to receive or not to receive one or more interventions that are being compared. The results are assessed by comparing outcomes in the different groups. Through randomisation, the groups should be similar in all aspects apart from the treatment they receive during the study.

Rapid tranquillisation   The use of drug treatment to achieve rapid, short-term behavioural control of extreme agitation, aggression and potentially violent behaviour that places the individual or those around them at risk of physical harm. The aim of rapid tranquillisation is to achieve sedation sufficient to minimise the risk posed to the person themselves or to others.

Relapse   The definitions of relapse used in this review were those adopted by the individual studies. This definition varied between studies. For example, four studies (Essock et al, 1996; Tran et al, 1998) defined relapse as hospitalisation for psychopathology, one study (Speller et al, 1997) required an increase of three or more BPRS positive symptom items that did not respond to a dose increase, while another study (Csernansky & Okamoto, 2000) required one of the following: hospitalisation for schizophrenia; increased level of care and 20% PANSS increase; self-injury, suicide or homicidal ideation or violent behaviour; or CGI >6. These varying definitions require that caution be exercised in the interpretation of the results.

Relative risk   Also known as risk ratio; the ratio of risk in the intervention group to the risk in the control group. The risk (proportion, probability or rate) is the ratio of people with an event in a group to the total in the group. A relative risk (RR) of 1 indicates no difference between comparison groups. For undesirable outcomes, an RR of less than 1 indicates that the intervention was effective in reducing the risk of that outcome.

Risk ratio   Relative risk.

Social skills training   For the purposes of this guideline, this is defined as any structured psychosocial intervention, group or individual or both, aimed at enhancing social performance and reducing distress and difficulty in social situations. The key components are: (1) careful behaviourally based assessment of a range of social and interpersonal skills; (2) an importance placed upon both verbal and non-verbal communication; (3) training focused upon an individual's perception and processing of relevant social cues, and ability to provide appropriate social reinforcement; and (4) an emphasis on homework tasks as well as clinic-based interventions.

Standard dosage   The recommended dosage range listed in the *British National Formulary;* this normally reflects the information contained in the manufacturers' Summary of Product Characteristics as well as advice from an external panel of experts.

Supported employment   An approach to vocational rehabilitation that attempts to place clients immediately in competitive employment.

Tardive dyskinesia   Abnormal involuntary movements of the lips, jaw, tongue and facial muscles, and sometimes the limbs and trunk; a side-effect of antipsychotic drug treatment.

Treatment-resistant schizophrenia   A variably defined condition. A reasonable and fairly practical definition, one used for the NICE Technology Appraisal of atypical antipsychotics, is 'a lack of a satisfactory clinical improvement despite the sequential use of the recommended doses for 6–8 weeks of at least two antipsychotics, at least one of which should be an atypical'.

Vocational rehabilitation   Work and employment schemes designed to assist service users to develop skills and gain the confidence to re-enter competitive employment.

Weighted mean difference   A method of meta-analysis used to combine measures on continuous scales (such as weight), where the mean, standard deviation and sample size in each group are known. The weight given to each study (e.g. how much influence each study has on the overall results of the meta-analysis) is determined by the precision of its estimate of effect and, in the statistical software used by the NCCMH, is equal to the inverse of the variance. This method assumes that all of the trials have measured the outcome on the same scale.

Appendices

Appendix 1
Scope for the development of a clinical guideline for schizophrenia

1 Preamble

The National Institute for Clinical Excellence is responsible for developing and disseminating clinical guidelines to provide advice on best practice for patients and health professionals in the NHS in England and Wales.

2 Title

The Management of Schizophrenia

(The management of symptoms and experiences of schizophrenia in primary and secondary care in the NHS.)

3 Summary

The guideline will be relevant to all adult patients with a diagnosis of schizophrenia, with the exception of very-late onset schizophrenia (that is, where the age of onset of the disorder is 60 years or greater). The guideline will cover the clinical aspects of primary and secondary care. It will cover pharmacological, psychological and service level interventions.

4 Status

This scoping statement has been subject to a period of consultation and discussed with stakeholders. It has been approved by the Guidelines Advisory Committee and the Institute's Guidance Executive and will be posted on the Institute's website along with details of the commission and the developers of the guideline.

5 Issues and objectives

There are a number of issues relevant to this guideline.

This guideline will focus on the clinical aspects of care, while recognising that mental healthcare is more wide-ranging than this. The guideline will describe clinical "best practice" that will underpin aspects of the Mental Health NSF and map to it. In particular, local protocols will be linked to these guidelines.

The guideline will cover a very broad range of care services, and the developers will need to assess how best to approach this.

This is an NHS guideline. While it will comment on the interface with other services, such as those provided by social services, secure settings and the voluntary sector, it will not include services exclusive to these sectors.

Guideline developers will need to consider the extent to which the previously commissioned guidelines work on atypical antipsychotics and on psychosocial interventions should be used to inform the development of this guideline.

The guideline will incorporate the findings of the Institute's Health Technology Appraisal on the use of the newer (atypical) antipsychotic drugs in treatment of schizophrenia.

Service users and carers will have an interest in the clinical, social and environmental aspects of the condition and its management. The guideline developers will need to work closely with service users to establish clear boundaries for the guideline.

6   Inclusions and exclusions

6.1 Disease or condition

The guideline should offer best practice advise on the care of adult patients (>18 years) who have a clinical working diagnosis of schizophrenia. Those with an established diagnosis of schizophrenia (with onset <60 years) who require treatment beyond 60 will be included but the guideline will not address very-late-onset schizophrenia.

The boundaries of the condition with other psychotic illnesses will need to be defined, including the entry point for management with this guideline.

Acute phase, stabilisation and maintenance/rehabilitation including later acute episodes/relapses will be covered.

The following will not be included in the scope of this guideline:
- diagnosis
- primary prevention
- assessment, except where it concerns patients with a diagnosis of schizophrenia
- management of schizophrenia in conjunction with learning difficulties
- management of schizophrenia in conjunction with significant physical or sensory difficulties.

6.2. Professions and health care setting

The guideline will cover the care that is received from health care professionals who have direct contact with and make decisions concerning the care of patients with schizophrenia.

The guideline will also be relevant to the work but will not cover the practice of A&E departments, paramedic services, prison medical services, the police and those who work in the criminal justice and education sectors.

The guideline will consider care in the context of the following service delivery systems:

- home treatment/crisis teams
- assertive community treatments
- intensive care management
- primary/secondary care interface
- early intervention programmes
- vocational rehabilitation.

The guideline will be useful in the management of rough sleepers with schizophrenia but will not specifically address this area.

7 Interventions and treatment modalities

The guideline will cover the full range of care routinely made available by the NHS.

Guidance to ensure that patients have the information they need and the opportunities to discuss with their clinicians the benefits and potential side-effects of treatment so that they can make informed choices about their treatment options.

The guideline will incorporate any relevant technology appraisals undertaken by the Institute, which are made available before the publication date of the guideline.

7.1 Appropriate use of mainstream pharmacological treatments

- type
- dose
- duration
- polypharmacy
- depot
- rapid tranquillisation
- benzopdiazipenes
- side-effects

7.2 Appropriate use of psychological interventions

- cognitive behavioural treatments
- family interventions
- social skills
- life skills
- cognitive rehabilitation
- other psychological therapies

Appendix 2
Special advisors to the Guideline Development Group

Sarah Davenport FRCPsych
Ashworth Hospital
Merseycare NHS Trust

Richard Gray RN PhD
Medical Research Council Fellow
Institute of Psychiatry

Robert Kerwin MA PhD MB BChir DSc FRCPsych
Professor of Clinical Neuropharmacology
Institute of Psychiatry

Frank Margison MD FRCPsych
Manchester Mental Health and Social Care Trust

Rob Poole MB BS FRCPsych
Consultant Psychiatrist
Mersey Care NHS Trust

Appendix 3
Stakeholders who responded to early requests for evidence

Association of the British Pharmaceutical Industry
AstraZeneca
Birmingham Specialist Community Health, Dental Services Directorate
Bristol-Myers Squibb Pharmaceuticals Ltd
British Dietetic Association
British Psychological Society
BUPA
Chartered Society of Physiotherapy
College of Occupational Therapists
Eli Lilly and Company Ltd
Inner Cities Mental Health Group
Lundbeck Ltd
Manic Depression Fellowship
MHF (Mental Health Foundation)
MIND (National Association for Mental Health)
National Schizophrenia Fellowship
Norton Health care
Novartis Pharmaceuticals UK Ltd
Pfizer Ltd
Pharmaceutical Schizophrenia Initiative
Royal College of Speech & Language Therapists
Schizophrenia Association of Great Britain
Zito Trust

Appendix 4
Stakeholders and experts who responded to the first consultation draft of the guideline

Stakeholders

All Wales Senior Nurses Advisory Group (Mental Health)
Association of the British Pharmaceutical Industry
AstraZeneca
British National Formulary
British Psychological Society
Chartered Society of Physiotherapy
College of Occupational Therapists
Department of Health & Welsh Assembly Government
Eli Lilly and Company Ltd
Independent Healthcare Association
Janssen Cilag
Lundbeck Ltd
MIND
National Voices Forum
NIMHE
Newcastle, North Tyneside & Northumberland Mental Health NHS Trust
Novartis Pharmaceuticals UK Ltd
Pfizer Ltd
PRODIGY
Rethink Severe Mental Illness
Royal College of Nursing
Royal College of Psychiatrists
Royal College of Speech & Language Therapists
Royal Pharmaceutical Society of Great Britain
SANE
Sainsbury Centre for Mental Health
Schizophrenia Association of Great Britain
UK Psychiatry Pharmacy Group

Experts who responded to the first draft of the guideline

Tony Armitage   Chesterfield Community Mental Health Team
Professor Max Birchwood   North Birmingham Early Intervention Service

Professor Terry Brugha   University of Leicester

Dr John Cookson   Consultant Psychiatrist and Honorary Senior Lecturer, Royal London Hospital

Leigh Dyson-Green   Occupational therapist, Chesterfield Community Mental Health Team

Nicola Fletcher   Occupational therapist, Chesterfield Community Mental Health Team

Bob Gardner   Nurse Consultant, Derbyshire Mental Health Services NHS Trust

David Glossop   Derbyshire Mental Health Services NHS Trust

Christopher Hill   Chesterfield Community Mental Health Team

Professor Robert Kerwin   Institute of Psychiatry

Professor David King   Queen's University Belfast

Professor David Kingdon   University of Southampton

Professor Elizabeth Kuipers   Institute of Psychiatry

Professor Shôn Lewis   University of Manchester

Dr Fiona MacMillan   Consultant Psychiatrist, West Midlands Primary Care Mental Health Lead, IRIS

Carol Paton   Chief Pharmacist, Bexley Hospital

Catherine Saxton   Derbyshire Mental Health Services NHS Trust

Professor Geoff Shepherd   Chief Executive, The Health Advisory Service (London)

Dr David Shiers   West Midlands Primary Care Mental Health, IRIS

Dr Jo Smith   Clinical Psychologist, Worcester, IRIS West Midlands Primary Health (Mental Health), IRIS

Kevan Taylor   Chief Executive, Community Health Sheffield

Professor Till Wykes   Institute of Psychiatry

Appendix 5
Researchers contacted to request information about unpublished or soon-to-be-published studies

Dr K Aitchison

Dr I Anderson

Professor H Ashton

Professor D Bakash

Dr D Baldwin

Dr E H Bennie

Professor M Birchwood

Dr I Bitter

Professor J Bobes

Professor G Bond

H D Brenner

G Buchkremer

Professor T Burns

S Byford

Professor C L Cazzullo

Dr S Cheeta

Dr J F Collins

Dr S Cooper

Professor T K J Craig

Professor S G Dahl

Professor A David

Professor M Davidson

Dr J Day

Professor B Deakin

Professor S J Dencker

Dr D Denney

Professor T Dinan

Dr R Drake

Dr R C Durham

Dr S Dursun

Professor L Farde

Professor N Ferrier

Dr W W Fleischhacker

Professor B Gallhofer

Dr J Gerlach

Dr A Gumley

Professor F A Henn

Professor S R Hirsch

Professor G E Hogarty

Dr A Hudson

Professor H Jackson

Dr J Jenner

Professor R S Kahn

Dr J M Kane

Professor S Kasper

Professor H Katschnig

Professor R Kerwin

Professor D King

Dr D Kingdon

Dr W Kissling

Professor M Knapp

Professor M Lader

Dr Tor K Larsen

Dr Y Lecrubier

Professor J Leff

Professor B Leonard

Professor S Lewis

Professor R P Liberman

Dr A Lingford-Hughes

Dr D H Linszen

Dr M G Livingston

Professor M Maj

Professor K Matthews

Dr H McAllister-Williams

Dr P McCrone

Dr P McGorr

Dr J McQuaid

Dr A Medalia

Professor H Möller

Dr K T Mueser

Professor B Müller-Oerlinghausen

Professor B Müller-Spahn

Professor R Murray

Professor D Naber

173

Professor C B Nemeroff

Dr M Nordentoft

Professor D Nutt

Dr S Nyberg

Professor C Pantelis

Dr B Park

Dr D L Penn

Dr R Perkins

Professor J Peuskens

Dr R M Pinder

Professor A Puech

Professor G Racagni

Dr J G C Rasmussen

Dr N A Rector

Professor I Reid

Dr W Rein

Professor A Reveley

Dr J L Scott

Dr T Sensky

Professor A Y Shalev

Professor W D Spaulding

Dr M J Startup

Dr D Stephenson

Professor N Tarrier

Mr D Taylor

Dr M Travis

Dr D Turkington

Professor P Tyrer

Professor M van Der Gaag

Professor J L Waddington

R Warner

Professor A Weizman

Professor F Wiesel

Professor D A Wirshing

Professor T Wykes

Professor A Young

Appendix 6
Clinical questions

Given the wide scope of the guideline, it was not possible with the time and resources available to address all of the clinical questions listed below. In prioritising the clinical questions the GDG considered the clinical importance of and the available evidence for each question. Questions that were not fully addressed by the guideline group may well be considered in future versions of this guideline.

1 Identification

- This is concerned with the early identification, prevention and diagnosis of schizophrenia
- It is outside the scope of the current guideline

2 Initial treatment

- This is concerned with appropriate treatment and management when a person first comes to the attention of services with a clinical picture indicating a probable diagnosis of schizophrenia

Aims

- Establishing an alliance with the service user
- Establishing an alliance with the carers/family
- Achieving full remission of symptoms
- Minimising stigma
- Minimising disruption
- Minimising acute side-effects
- Reducing risk

Questions

A6.2.1 General

A6.2.1.1 What pharmacological/psychological interventions are most likely to achieve improvements, including full remission?

A6.2.1.2 What are the effective service settings in which to provide the initial treatment?

A6.2.1.3 What if initial antipsychotic drug treatment is not fully effective? When do you decide to alter it?

A6.2.1.4 Are there any relevant factors (including service-user populations) that predict the nature and degree of response to initial treatment?

A6.2.1.5 What should be the dose/duration (and where relevant frequency) of initial treatment(s)?

A6.2.1.6 Are the identified treatments more acceptable (greater satisfaction, lower number of people leaving the study early) than comparator treatments? (plus: This relates to the alliance between service users/carers/mental health professionals)

A6.2.2 Pharmacological interventions

A6.2.2.1 When antipsychotic-naïve patients are started on antipsychotic drugs, are relatively low doses required for a therapeutic response?

A6.2.2.2 When antipsychotic-naïve patients are started on antipsychotic drugs, are they particularly susceptible to acute extrapyramidal side-effects?

A6.2.2.3 When antipsychotic-naïve patients are started on antipsychotic drugs are they particularly susceptible to side-effects other than extrapyramidal side-effects?

A6.2.2.4 Is there evidence for a particular antipsychotic(s) having optimal risk:benefit at initiation of treatment?

A6.2.3 Psychological interventions

A6.2.3.1 Does the specified treatment produce benefit over and above other psychological interventions?

A6.2.3.2 What are the most effective formats for treatment in initial treatment (e.g. group or individual)?

A6.2.3.3 Are there any advantages of combining the specific intervention either concurrently or sequentially with other psychological interventions?

A6.2.4 Service interventions

A6.2.4.1 What service configuration(s) best promotes good outcomes in early intervention?

A6.2.4.2 For those who may require admission, are there effective alternatives?

3 Acute treatment

- This is concerned with the management and treatment of any acute exacerbation or recurrence of schizophrenia

Aims

- Maintaining/re-establishing the relationship
- Minimizing harm & disruption (social situation, work, relationships, family)
- Achieving rapid and full remission of symptoms
- Minimising acute side-effects
- Reducing risk
- Establishing and addressing the causes of relapse

Questions

A6.3.1 General

A6.3.1.1 What pharmacological/psychological interventions are most likely to achieve improvements, including full remission?

A6.3.1.2 What are the effective service settings in which to provide treatment?

A6.3.1.3 What if antipsychotic drug treatment is not fully effective? When do you decide to alter it?

A6.3.1.4 Are there any relevant factors (including patient populations) that predict the nature and degree of response to treatment?

A6.3.1.5 What should be the dose/duration (and where relevant frequency) of treatment(s)?

A6.3.1.6 Are the identified treatments more acceptable (greater satisfaction, lower number of people leaving the study early) than comparator treatments? (plus: This relates to the alliance between service users/carers/mental health professionals)

A6.3.2 Pharmacological interventions

A6.3.2.1 Is there evidence that any particular antipsychotic drug is or more or less effective for the management of acute psychotic episodes?

A6.3.2.2 Is there evidence for improved compliance with any particular antipsychotic drug when treating an acute psychotic episode?

A6.3.2.3 For the treatment of acute psychotic episodes, has an optimal dose range for antipsychotic drugs been established (e.g. in chlorpromazine equivalents, mg a day for conventional antipsychotics and on a drug-by-drug basis for the newer 'atypical' drugs)?

A6.3.2.4 Does rapid escalation of dosage/relatively high dosage yield any advantage in terms of speed of onset or degree of therapeutic response?

A6.3.2.5 Is there evidence for a lower liability for acute extrapyramidal side-effects for any antipsychotic drug, administered within the recommended dose range?

A6.3.2.6 Is there evidence for a lower liability for weight gain for any antipsychotic, administered within the recommended dose range?

A6.3.2.7　Is there evidence for a lower liability of sedation/fatigue for any antipsychotic, administered within the recommended dose range?

A6.3.2.8　Is there evidence for a lower liability of sexual dysfunction for any antipsychotic, administered within the recommended dose range?

A6.3.2.9　Is there evidence for a lower liability for diabetes/disturbance of glucose homeostasis for any antipsychotic, administered within the recommended dose range?

A6.3.2.10 Is there evidence for a lower liability for increased prolactin with any antipsychotic, administered within the recommended dose range?

A6.3.2.11 Is there evidence for a lower liability of cardiotoxicity for any antipsychotic, administered within the recommended dose range?

A6.3.2.12 Is there evidence that any particular antipsychotic drug has a better risk:benefit in the management of acute psychotic episodes?

A6.3.2.13 Is there an optimal drug treatment (in terms of risk:benefit) for acute behavioural disturbance? (Rapid tranquillisation.)

A6.3.3 Psychological interventions

A6.3.3.1　Does the specified treatment produce benefit over and above other psychological treatments?

A6.3.3.2　What are the most effective formats for treatment (e.g. group or individual)?

A6.3.3.3　Are there any advantages of combining the specific intervention either concurrently or sequentially with other psychological interventions?

A6.3.4 Service level interventions

A6.3.4.1　What service configuration(s) best promotes good outcomes in crisis/acute intervention?

A6.3.4.2　For those who may require admission, are there effective alternatives?

4 Promoting recovery

- This is concerned with the continuing management and treatment of schizophrenia

Aims

- Maintaining contact
- Achieving partnership in the management of the illness autonomy
- Preventing relapse
- Managing residual symptoms (including depression)
- Achieving full potential in vocational roles and accommodation
- Supporting families and carers

- Reducing risk
- Minimizing long-term side-effects/harm

Questions

A6.4.1 General

A6.4.1.1 What pharmacological/psychological interventions are most likely to achieve improvements, including interventions for people with treatment-resistant schizophrenia?

A6.4.1.2 What are the effective service interventions that are best placed to help individuals reach their full potential and prevent relapse?

A6.4.1.3 What if antipsychotic drug treatment is not fully effective? When do you decide to alter it?

A6.4.1.4 Are there any relevant factors (including service-user populations) that predict the nature and degree of response to treatment?

A6.4.1.5 What should be the dose/duration (and where relevant, frequency) of treatment(s)?

A6.4.1.6 Are the identified treatments more acceptable (greater satisfaction, lower number of people leaving the study early) than comparator treatments? (plus: This relates to the alliance between service users/carers/mental health professionals)

A6.4.2 Pharmacological interventions

A6.4.2.1 Is any antipsychotic drug(s) more or less effective at preventing relapse in the long-term, when prescribed in the recommended maintenance dose range?

A6.4.2.2 How long should antipsychotic drug treatment be continued for prevention of relapse?

A6.4.2.3 Is any antipsychotic drug(s) associated with improved or reduced compliance when prescribed at the recommended dosage?

A6.4.2.4 Does depot antipsychotic drug treatment show any advantage over oral antipsychotic treatment in relapse prevention over time?

A6.4.2.5 Are there differences between depot antipsychotic preparations in risk:benefit?

A6.4.2.6 With long-term medication, is there evidence that service users' have a preference for either depot or oral preparations?

A6.4.2.7 Do high (mega) doses of antipsychotic drugs offer any therapeutic advantage over standard (recommended) dosage?

A6.4.2.8 Is there evidence that clozapine is more effective than other antipsychotics for treatment-resistant schizophrenia?

A6.4.2.9 Is there evidence that any antipsychotic(s) other than clozapine has superior efficacy in any people with schizophrenia?

A6.4.2.10 Is the augmentation of an antipsychotic drug with another antipsychotic (combined antipsychotics) associated with an enhanced therapeutic response?

A6.4.2.11 In service users with comorbid depressive features, is there evidence for any particular benefit with any particular antipsychotic drug?

A6.4.2.12 In service users with comorbid depressive features, is there evidence that augmentation of antipsychotic drugs with an antidepressant is an effective treatment strategy?

A6.4.2.13 Are there any effective drug treatments (including adjunctive treatments) for persistent negative symptoms?

A6.4.2.14 Are there any effective drug treatments (including augmentation strategies) for service users with persistent symptoms of irritability, hostility and aggression?

A6.4.2.15 Is there evidence that some antipsychotic drugs are able to improve cognitive function in relevant domains?

A6.4.2.16 Is there evidence for a lower liability for tardive dyskinesia with any particular antipsychotic drug(s)?

A6.4.2.17 Is there evidence that switching to any particular antipsychotic is associated with a therapeutic effect on existing tardive dyskinesia?

A6.4.2.18 Is there evidence that combinations of antipsychotics are associated with an increased risk of/severity of side-effects?

A6.4.3 Psychological interventions

A6.4.3.1 Does the specified treatment produce benefit over and above other psychological treatments?

A6.4.3.2 What are the most effective formats for treatment (e.g. group or individual)?

A6.4.3.3 Are there any advantages of combining the specific intervention either concurrently or sequentially with other psychological interventions?

A6.4.4 Service level interventions

A6.4.4.1 What service configuration(s) best promotes and sustains recovery?

A6.4.4.2 What model of service delivery promotes placement in gainful employment?

Appendix 7
Drug names and definitions of interventions reviewed

Pharmacological topic area

The source used for drug and preparation names and details is the 42nd issue (September 2001) of the *British National Formulary*.

Atypical antipsychotics

- AMISULPRIDE – Solian®
- CLOZAPINE – Clozaril®
- OLANZAPINE – Zyprexa®
- QUETIAPINE – Seroquel®
- RISPERIDONE – Risperdal®
- ZOTEPINE – Zoleptil®

Conventional antipsychotics

- BENPERIDOL – Anquil®
- CHLORPROMAZINE HYDROCHLORIDE – Chlorpromazine, Largactil®
- FLUPENTIXOL (Flupenthixol) – Depixol®
- FLUPHENAZINE HYDROCHLORIDE – Moditen®, Modecate®
- HALOPERIDOL – Haloperidol, Dozic®, Haldol®, Serenace®
- LEVOMEPROMAZINE/METHOTRIMEPRAZINE – Nozinan®
- LOXAPINE – Loxapac®
- OXYPERTINE – Oxypertine
- PERICYAZINE (Periciazine) – Neulactil®
- PERPHENAZINE – Fentazin®
- PIMOZIDE – Orap®
- PROCHLORPERAZINE
- PROMAZINE HYDROCHLORIDE – Promazine
- SULPIRIDE – Sulpiride, Dolmatil®, Sulparex®, Sulpitil®
- THIORIDAZINE – Thioridazine, Melleril®
- TRIFLUOPERAZINE – Trifluoperazine, Stelazine®

- ZUCLOPENTHIXOL ACETATE – Clopixol Acuphase®
- ZUCLOPENTHIXOL DIHYDROCHLORIDE – Clopixol®

Depot injections

- FLUPENTIXOL DECANOATE (Flupenthixol Decanoate) – Depixol®, Depixol Conc.®, Depixol Low Volume®
- FLUPHENAZINE DECANOATE – Modecate®, Modecate Concentrate®
- HALOPERIDOL DECANOATE – Haldol Decanoate®
- PIPOTHIAZINE (PIPOTIAZINE) PALMITATE – Piportil Depot®
- ZUCLOPENTHIXOL DECANOATE – Clopixol®, Clopixol Conc.®

Benzodiazepines (anxiolytics for tranquillisation and sedation)

Hypnotics

- NITRAZEPAM
- FLUNITRAZEPAM
- FLURAZEPAM
- LOPRAZOLAM
- LORMETAZEPAM
- TEMAZEPAM
- ZOLPIDEM
- ZOPICLONE

Anxiolytics (anti-anxiety drugs)

- DIAZEPAM
- ALPRAZOLAM
- BROMAZEPAM
- CHLORDIAZEPOXIDE
- CLORAZEPATE DIPOTASSIUM
- LORAZEPAM
- OXAZEPAM

Anti-depressants and mood stabilisers

Tricyclic antidepressants

- AMITRIPTYLINE HYDROCHLORIDE
- AMOXAPINE
- CLOMIPRAMINE HYDROCHLORIDE
- DOSULEPIN HYDROCHLORIDE/DOTHIEPIN HYDROCHLORIDE
- DOXEPIN
- IMIPRAMINE HYDROCHLORIDE

- LOFEPRAMINE
- NORTRIPTYLINE
- TRIMIPRAMINE

SSRIs

- CITALOPRAM
- FLUOXETINE
- FLUVOXAMINE MALEATE
- PAROXETINE
- SERTRALINE

MAO-Inhibitors

- PHENELZINE
- ISOCARBOXAZID
- TRANYLCYPROMINE
- MOCLOBEMIDE

Other antidepressants

- FLUPENTIXOL
- MIRTAZAPINE
- NEFAZODONE HYDROCHLORIDE
- REBOXETINE
- TRYPTOPHAN
- VENLAFAXINE XL

Mood stabilisers

- LITHIUM CARBONATE
- LAMOTRIGINE
- CARBAMAZEPINE
- OXYCARBAZEPINE
- SODIUM VALPROATE
- PHENYTOIN

Other interventions (including those used in the management of side-effects)

- CARBAMAZEPINE
- OXYCARBAZEPINE

Beta-adrenoceptor blocking drugs

- PROPRANOLOL HYDROCHLORIDE
- ACEBUTOLOL

- ATENOLOL
- BETAXOLOL HYDROCHLORIDE
- BISOPROLOL FUMARATE
- CARVEDILOL
- CELIPROLOL HYDROCHLORIDE
- ESMOLOL HYDROCHLORIDE
- LABETALOL HYDROCHLORIDE
- METOPROLOL TARTRATE
- NADOLOL
- NEBIVOLOL
- OXPRENOLOL HYDROCHLORIDE
- PINDOLOL
- SOTALOL HYDROCHLORIDE
- TIMOLOL MALEATE

Antimuscarinic drugs (less correctly termed 'anticholinergics')

- BENZATROPINE MESYLATE (Benztropine mesylate)
- BIPERIDEN HYDROCHLORIDE
- ORPHENADRINE HYDROCHLORIDE
- PROCYCLIDINE HYDROCHLORIDE
- TRIHEXYPHENIDYL HYDROCHLORIDE/BENZHEXOL HYDROCHLORIDE

Non-benzodiazepine GABA agonists

- BACLOFEN
- DIVALPROEX
- GAMMA-ACETYLENIC-GABA
- GAMMA-VINYL-GABA
- MUSCIMOL
- PROGABIDE
- SODIUM VALPROATE
- THIP
- VALPROIC ACID

Calcium channel blockers

- DILTIAZEM HYDROCHLORIDE
- NIFEDIPINE
- NIMODIPINE
- VERAPAMIL HYDROCHLORIDE

Cholinergics

- ARECOLINE
- CHOLINE

- DEANOL
- LECITHIN
- MECLOFENOXATE
- PHYSOSTIGMINE
- RS 86

Miscellaneous

- DIMETHYLAMINOETHANOL
- ENDORPHIN
- ESTROGEN
- ESSENTIAL FATTY ACID
- EX 11-582A
- GANGLIOSIDE GM1
- LITHIUM
- METHYLPHENIDATE
- NALOXONE
- NALTREXONE
- PERIACTIN
- PHENYLALANINE
- PIRACETAM
- STEPHOLIDINE
- TRYPTOPHAN
- VITAMIN E (TOCOPHEROL)

Psychological topic area

Cognitive–behavioural therapy (CBT)

Cognitive–behavioural therapy was defined as a discrete psychological intervention where:

1 Recipients establish links between their thoughts, feelings or actions with respect to the current or past symptoms; and

2 The re-evaluation of their perceptions, beliefs or reasoning relate to the target symptoms.

In addition, a further component of the intervention should involve the following:

1 Recipients' monitor their own thoughts, feelings or behaviours with respect to the symptom; and/or

2 The promotion of alternative ways of coping with the target symptom, and/or

3 The reduction of distress.

Cognitive remediation

Cognitive remediation was defined as:

1 An identified procedure that is specifically focused on primary-level cognitive function, and

2 The procedure is implemented with the specific intention of bringing about an improvement in the level of performance on that specified cognitive function or other primary-level functions.

Counselling and supportive therapy

Counselling or supportive therapy was a discrete psychological intervention where:

1 The intervention is facilitative, non-directive and/or relationship focused, with the content largely determined by the service user; and

2 The intervention does not fulfil the criteria for any other psychological intervention.

Family interventions

Family Interventions were defined as:

1 Family sessions with a specific supportive or treatment function based on systemic, cognitive behavioural or psychoanalytic principles, and must contain at least one of the following components:

    (a)   Psychoeducational intervention, or

    (b)   Problem-solving/crisis management work, or

    (c)   Intervention with the identified service user.

Psychoanalytic psychotherapy

Psychodynamic interventions were defined as:

1 Regular therapy sessions based on a psychodynamic or psychoanalytic model, and

2 Sessions could rely on a variety of strategies, including explorative insight-oriented, supportive or directive activity, applied flexibly; and

3 To be considered well-defined psychodynamic psychotherapy, the intervention needed to include working with transference and unconscious processes.

Psychoanalytic Interventions were defined as:

1 Regular, individual sessions planned to continue for at least one year; and

2 Analysts were required to adhere to a strict definition of psychoanalytic technique, and

3 To be considered as well-defined psychoanalysis, the intervention needed to involve working with the unconscious and early child/adult relationships.

Psychoeducation

Psychoeducational interventions were defined as:

1   Any programme involving interaction between information provider and service user or family. These programmes address the disorder from multidimensional viewpoints, including the following perspectives:

(a)   Familial, or

(b)   Social, or

(c)   Biological, or

(d)   Pharmacological.

2   Service users or families are provided with support, information and management strategies.

3   To be considered as well defined, the educational strategy should be tailored to the need of individuals or families.

Social skills training

Social skills training was defined as:

1   A structured psychosocial intervention (group or individual) that aims to:

(a)   Enhance social performance, and

(b)   Reduce distress and difficulty in social situations.

2   The intervention must:

(a)   Include behaviourally based assessments of a range of social and interpersonal skills, and

(b)   Place importance on both verbal and non-verbal communication, the individual's ability to perceive and process relevant social cues, and to respond to and provide appropriate social reinforcement.

Multimodal interventions

To be classified as multimodal, an intervention needed to be composed of the following:

1   A treatment programme where one or more specific psychological interventions (as defined above) were combined in a systematic and programmed way, and

2   The intervention was conducted with the specific intention of producing a benefit over and above that which might achieved by a single intervention alone.

In addition, multimodal treatments could provide specific interventions, either concurrently or consecutively.

Service-level topic area

Vocational rehabilitation

There are three aspects to vocational rehabilitation:

1   Pre-vocational training. In this approach individuals undergo a period of preparation prior to being encouraged to seek open employment. This may

involve activity in a sheltered environment, some form of pre-employment training, or transitional employment, and

2   Supported employment. This is defined as an activity that attempted to place individuals in competitive employment without preparation, but provides ongoing support in seeking work and when in post, and

3   Maintaining employment/education.

Alternatives to admission

There are two broad alternatives to admission:

1   Treatment at home, either from a residential crisis team, or from a generic CMHT with a home treatment component, and

2   Alternative non-hospital environments such as respite accommodation, or day hospital care.

Assertive community treatment (assertive outreach teams)

Assertive community treatment (commonly known as assertive outreach teams in the UK) was defined as a multi-disciplinary team-based approach to the treatment and management of people with severe mental illness. Assertive Community Treatment was characterised by:

1   Team members sharing responsibility for service users.

2   Low caseloads, typically between 10 and 15.

3   Provision of a range of services by the team, including psychiatric and social care within the team context.

4   Assertive outreach aimed at promoting engagement with services.

5   Contact with the team, which is usually expected to be at least on a weekly basis.

Case management

Case management was defined as a method for the coordination of care of people with severe mental illness. It places responsibility on individual workers to coordinate and, where necessary, provide care to individuals. Case management can be provided in a number of ways, as set out below:

1   Intensive case management. This is where an individual has responsibility for the care and coordination of an individual. Typically this will be with caseloads of not greater than 15. Contact with the team is usually expected to be at least on a weekly basis, or

2   Brokerage-based case management. In this model the case manager specifically eschews any direct provision of clinical services to the individual, merely acting as a coordinator and possible funder of services provided, or

3   User-based case management. In this circumstance, a user (patient) is responsible for the care and coordination of another service user.

These should be distinguished from assertive community treatment where the emphasis is on team-based provision of services as opposed to individual-based provision of services.

Early intervention services were defined as a service approach with focus on the care and treatment of individuals in the early phase (usually up to 5 years) and including the prodromal phase of the disorder. The service may be provided by a team or a specialised element of a team, which has designated responsibility for at least two of the following functions:

1   Early identification and therapeutic engagement of people in the prodromal phase, and/or

2   Provision of specialised pharmacological and psychosocial interventions during or immediately following a first episode of psychosis, and/or

3   Educating the wider community to reduce obstacles to early engagement in treatment.

Appendix 8
Detailed clinical review process

Systematic reviews

The first stage of the search process involved searching for systematic reviews published or updated since 1996. The use of a time limit was based on the rationale that, compared to earlier reviews, more recently published systematic reviews would be of better quality (e.g. used a more comprehensive and systematic search strategy). Searches were carried out in August 2001 to capture newly indexed records. (A further search for systematic reviews covering the pharmacological topic area was made in February 2002.) If no relevant systematic reviews were identified, the search was extended by five years. If still no systematic reviews were detected, the review team conducted a new review where possible.

Randomised controlled trials

Where an existing systematic review answered a clinical question, a systematic search was made for RCTs with a publication date too recent to be included in the review. If a review did not specify the search date, the literature was searched back to three years before the review's publication date. Where a new systematic review was undertaken, the literature was searched back as far as possible.

Search strings

Electronic databases were searched using a combination of subject heading and free-text phrases (see Box A8.1). The search filter for schizophrenia was adapted from that suggested by the Cochrane Schizophrenia Group (May 2001). On the advice of a member of the GDG, the term 'anti-psychotic' was added, but this did not produce any further references, so it was not used as a search term. The search filter for systematic reviews was adapted from that used by Clinical Evidence (BMJ Publishing Group, 2001). Search strings were modified according to the syntax required for the interface and database being used (see Appendix 9 for each strategy).

Additional searches were made of the reference lists of all eligible systematic reviews and RCTs, and the list of evidence submitted by stakeholders. Known experts in the field (Appendix 5), based both on the references identified in early steps and on advice from GDG members were sent letters requesting systematic reviews or RCTs that were in the process of being published. Unpublished full trial reports were also accepted where sufficient information was available to judge eligibility and quality. Finally, the tables of contents (August 2001 and February 2002) of those journals identified as having published more than one appropriate review, or known to publish reviews, were searched (i.e. *Acta Psychiatrica Scandinavica*, *American Journal of Psychiatry*, *Annals of Pharmacotherapy*, *Archives of General Psychiatry*, *British Journal of Psychiatry*,

Identification of papers concerning schizophrenia spectrum disorders

Schizophrenia; paranoid disorders; schizo$; hebephreni$; oligophreni$; psychotic$; psychosis; psychoses; (chronic$ or sever$) mental$ (ill$ or disorder$); tardiv$ dyskine$; akathisi$; acathisi$; neuroleptic$ malignant syndrome; neuroleptic movement disorder; parkinsoni$; neuroleptic-induc$; *not* parkinsons disease; drug-induced dyskinesia; drug-induced akathisia; schizophrenia and disorders with psychotic features

Identification of systematic reviews or meta-analyses

Meta-analysis; review; tutorial review; academic review; *not* comment or letter; medline; medlars; embase; scisearch; psychinfo; psychlit; psyclit; cinahl; cochrane; hand search; manual search; electronic database; bibliographic database; pooling; pooled analysis; peto; der simonian; dersimonian; random effect; fixed effect; mantel haenzel; systematic review; systematic overview; quantitative review; quantitative overview; methodologic$ review; methodologic$ overview; integrative research review; research integration; quantitative synthesis; data synthesis

Identification of randomised controlled trial

Experimental design; experimentation; prospective studies, experiment controls; experimental subjects; empirical methods; random; trial; control; controlled; controls; randomisation; randomly; randomised; trials; triallist; placebo; blinded; blind; double; single; treble; triple; empirical study

The symbol "$" is used to denote unlimited truncation.

Clinical Therapeutics, European Archives of Psychiatry & Clinical Neuroscience, European Psychiatry, International Clinical Psychopharmacology, International Journal of Psychiatry in Clinical Practice, Journal of Clinical Pharmacy and Therapeutics, Journal of Clinical Psychiatry, Journal of Psychiatry & Neuroscience, Journal of Psychopharmacology, Journal of the American Medical Association, Lancet, New England Journal of Medicine, Psychological Medicine, Schizophrenia Bulletin, Schizophrenia Research).

Study selection (eligibility criteria)

Specific inclusion criteria (see Box A8.3) and exclusion criteria (see Box A8.4) were evaluated using a standardised form (Appendix 10). In the case of primary research, all trials used in the review or added to an existing review had to be concerned with a specific drug or meet our definition of an appropriate intervention (Appendix 7). Reports were specifically excluded if they concerned treatment options or populations outside the scope of the guideline (see Box A8.4). In addition, an attempt was made to include non-English-language papers. However, for the purpose of initial study selection, the title and abstract of the paper had to be available in English.

Duplicate publications (i.e. papers that report about trials using the same sample of participants or systematic reviews published in different journals) were identified at the time of data extraction. Factors used in the identification of duplicates included the authors' names, geographic locations of studies, study design (including which interventions were studied), numbers of participants, study lengths, and outcome measures used (US Department of Health and Human Services, 1999). When the reviewers could not determine whether a publication represented duplication, the author was contacted for clarification.

Quality assessment of studies

The methodological quality of each systematic review was evaluated using dimensions adapted from SIGN (Scottish Intercollegiate Guidelines Network, 2001) (see Box A8.5). SIGN originally adapted their quality criteria from checklists developed in Australia (Liddel, Williamson, & Irwig, 1996). Both groups reportedly undertook extensive development and validation procedures when creating their quality criteria. The quality assessment of each RCT was based on suggestions made in the Cochrane Collaboration Handbook (Clarke & Oxman, 2000) (see Box A8.5).

After considering each criterion, an overall assessment of the risk of bias was made using the three quality categories as described in the Cochrane Collaboration Handbook (see Box A8.6) (Clarke & Oxman, 2000). Checklists were used to maintain consistency and aid with cross-checking (see Appendix 11).

With respect to RCTs, the following criteria were also used to address quality issues: identification of co-interventions, reporting of eligibility criteria, adequacy of blinding, comparability of groups at baseline, attrition rate, adequacy of description of withdrawals, adequacy of intention to treat analysis, appropriate dose of comparator drug, adequate washout period (defined as 7 days or more). Threats to validity were assessed using sensitivity analyses where possible.

Reviews and studies with a high risk of bias were excluded from further analysis. The overall rating, coupled with notes addressing the quality criteria, were used to decide the level of evidence that a study provides. This information was presented to the TG members as part of an evidence table.

For methodological reasons (i.e., to avoid attrition bias), data from continuous outcome measures were excluded where more than 50% of participants in any group were lost to follow-up. In addition, studies of family interventions were excluded if the number of sessions was very short (i.e., less than six sessions). Unpublished scales have been shown to be a source of bias in trials of treatments for schizophrenia (Marshall *et al*, 2000). Thus, continuous data from unpublished scales or from a subset of items from a scale were excluded.

Confirmation of eligibility/quality assessment process

To confirm the eligibility and quality assessment process was satisfactory, the topic group (TG) members were sent examples of reviews relevant to their topic area along with copies of the completed checklists. Each TG member was sent examples of two

Box A8.2 Electronic searches

Database	Interface	Searched for RCTs	Searched for Systematic Reviews
MEDLINE	OVID (Release 4.1.1)	Yes	Yes
PsycINFO	OVID	Yes	Yes
Cumulative Index to Nursing and Allied Health Literature (CINAHL)	OVID	Yes	Yes
Excerpta Medica Database (EMBASE)	WebSPIRS	Yes	Yes
Cochrane Database of Systematic Reviews	OVID/Cochrane Library		Yes
Science Citation Index (SCI)/ Social Science Citation Index (SSCI)	Web of Science		Yes
PubMed *in-process**	National Library of Medicine website	Yes	Yes
Evidence-Based Mental Health (EBMH)	Website	Yes	Yes
NHS R&D Health Technology Assessment (HTA)	Website		Yes
Medical Matrix	Website		Yes
Clinical Evidence (Issue 5)	Website		Yes
Cochrane Controlled Trials Register	Website	Yes	
National Research Register	Website	Yes	
ClinicalTrials.gov	Website	Yes	

PubMed's in-process records provide basic citation information and abstracts before the citations are indexed with the US National Library of Medicine's MeSH Terms and added to MEDLINE.

eligible papers (one coded as having a low risk of bias and the other coded as having a high risk of bias) and a paper that was coded as not eligible. Each TG member also received information about the number of papers found and their eligibility/quality rating. A discussion was then initiated to form a view of the extent and quality of the studies. This process allowed changes to the focus of the review or the eligibility criteria to be made if necessary. In light of any changes, the proposal for the analysis and synthesis of the studies was discussed. This included what sensitivity analyses were required. Finally, any issues that had arisen relating to the format of the report were

Box A8.3 Inclusion criteria for systematic reviews and randomised controlled trials

---

Population

- Reported results from patients with a diagnosis of a schizophrenia spectrum disorder (including schizotypal, schizoaffective and schizophreniform disorders), or in which the effects of treatment could be estimated separately for these patients (a population described as severe mentally ill [*or similar term*] was taken as a proxy for schizophrenia)

Intervention

And reported results from one of the following **pharmacological** topic areas:

- antidepressants/mood stabilisers
- atypical antipsychotics*
- Benzodiazepines
- conventional antipsychotics
- depot injections
- other compounds (including those used in the management of side-effects).

Or reported results from one of the following **psychological** topic areas:

- cognitive–behavioural therapy
- cognitive remediation
- counselling and supportive therapy
- family interventions
- multimodal interventions
- psychoanalytic psychotherapy
- psychoeducation
- social skills training.

Or reported results from one of the following **service system** topic areas:

- assertive community treatment
- alternatives to admission
- case management (intensive, standard, user-led)
- early intervention services
- vocational rehabilitation.

---

*The evidence for the cost-effectiveness of atypical antipsychotics used in this guideline was taken in the first instance from the work of the NICE Health Technology Appraisal (HTA) programme.

discussed. Each TG then reported back to the wider GDG for approval of the assessment process.

Prioritisation and selection of studies

For some clinical questions, it was necessary to prioritise the evidence with respect to the UK context. To make this process explicit, the TGs took into account the following factors when assessing the evidence:

Outcomes

And reported results from at least one of the following outcomes:

- adverse effects of treatment
- carer/family outcomes
- cognitive functioning
- compliance with:
  - (a) drug treatment
  - (b) other non-drug treatments
- death (any cause and sudden unexpected death or suicide)
- economic outcomes
- engagement
- hospital admission
- involvement with criminal justice system
- mental state:
  - (a) criterion-based improvement (as defined in individual studies) with reference to the positive and negative symptoms of schizophrenia
  - (b) continuous measures of mental state
- occupational status
- other intervention-specific outcomes
- patient satisfaction
- psychological well-being:
  - (a) criterion-based improvement (as defined in individual studies) with respect to general psychological well-being, such as self-esteem or distress
  - (b) continuous measures of psychological well-being
- quality of life
- relapse (as defined in the individual studies)
- social functioning
- any other unexpected or unwanted effect.

Box A8.4 Exclusion criteria for systematic reviews and research reports

- Only concerned the initial diagnosis and assessment of schizophrenia
- *Or* only concerned very-late onset schizophrenia (i.e., where the age of onset of the disorder is 60 years or greater)
- *Or* only concerned children with schizophrenia (i.e., where the age of the patient was under 18)
- *Or* only concerned the management of schizophrenia in conjunction with learning difficulties
- *Or* only concerned the management of schizophrenia in conjunction with significant physical or sensory impairment

Box A8.5 Quality criteria

For systematic reviews:

- Does the review address an appropriate and clearly focused question?
- Does the review include a description of the methodology used?
- Was the literature search sufficiently rigorous to identify relevant studies?
- Was study quality assessed and taken into account?

For randomised controlled trials:

- Was the assignment of subjects to treatment groups randomised?
- Was an adequate concealment method used?

Box A8.6 Categories for the overall assessment of methodological quality

A Low risk of bias	Plausible bias unlikely to seriously alter the results
B Moderate risk of bias	Plausible bias that raises some doubt about the results
C High risk of bias	Plausible bias that seriously weakens confidence in the results

1   Participant factors (e.g., gender, age, ethnicity)
2   Provider factors (e.g., model fidelity, the conditions under which the intervention was performed, the availability of experienced staff to undertake the procedure)
3   Cultural factors (e.g., differences in standard care, differences in the welfare system)

It was the responsibility of each TG to decide which prioritisation factors were relevant to each clinical question in light of the UK context, and then decide to how they should modify their recommendations.

Presentation of data to the GDG

Forest plots: In presenting data to the GDG, forest plots were organised so that display of data in the area to the left of the 'line of no effect' indicated a 'favourable' outcome for the treatment in question. Dichotomous outcomes were presented as a standard estimation of the odds ratio (OR) and its 95% confidence interval. The relative risk (RR) and, where appropriate, the number needed to treat (NNT) or number needed to harm (NNH), were also calculated on an intention-to-treat basis (i.e. a 'once randomised-always-analyse' basis). This assumes that those participants who ceased to engage in the study – from whatever group – had an unfavourable outcome (with the exception of the outcome of 'death').

The chi-squared test of heterogeneity (*P*<0 .10) was used, as well as visual inspection of graphs, to look for the possibility of heterogeneity. Where no heterogeneity was detected, a fixed-effects model was used to summarise the results. Where heterogeneity was present, an attempt was made to explain the variation. If studies with heterogeneous results were found to be comparable, a random-effects model was used to synthesise the results (DerSimonian & Laird, 1986). In the random-effects analysis, heterogeneity is accounted for both in the width of confidence intervals and the estimate of the treatment effect. With decreasing heterogeneity, the random-effects approach moves asymptotically towards a fixed-effects model.

Appendix 9
Search strategies for the identification of clinical studies

Schizophrenia search filters

CINAHL – OVID interface

(exp Psychotic disorders/ or (SCHIZO$ or HEBEPHRENI$ or OLIGOPHRENI$ or
PSYCHOTIC$ or PSYCHOSIS or PSYCHOSES or ((CHRONIC$ or SEVER$) and MENTAL$
and (ILL$ or DISORDER$))) or ((((TARDIV$ and DYSKINE$) or AKATHISI$ or ACATHISI$ or
(NEUROLEPTIC$ and (MALIGNANT and SYNDROME)) or (NEUROLEPTIC and
MOVEMENT and DISORDER) or PARKINSONI$ or NEUROLEPTIC-INDUC$) or exp
Movement disorders/ or Akathisia, drug-induced/ or Dyskinesia, drug-induced/ or exp
Neuroleptic malignant syndrome/) not (PARKINSON$ and DISEASE).ti.))

Cochrane Database of Systematic Reviews – OVID interface

(SCHIZO$ or HEBEPHRENI$ or OLIGOPHRENI$ or PSYCHOTIC$ or PSYCHOSIS or
PSYCHOSES or ((CHRONIC$ or SEVER$) and MENTAL$ and (ILL$ or DISORDER$)) or
((TARDIV$ and DYSKINE$) or AKATHISI$ or ACATHISI$ or (NEUROLEPTIC$ and
(MALIGNANT and SYNDROME)) or (NEUROLEPTIC and MOVEMENT and DISORDER) or
PARKINSONI$ or NEUROLEPTIC-INDUC$)) not (PARKINSONS and DISEASE).ti.

Cochrane Controlled Trials Register – Cochrane Library

(SCHIZO$ or HEBEPHRENI$ or OLIGOPHRENI$ or PSYCHOTIC$ or PSYCHOSIS or
PSYCHOSES or ((CHRONIC$ or SEVER$) and MENTAL$ and (ILL$ or DISORDER$)) or
((TARDIV$ and DYSKINE$) or AKATHISI$ or ACATHISI$ or (NEUROLEPTIC$ and
(MALIGNANT and SYNDROME)) or (NEUROLEPTIC and MOVEMENT and DISORDER) or
PARKINSONI$ or NEUROLEPTIC-INDUC$)) not (PARKINSONS and DISEASE).ti.

Database of Reviews of Effectiveness – OVID interface

(SCHIZO$ or HEBEPHRENI$ or OLIGOPHRENI$ or PSYCHOTIC$ or PSYCHOSIS or
PSYCHOSES or ((CHRONIC$ or SEVER$) and MENTAL$ and (ILL$ or DISORDER$)) or
((TARDIV$ and DYSKINE$) or AKATHISI$ or ACATHISI$ or (NEUROLEPTIC$ and

(MALIGNANT and SYNDROME)) or (NEUROLEPTIC and MOVEMENT and DISORDER) or PARKINSONI$ or NEUROLEPTIC-INDUC$)) not (PARKINSONS and DISEASE).ti.

EMBASE – WebSPIRS interface

(((explode 'SCHIZOPHRENIA' / all subheadings) or (explode 'PARANOID-PSYCHOSIS' / all subheadings) or (SCHIZO*) or (HEBEPHRENI*) or (OLIGOPHRENI*) or (PSYCHOTIC*) or (PSYCHOS?S) or (((CHRONIC* or SEVER*) near2 MENTAL*) near2 (ILL* or DISORDER*)) or (TARDIV* near2 DYSKINE*) or (AKATHISI*) or (ACATHISI*) or (NEUROLEPTIC* and (MALIGNANT near2 SYNDROME)) or (NEUROLEPTIC and MOVEMENT and DISORDER) or (PARKINSONI*) or (NEUROLEPTIC-INDUC*) or ('NEUROLEPTIC-MALIGNANT-SYNDROME'/ all subheadings)) not (PARKINSON'S near1 (DISEASE in TI)))

Evidence-Based Mental Health – Website

(SCHIZO* or HEBEPHRENI* or OLIGOPHRENI* or PSYCHOTIC* or PSYCHOSIS or PSYCHOSES or ((CHRONIC* or SEVER*) and MENTAL* and (ILL* or DISORDER*)) or (TARDIV* and DYSKINE*) or AKATHISI* or ACATHISI* or (NEUROLEPTIC* and (MALIGNANT and SYNDROME)) or (NEUROLEPTIC and MOVEMENT and DISORDER) or PARKINSONI* or NEUROLEPTIC-INDUC* or (drug-induced and Dyskinesia) or (drug-induced and Akathisia))

MEDLINE – OVID interface

(exp Schizophrenia/ or exp Paranoid disorders/ or (SCHIZO$ or HEBEPHRENI$ or OLIGOPHRENI$ or PSYCHOTIC$ or PSYCHOSIS or PSYCHOSES or ((CHRONIC$ or SEVER$) and MENTAL$ and (ILL$ or DISORDER$))) or (((TARDIV$ and DYSKINE$) or AKATHISI$ or ACATHISI$ or (NEUROLEPTIC$ and (MALIGNANT and SYNDROME)) or (NEUROLEPTIC and MOVEMENT and DISORDER) or PARKINSONI$ or NEUROLEPTIC-INDUC$) not (PARKINSON$ and DISEASE).ti.) or (exp Movement disorders/ or Akathisia, drug-induced/ or Dyskinesia, drug-induced/ or exp Neuroleptic malignant syndrome/ or (exp schizrenia/ and disorders with psychotic features/)))

NHS R&D Health Technology Assessment Programme – Website

(SCHIZO* or HEBEPHRENI* or OLIGOPHRENI* or PSYCHOTIC* or PSYCHOSIS or PSYCHOSES or ((CHRONIC* or SEVER*) and MENTAL* and (ILL* or DISORDER*)) or (TARDIV* and DYSKINE*) or AKATHISI* or ACATHISI* or (NEUROLEPTIC* and (MALIGNANT and SYNDROME)) or (NEUROLEPTIC and MOVEMENT and DISORDER) or PARKINSONI* or NEUROLEPTIC-INDUC* or (drug-induced and Dyskinesia) or (drug-induced and Akathisia))

PsycINFO – OVID interface

(exp Schizophrenia/ or (SCHIZO$ or HEBEPHRENI$ or OLIGOPHRENI$ or PSYCHOTIC$ or PSYCHOSIS or PSYCHOSES or ((CHRONIC$ or SEVER$) and MENTAL$ and (ILL$ or DISORDER$))) or ((((TARDIV$ and DYSKINE$) or AKATHISI$ or ACATHISI$ or

(NEUROLEPTIC$ and (MALIGNANT and SYNDROME)) or (NEUROLEPTIC and MOVEMENT and DISORDER) or PARKINSONI$ or NEUROLEPTIC-INDUC$) or exp "side effects (drug)"/ or exp neuroleptic malignant syndrome/) not (PARKINSON$ and DISEASE).ti.))

PubMed – Website (in process 2001)

(SCHIZO* or HEBEPHRENI* or OLIGOPHRENI* or PSYCHOTIC* or PSYCHOSIS or PSYCHOSES or ((CHRONIC* or SEVER*) and MENTAL* and (ILL* or DISORDER*)) or (TARDIV* and DYSKINE*) or AKATHISI* or ACATHISI* or (NEUROLEPTIC* and (MALIGNANT and SYNDROME)) or (NEUROLEPTIC and MOVEMENT and DISORDER) or PARKINSONI* or NEUROLEPTIC-INDUC* or (drug-induced and Dyskinesia) or (drug-induced and Akathisia))

Science Citation Index/Social Science Citation Index – Web of Science interface

(SCHIZO* or HEBEPHRENI* or OLIGOPHRENI* or PSYCHOTIC* or PSYCHOSIS or PSYCHOSES or ((CHRONIC* or SEVER*) and MENTAL* and (ILL* or DISORDER*)) or (TARDIV* and DYSKINE*) or AKATHISI* or ACATHISI* or (NEUROLEPTIC* and (MALIGNANT and SYNDROME)) or (NEUROLEPTIC and MOVEMENT and DISORDER) or PARKINSONI* or NEUROLEPTIC-INDUC* or (drug-induced and Dyskinesia) or (drug-induced and Akathisia))

Systematic review search filters

CINAHL – OVID interface

((meta analysis or literature review or research review).fc. and ((medline or medlars or embase or scisearch or psychinfo or psycinfo or psychlit or psyclit or cinahl or cochrane).ti,ab,sh. or (hand search$ or manual search$ or electronic database$ or bibliographic database$ or POOLING or POOLED ANALYSIS or PETO or DER SIMONIAN or DERSIMONIAN or FIXED EFFECT or RANDOM EFFECT or (MANTEL adj2 HAENZEL)).tw.)) or (exp meta analysis/ or (meta-analy$ or metaanaly$ or meta analy$ or (systematic$ adj25 review$) or (systematic$ adj25 overview) or (QUANTITATIVE$ adj25 REVIEW) or (QUANTITATIVE$ adj25 OVERVIEW) or (METHODOLOGIC$ adj25 REVIEW) or (METHODOLOGIC$ adj25 OVERVIEW) or INTEGRATIVE RESEARCH REVIEW$ or RESEARCH INTEGRATION or QUANTITATIVE$ SYNTHESIS).mp. or DATA SYNTHESIS.tw.)

EMBASE – WebSPIRS interface

(((systematic near1 review*) or (data near1 synthesis) or ((published near1 studies) in ab) or (meta?analys*)) not (((letter in pt) or (editorial in pt)) or ('animal' / all subheadings not ('animal' / all subheadings and 'human' / all subheadings))))

MEDLINE – OVID interface

((meta analysis or literature review or research review).fc. and ((medline or medlars or embase or scisearch or psychinfo or psycinfo or psychlit or psyclit or cinahl or cochrane).ti,ab,sh. or (hand search$ or manual search$ or electronic database$ or bibliographic database$ or POOLING or POOLED ANALYSIS or PETO or DER SIMONIAN or DERSIMONIAN or FIXED EFFECT or RANDOM EFFECT or (MANTEL adj2 HAENZEL)).tw.)) or (exp meta analysis/ or (meta-analy$ or metaanaly$ or meta analy$ or (systematic$ adj25 review$) or (systematic$ adj25 overview) or (QUANTITATIVE$ adj25 REVIEW) or (QUANTITATIVE$ adj25 OVERVIEW) or (METHODOLOGIC$ adj25 REVIEW) or (METHODOLOGIC$ adj25 OVERVIEW) or INTEGRATIVE RESEARCH REVIEW$ or RESEARCH INTEGRATION or QUANTITATIVE$ SYNTHESIS).mp. or DATA SYNTHESIS.tw.)

PsycINFO – OVID interface

((review or review, tutorial or review, academic).pt. and ((medline or medlars or embase or scisearch or psychinfo or psycinfo or psychlit or psyclit or cinahl or cochrane).ti,ab,sh. or (hand search$ or manual search$ or electronic database$ or bibliographic database$ or pooling or pooled analys$ or fixed effect or random effect or (mantel adj2 haenzel) or peto or der?simonian).tw.)) or (meta-analysis.pt,sh. or (meta-analy$ or metaanaly$ or meta analy$ or (systematic$ adj25 review$) or (systematic$ adj25 overview) or (quantitative$ adj25 review) or (quantitative$ adj25 overview) or (methodologic$ adj25 review) or (methodologic$ adj25 overview) or integrative research review$ or research integration or quantitative$ synthesis or data synthesis).tw.)

Science Citation Index/Social Science Citation Index – Web of Science interface

(meta-analy* or metaanaly* or meta analy* or (systematic* and review*) or (systematic* and overview) or (systematic* and overview) or (quantitative* and review) or (quantitative* and overview) or (methodologic* and review) or (methodologic* and overview) or (integrative research review*) or (research integration) or (quantitative* synthesis) or (data synthesis)); DocType=All document types; Language=All languages; Databases=SCI-EXPANDED, SSCI

Randomised controlled trials search filters

EMBASE – WebSPIRS interface

((CLIN*) near (TRIAL*)) or (((SINGL*) or (DOUBL*) or (TREBL*) or (TRIPL*)) near ((BLIND*) or (MASK*))) or (RANDOMI*) or ((RANDOM*) near ((ALLOCAT*) or (ASSIGN*))) or (CROSSOVER) or (explode 'RANDOMIZED-CONTROLLED-TRIAL'/ all subheadings) or (explode 'DOUBLE-BLIND-PROCEDURE'/ all subheadings) or (explode 'CROSSOVER-PROCEDURE'/ all subheadings) or (explode 'SINGLE-BLIND-PROCEDURE'/ all subheadings) or (explode 'RANDOMIZATION'/ all subheadings)

MEDLINE – OVID interface

(exp Clinical Trials/ or exp Randomized Controlled Trials/ or exp Double-Blind Method/ or exp Random Allocation/ or exp Double-Blind Method/ or exp Single-Blind Method/ or exp Cross-Over Studies/ or exp Placebos/ or exp Treatment Outcome/ or exp Follow-Up Studies/ or exp Program Evaluation/)

PsycINFO – OVID interface

(crossover or placebo$ or ((crossover or random$ or control$) adj trial) or (random$ adj control$ adj trial$) or (clin$ adj trial$) or ((sing$ or doubl$ or trebl$ or tripl$) adj (blind$ or mask$)) or (control$ adj clin$ adj trial$) or (random$ adj (alloc$ or assign$))) or (exp treatment effectiveness evaluation/ or exp mental health program evaluation/ or exp treatment outcomes/ or exp placebo/)

CINAHL – OVID interface

(exp Clinical Trials/ or exp Double-Blind Studies/ or exp Treatment Outcomes/ or exp Placebos/ or exp Single-Blind Studies/ or exp crossover design/ or exp Placebos/ or exp Treatment Outcomes/ or exp Prospective Studies/ or exp PROGRAM EVALUATION/ or exp SUMMATIVE EVALUATION RESEARCH/ or exp EVALUATION/ or exp EVALUATION RESEARCH/ or exp FORMATIVE EVALUATION RESEARCH/)

Family intervention search filters

The Cochrane Controlled Trials Register (October 2001) was searched using the search filter for schizophrenia (see above) combined with:

[and (famil*)]

EMBASE (2000 – September 2001) was searched using the search filter for schizophrenia and the search filter for RCTs (see above) combined with:

[and (famil* near (therap* or intervent*))]

MEDLINE (2000 – September 2001) was searched using the search filter for schizophrenia and the search filter for RCTs (see above) combined with:

[and ((exp Family Therapy/) or (exp Family/ and (therap$ or intervent$)) or (famil$ and (therap$ or intervent$)))]

PsycINFO (2000 – October 2001) was searched using the search filter for schizophrenia and the search filter for RCTs (see above) combined with:

[and ((exp Family Therapy/) or (exp Family/ and (therap$ or intervent$)) or (famil$ and (therap$ or intervent$)))]

CINAHL (2000 – September 2001) was searched using the search filter for schizophrenia and the search filter for RCTs (see above) combined with:

[and ((exp Family Therapy/) or (famil$ and (therap$ or intervent$)))]

Cognitive Behavioural Therapy search filters

The Cochrane Controlled Trials Register (October 2001) was searched using the search filter for schizophrenia (see above) combined with:

[and (COGNITIV* and BEHAVIO* and THERAP*)]

EMBASE (2000 – September 2001) was searched using the search filter for schizophrenia and the search filter for RCTs (see above) combined with:

[and ((COGNITIV* and BEHAVIO* and THERAP*) or (COGNITI* and (TECHNIQUE* or THERAP* or RESTRUCTUR* or CHALLENG*)) or (ATTRIBUTION* or (SELF and (INSTRUCT* or MANAGEMENT* or ATTRIBUTION*))) or (RET or (RATIONAL and EMOTIV*)) or ('COGNITIVE-THERAPY'/ all subheadings))]

MEDLINE (2000 – September 2001) was searched using the search filter for schizophrenia and the search filter for RCTs (see above) combined with:

[and ((COGNITIV$ and BEHAVIO$ and THERAP$) or (COGNITI$ and (TECHNIQUE$ or THERAP$ or RESTRUCTUR$ or CHALLENG$)) or (ATTRIBUTION$ or (SELF and (INSTRUCT$ or MANAGEMENT$ or ATTRIBUTION$)) or (RET or (RATIONAL and EMOTIV$)))]

PsycINFO (2000 – October 2001) was searched using the search filter for schizophrenia and the search filter for RCTs (see above) combined with:

[and ((COGNITIV$ and BEHAVIO$ and THERAP$) or (COGNITI$ and (TECHNIQUE$ or THERAP$ or RESTRUCTUR$ or CHALLENG$)) or (ATTRIBUTION$ or (SELF and (INSTRUCT$ or MANAGEMENT$ or ATTRIBUTION$))) or (RET or (RATIONAL and EMOTIV$))) or (exp Cognitive Therapy/)]

CINAHL (2000 - August 2001) was searched using the search filter for schizophrenia and the search filter for RCTs (see above) combined with:

[and ((COGNITIV$ and BEHAVIO$ and THERAP$) or (COGNITI$ and (TECHNIQUE$ or THERAP$ or RESTRUCTUR$ or CHALLENG$)) or (ATTRIBUTION$ or (SELF and (INSTRUCT$ or MANAGEMENT$ or ATTRIBUTION$)) or (RET or (RATIONAL and EMOTIV$)))]

Social Skills Training search filters

The Cochrane Controlled Trials Register (October 2001) was searched using the search filter for schizophrenia (see above) combined with:

[and ((social* or personal or interpersonal) and (skills* or program* or training*))]

EMBASE (2000 – September 2001) was searched using the search filter for schizophrenia and the search filter for RCTs (see above) combined with:

[and ((social or personal or interpersonal or socialisation) and (skills* or program* or training*))]

MEDLINE (2000 – September 2001) was searched using the search filter for schizophrenia and the search filter for RCTs (see above) combined with:

[and ((social or personal or interpersonal or socialisation) and (skills$ or program$ or training$))]

PsycINFO (2000 – October 2001) was searched using the search filter for schizophrenia and the search filter for RCTs (see above) combined with:

[and ((social or personal or interpersonal or socialisation) and (skills$ or program$ or training$))]

CINAHL (2000 - August 2001) was searched using the search filter for schizophrenia and the search filter for RCTs (see above) combined with:

[and ((social or personal or interpersonal or socialisation) and (skills$ or program$ or training$))]

Cognitive Remediation search filters

The Cochrane Controlled Trials Register (October 2001) was searched using the Cochrane Schizophrenia Group's filter for schizophrenia (see Group Module) combined with the phrase:

[and ((COGNITIV* or NEURO* or MEMORY) and REMEDIAT*) or (COGNITI* and (TRAIN* or FUNCTION* or MODIF*)) or (ATTENTION* and (TRAIN* or MANAGEMENT* or REMEDIAT*)) or (MEMORY or (TRAIN* and REMED*))]

EMBASE (2000 – September 2001) was searched using the search filter for schizophrenia and the search filter for RCTs (see above) combined with:

[and (((COGNITIV* or NEURO* or MEMORY) and REMEDIAT*) or (COGNITI* and (TRAIN* or FUNCTION* or MODIF*)) or (ATTENTION* and (TRAIN* or MANAGEMENT* or REMEDIAT*)) or (MEMORY or (TRAIN* and REMED*)) or (cognitiv* and rehab*))]

MEDLINE (2000 – September 2001) was searched using the search filter for schizophrenia and the search filter for RCTs (see above) combined with:

[and (((COGNITIV$ or NEURO$ or MEMORY) and REMEDIAT$) or (COGNITI$ and (TRAIN$ or FUNCTION$ or MODIF$)) or (ATTENTION$ and (TRAIN$ or MANAGEMENT$ or REMEDIAT$)) or (MEMORY or (TRAIN$ and REMED$)) or (cognitiv$ adj rehab$)))]

PsycINFO (2000 – October 2001) was searched using the search filter for schizophrenia and the search filter for RCTs (see above) combined with:

[and (((COGNITIV$ or NEURO$ or MEMORY) and REMEDIAT$) or (COGNITI$ and (TRAIN$ or FUNCTION$ or MODIF$)) or (ATTENTION$ and (TRAIN$ or MANAGEMENT$ or REMEDIAT$)) or (MEMORY or (TRAIN$ and REMED$)) or (cognitiv$ adj rehab$)))]
CINAHL (2000 - August 2001) was searched using the search filter for schizophrenia and the search filter for RCTs (see above) combined with:

[and (((COGNITIV$ or NEURO$ or MEMORY) and REMEDIAT$) or (COGNITI$ and (TRAIN$ or FUNCTION$ or MODIF$)) or (ATTENTION$ and (TRAIN$ or MANAGEMENT$ or REMEDIAT$)) or (MEMORY or (TRAIN$ and REMED$)) or (cognitiv$ adj rehab$)))]

Psychoeducation search filters

The Cochrane Controlled Trials Register (October 2001) was searched using the search filter for schizophrenia (see above) combined with:

[and ((patient and (education or instruction)) or psychoeducat*)]

EMBASE (1999 – September 2001) was searched using the search filter for schizophrenia and the search filter for RCTs (see above) combined with:

[and ((patient near (education or teaching or instruction or information or knowledge)) or (educational near (program* or intervention*)) or (psychoeducat*))]

MEDLINE (1999 – September 2001) was searched using the search filter for schizophrenia and the search filter for RCTs (see above) combined with:

[[and ((psychoeducation or exp Patient Education/) or (patient adj (education or teaching or instruction or information or knowledge)) or (educational adj (program$ or intervention$)))]

PsycINFO (1999 – October 2001) was searched using the search filter for schizophrenia and the search filter for RCTs (see above) combined with:

[and (psychoeducation or exp Client Education/ or (patient adj (education or teaching or instruction or information or knowledge)) or (educational adj (program$ or intervention$)) or exp psychoeducation/)]

CINAHL (1999 – September 2001) was searched using the search filter for schizophrenia and the search filter for RCTs (see above) combined with:

[[and ((psychoeducation or exp Patient Education/) or (patient adj (education or teaching or instruction or information or knowledge)) or (educational adj (program$ or intervention$)))]

Counselling and supportive therapy search filters

The Cochrane Controlled Trials Register (October 2001) was searched using the search filter for schizophrenia (see above) combined with:

[and ((counsel*) or (support* and (therap* or psychotherapy)))]

EMBASE (1980 – October 2001) was searched using the search filter for schizophrenia and the search filter for RCTs (see above) combined with:

[and (((counsel*) or (support* near (therap* or psychotherapy)) or ('counseling-' / all subheadings)))]

MEDLINE (1966 – September 2001) was searched using the search filter for schizophrenia and the search filter for RCTs (see above) combined with:

[and (counsel$ or (support$ adj (therap$ or psychotherapy)) or exp counseling/)]

PsycINFO (1872 – October 2001) was searched using the search filter for schizophrenia and the search filter for RCTs (see above) combined with:

[and (counsel$ or (support$ adj (therap$ or psychotherapy)) or exp Counseling/ or exp Supportive Psychotherapy/)]

CINAHL (1982 – September 2001) was searched using the search filter for schizophrenia and the search filter for RCTs (see above) combined with:

[and (counsel$ or (support$ adj (therap$ or psychotherapy)) or exp counseling/)]

Psychoanalytic psychotherapy search filters

The Cochrane Controlled Trials Register (October 2001) was searched using the search filter for schizophrenia (see above) combined with:

[and (PSYCHOANALY* or ((ANALYTIC* or DYNAMIC* or PSYCHODYNAMIC*) and (THERAP* or PSYCHOTHERAP*)))]

EMBASE (2000 – September 2001) was searched using the search filter for schizophrenia and the search filter for RCTs (see above) combined with:

[and ((psychoanaly*) or ((analytic* or dynamic* or psychodynamic*) near2 (therap* or psychotherap*))or ('PSYCHOANALYSIS-'/ all subheadings))]

MEDLINE (2000 – September 2001) was searched using the search filter for schizophrenia and the search filter for RCTs (see above) combined with:

[and ((exp PSYCHOANALYSIS/ or exp Psychoanalytic Therapy/) or (psychoanaly$ or ((analytic$ or dynamic$ or psychodynamic$) adj2 (therap$ or psychotherap$)))]

PsycINFO (2000 – October 2001) was searched using the search filter for schizophrenia and the search filter for RCTs (see above) combined with:

[and (exp Psychoanalysis/ or (psychoanaly$ or ((analytic$ or dynamic$ or psychodynamic$) adj2 (therap$ or psychotherap$))))]

CINAHL (2000 – August 2001) was searched using the search filter for schizophrenia and the search filter for RCTs (see above) combined with:

[and ((exp PSYCHOANALYSIS/ or exp Psychoanalytic Therapy/) or (psychoanaly$ or ((analytic$ or dynamic$ or psychodynamic$) adj2 (therap$ or psychotherap$)))]

Depot search filters

Depot OVID filters

Flupenthixol decanoate filter

[and ((FLUPENT$ ADJ1 DECANOATE) or ((DEPOT$ or (LONG ADJ4 ACTING) or (DELAY ADJ2 ACTION)) adj (FLUPENT$ or FLUANXOL$ or DEPIXOL$ or LU 7105$ or LU 5-110))) or (exp "FLUPENTHIXOL"/)]

Fluphenazine decanoate filter

[and (FLUPHENAZINE OR MODEC$ OR MODITEN$ OR exp "FLUPHENAZINE"/) and (DEPOT or (LONG and ACTING) OR (DELAY$ AND ACTION))] [and (HAL$ ADJ1 DECANOATE) or ((DEPOT$ or (LONG ADJ4 ACTING) or (DELAY$ ADJ2 ACTION)) adj (HALO$ or HALDOL or SEREN$ or SIGAPERIDOL or BROTOPON or EINALON or LINTON or PELUCES))]

[and ((PIPOTHIA$ ADJ1 PALMITATE) or ((DEPOT$ or (LONG ADJ4 ACTING) or (DELAY$ ADJ2 ACTION)) adj (PIPOTHIA$ or PIPORTIL$ or DECANOATE$ or PIPORTYL$ or PALMITATE$ or LONSEREN$)))]

[and (ZUCLOPENTHIXOL or CIATYL or CISORDINOL$ or CLOPIXOL$ or SORDINOL) or (exp "ZUCLOPENTHIXOL"/)]

The Cochrane Controlled Trials Register (October 2001) was searched using the search filter for schizophrenia combined with the depot OVID filters (see above).

EMBASE (2000 – September 2001) was searched using the search filter for schizophrenia and the search filter for RCTs combined with the depot WebSPIRS filters (see above).

MEDLINE (2000 – September 2001) was searched using the search filter for schizophrenia and the search filter for RCTs combined with the depot OVID filters (see above).

PsycINFO (2000 – October 2001) was searched using the search filter for schizophrenia and the search filter for RCTs combined with the depot OVID filters (see above).

CINAHL (2000 – August 2001) was searched using the search filter for schizophrenia and the search filter for RCTs combined with the depot OVID filters (see above).

Rapid tranquillisation search filters

Rapid tranquillisation OVID filter

((((psychiatric adj3 emergenc$) or (emergency services, psychiatric/) or ((rapid$ or acute or short-acting or fast-acting or emergenc$ or urgent) adj3 (sedat$ or tranquil$)) or ((chemical$ or pharmacological) adj3 restrain$) or (acute adj3 agitation)) or ((haloperidol/ or Promazine/ or lorazepam/ or diazepam/ or flunitrazepam/ or clonazepam/ or midazolam/ or prochlorperazine/ or exp benzodiazepines/ or exp benzodiazepinones/ or chlorpromazine/ or Clopenthixol/ or exp antipsychotic agents/) and (emergenc$ or emergency service, hospital/ or agitat$ or aggress$ or distress$ or (acute adj3 psycho$) or (acut$ adj2 disturb$)))) not (animal/ or (Dementia or (brain adj3 injur$) or epilepsy or seizure or elderly or aged or (mental adj3 retard$) or anaesthetic or anesthetic or (alcohol adj3 withdrawal) or intubation or ventilation or (status adj3 epilepticus)).ti.)

Rapid tranquillisation WebSPIRS filter

(((psychiatric near3 emergenc*) or ('emergency-health-service' / all subheadings) or ((rapid* or acute or short-acting or fast-acting or emergenc* or urgent) near3 (sedat* or tranquil*)) or ((chemical* or pharmacological) near3 restrain*) or (acute near3 agitation)) or (('haloperidol-' / all subheadings or 'promazine-' / all subheadings or 'lorazepam-' / all subheadings or 'diazepam-' / all subheadings or 'flunitrazepam-' / all subheadings or 'clonazepam-' / all subheadings or 'midazolam-' / all subheadings or 'prochlorperazine-' / all subheadings or explode 'benzodiazepine-derivative' / all subheadings or 'chlorpromazine-' / all subheadings or 'clopenthixol-' / all subheadings or explode 'neuroleptic-agent' / all subheadings) and (emergenc* or 'emergency-health-service' / all subheadings or agitat* or aggress* or distress* or (acute near3 psycho*) or (acut* near2 disturb*)))) not ('animal-' / all subheadings or (Dementia or (brain near3 injur*) or epilepsy or seizure or elderly or aged or (mental near3 retard*) or anaesthetic or anesthetic or (alcohol near3 withdrawal) or intubation or ventilation or (status near3 epilepticus)) in TI)

The Cochrane Controlled Trials Register (1st Quarter, 2002) was searched using the search filter for schizophrenia combined with the rapid tranquillisation OVID filter (see above).

EMBASE (1980 – 2002) was searched using the search filter for schizophrenia and the search filter for RCTs combined with the rapid tranquillisation WebSPIRS filter (see above).

MEDLINE (1966 – October 2001) was searched using the search filter for schizophrenia and the search filter for RCTs combined with the rapid tranquillisation OVID filter (see above).

PsycINFO (1984 – February 2002) was searched using the search filter for schizophrenia and the search filter for RCTs combined with the rapid tranquillisation OVID filter (see above).

CINAHL (1982 – February 2002) was searched using the search filter for schizophrenia and the search filter for RCTs combined with the rapid tranquillisation OVID filter (see above).

Oral antipsychotic search filters

A specific filter was developed for each antipsychotic drug using a similar structure for each. Owing to the size of the filters, only chlorpromazine is presented here.

Chlorpromazine OVID filter

1. (benperidol or benperidolo or benperidolum or benzperidol or cb-8089 or "cb 8089" or "8089 cb" or mcn-jr-4584 or "mcn jr 4584" or r-4584 or "r 4584" or benperidone or benzoperidol or frenactyl or glianimon or phenactil or frenactil or anquil or psichoben).mp. or exp benperidol/ or ((flupentixol or flupenthixol or depixol).mp. or exp flupentixol/) or ((fluphenazine or moditen or modecate).mp. or exp

fluphenazine/) or ((haloperi$ or r-1625 or haldol$ or alased$ or aloperidi$ or bioperido$ or buterid$ or ceree$ or dozic$ or duraperido$ or fortuna$ or serena$ or serenel$ or seviu$ or sigaperid$ or sylad$ or zafri$).mp. or exp haloperidol/) or ((levomepromazine or methotrimeprazine or nozinan).mp. or exp levomepromazine/ or exp methotrimeprazine/) or ((loxapine or lw-3170 or sum-3170 or cl-71563 or loxpac or loxapac or loxitane or desconex or oxilapine).mp. or exp loxapine/) or oxypertine.mp. or ((perphenazine or fentazin).mp. or exp perphenazine/) or ((pimozide or orap or antalon or opiran or pirium).mp. or exp pimozide/) or (prochlorperazine.mp. or exp prochlorperazine/) or (promazine.mp. or exp promazine/) or ((abilit or championyl or coolspan or col-sulpir or digton or dixibon or dobren or dogmatil or dolmatil or drominetas or eglonyl or equilid or eusulpid or guastil or isnamid or kapiride or lavodina or lebopride or lusedan or miradol or mirbanil or misulvan or neuromyfar or normum or omperan or psicocen or quiridil or sato or sernevin or sicofrenol or sulparex or sulpiride or sulpisedan or sulpitil or suprium or sursumid or tepavil or tonofit or ulpir or vipral).mp. or exp sulpiride/) or ((thioridazine or meleril or mellaril or melleril or melleryl or melleretten or mallorol or elperil or flaracantyl or mefurine or orsanil or ridazine or sonapax or stalleril or tirodil or visergil).mp. or exp thioridazine/) or ((trifluoperazine or stelazine).mp. or exp trifluoperazine/) or ((clopenthixol or zuclopenthixol or clopixol or acuphase).mp. or exp zuclopenthixol/) [mp=ti, ab, rw, sh, it, ot, hw, kw, ty, id]

2. (benperidol or benperidolo or benperidolum or benzperidol or cb-8089 or "cb 8089" or "8089 cb" or mcn-jr-4584 or "mcn jr 4584" or r-4584 or "r 4584" or benperidone or benzoperidol or frenactyl or glianimon or phenactil or frenactil or anquil or psichoben or (flupentixol or flupenthixol or depixol)).mp. or ((fluphenazine or moditen or modecate).mp. or exp fluphenazine/) or ((haloperi$ or r-1625 or haldol$ or alased$ or aloperidi$ or bioperido$ or buterid$ or ceree$ or dozic$ or duraperido$ or fortuna$ or serena$ or serenel$ or seviu$ or sigaperid$ or sylad$ or zafri$).mp. or exp haloperidol/) or (levomepromazine or methotrimeprazine or nozinan).mp. or (loxapine or lw-3170 or sum-3170 or cl-71563 or loxpac or loxapac or loxitane or desconex or oxilapine).mp. or oxypertine.mp. or (pericyazine or periciazine or neulactil).mp. or (perphenazine or fentazin).mp. or (pimozide or orap or antalon or opiran or pirium).mp. or (prochlorperazine.mp. or exp prochlorperazine/) or promazine.mp. or (abilit or championyl or coolspan or col-sulpir or digton or dixibon or dobren or dogmatil or dolmatil or drominetas or eglonyl or equilid or eusulpid or guastil or isnamid or kapiride or lavodina or lebopride or lusedan or miradol or mirbanil or misulvan or neuromyfar or normum or omperan or psicocen or quiridil or sato or sernevin or sicofrenol or sulparex or sulpiride or sulpisedan or sulpitil or suprium or sursumid or tepavil or tonofit or ulpir or vipral).mp. or ((thioridazine or meleril or mellaril or melleril or melleryl or melleretten or mallorol or elperil or flaracantyl or mefurine or orsanil or ridazine or sonapax or stalleril or tirodil or visergil).mp. or exp thioridazine/) or (trifluoperazine or stelazine).mp. or (clopenthixol or zuclopenthixol or clopixol or acuphase).mp. [mp=ti, ab, rw, sh, it, ot, hw, kw, ty, id]

3. (benperidol or benperidolo or benperidolum or benzperidol or cb-8089 or "cb 8089" or "8089 cb" or mcn-jr-4584 or "mcn jr 4584" or r-4584 or "r 4584" or benperidone or benzoperidol or frenactyl or glianimon or phenactil or frenactil or anquil or psichoben or (flupentixol or flupenthixol or depixol) or (fluphenazine or moditen or modecate) or (haloperi$ or r-1625 or haldol$ or alased$ or aloperidi$ or bioperido$ or buterid$ or ceree$ or dozic$ or duraperido$ or fortuna$ or serena$ or serenel$ or seviu$ or sigaperid$ or sylad$ or zafri$) or (levomepromazine or

methotrimeprazine or nozinan) or (loxapine or lw-3170 or sum-3170 or cl-71563 or loxpac or loxapac or loxitane or desconex or oxilapine) or oxypertine or (pericyazine or periciazine or neulactil) or (perphenazine or fentazin) or (pimozide or orap or antalon or opiran or pirium) or prochlorperazine or promazine or (abilit or championyl or coolspan or col-sulpir or digton or dixibon or dobren or dogmatil or dolmatil or drominetas or eglonyl or equilid or eusulpid or guastil or isnamid or kapiride or lavodina or lebopride or lusedan or miradol or mirbanil or misulvan or neuromyfar or normum or omperan or psicocen or quiridil or sato or sernevin or sicofrenol or sulparex or sulpiride or sulpisedan or sulpitil or suprium or sursumid or tepavil or tonofit or ulpir or vipral) or (thioridazine or meleril or mellaril or melleril or melleryl or melleretten or mallorol or elperil or flaracantyl or mefurine or orsanil or ridazine or sonapax or stalleril or tirodil or visergil) or (trifluoperazine or stelazine) or (clopenthixol or zuclopenthixol or clopixol or acuphase)).mp. [mp=ti, ab, rw, sh, it, ot, hw, kw, ty, id]

4. (benperidol or benperidolo or benperidolum or benzperidol or cb-8089 or "cb 8089" or "8089 cb" or mcn-jr-4584 or "mcn jr 4584" or r-4584 or "r 4584" or benperidone or benzoperidol or frenactyl or glianimon or phenactil or frenactil or anquil or psichoben or (flupentixol or flupenthixol or depixol)).mp. or ((fluphenazine or moditen or modecate).mp. or exp fluphenazine/) or ((haloperi$ or r-1625 or haldol$ or alased$ or aloperidi$ or bioperido$ or buterid$ or ceree$ or dozic$ or duraperido$ or fortuna$ or serena$ or serenel$ or seviu$ or sigaperid$ or sylad$ or zafri$).mp. or exp haloperidol/) or (levomepromazine or methotrimeprazine or nozinan).mp. or ((loxapine or lw-3170 or sum-3170 or cl-71563 or loxpac or loxapac or loxitane or desconex or oxilapine).mp. or exp loxapine/) or oxypertine.mp. or (pericyazine or periciazine or neulactil).mp. or ((perphenazine or fentazin).mp. or exp perphenazine/) or ((pimozide or orap or antalon or opiran or pirium).mp. or exp pimozide/) or (prochlorperazine.mp. or exp prochlorperazine/) or (promazine.mp. or exp promazine/) or ((abilit or championyl or coolspan or col-sulpir or digton or dixibon or dobren or dogmatil or dolmatil or drominetas or eglonyl or equilid or eusulpid or guastil or isnamid or kapiride or lavodina or lebopride or lusedan or miradol or mirbanil or misulvan or neuromyfar or normum or omperan or psicocen or quiridil or sato or sernevin or sicofrenol or sulparex or sulpiride or sulpisedan or sulpitil or suprium or sursumid or tepavil or tonofit or ulpir or vipral).mp. or exp sulpiride/) or ((thioridazine or meleril or mellaril or melleril or melleryl or melleretten or mallorol or elperil or flaracantyl or mefurine or orsanil or ridazine or sonapax or stalleril or tirodil or visergil).mp. or exp thioridazine/) or ((trifluoperazine or stelazine).mp. or exp trifluoperazine/) or (clopenthixol or zuclopenthixol or clopixol or acuphase).mp. [mp=ti, ab, rw, sh, it, ot, hw, kw, ty, id]

5. 1 or 2 or 3 or 4

6. (anadep or chloractil or chlorazin or chlorpromados or chlorpromazine or chlorprom-ez-ets or chlor p-z or chromedazine or cpz or elmarine or esmind or fenactil or hibanil or hibernal or klorazin or klorproman or klorpromez or largactil or megaphen or neurazine or plegomazine or procalm or promachel or promacid or promapar or promexin or promosol or prozil or psychozine or psylactil or (rp adj "4560") or serazone or sonazine or thoradex or thorazine or tranzine).mp. or exp chlorpromazine/ [mp=ti, ab, rw, sh, it, ot, hw, kw, ty, id]

7. (anadep or chloractil or chlorazin or chlorpromados or chlorpromazine or chlorprom-ez-ets or chlor p-z or chromedazine or cpz or elmarine or esmind or fenactil

or hibanil or hibernal or klorazin or klorproman or klorpromez or largactil or megaphen or neurazine or plegomazine or procalm or promachel or promacid or promapar or promexin or promosol or prozil or psychozine or psylactil or (rp adj "4560") or serazone or sonazine or thoradex or thorazine or tranzine).mp. [mp=ti, ab, rw, sh, it, ot, hw, kw, ty, id]

8. 6 or 7

9. 5 and 8

10. exp meta-analysis/

11. (amisulpride or solian or clozapine or clozaril or olanzapine or zyprexa or quetiapine or seroquel or risperidone or risperdal or zotepine or zoleptil).ti.

12. 9 not (10 or 11)

EMBASE (1980 – 2002) was searched using the search filter for schizophrenia and the search filter for RCTs combined with the OVID filter (see above).

MEDLINE (1966 – October 2001) was searched using the search filter for schizophrenia and the search filter for RCTs combined with the OVID filter (see above).

PsycINFO (1984 – February 2002) was searched using the search filter for schizophrenia and the search filter for RCTs combined with the OVID filter (see above).

CINAHL (1982 – February 2002) was searched using the search filter for schizophrenia and the search filter for RCTs combined with the OVID filter (see above).

Appendix 10
Clinical study eligibility checklist

Eligibility checklist	Report reference ID:		*Eligibility* Y N
Checklist completed by:	Date completed:		(circle one)
Topic Areas: 1 2 3 (circle all applicable)			
Overall assessment			
Comment			
Exclusion criteria			Code options Y N
Only concerned with:			
• The initial diagnosis and assessment of schizophrenia			
• Very-late onset schizophrenia (onset = 60 years old)			
• Children with schizophrenia (age < 18)			
• The management of schizophrenia in conjunction with learning difficulties			
• The management of schizophrenia in conjunction with significant physical or sensory impairment			
Inclusion criteria			
Population			
• Schizophrenia spectrum disorders (including schizotypal, schizoaffective and schizophreniform disorders)			
• *Or* reported results in which the effects of treatment could be estimated separately for these participants (a population described as severe mentally ill [*or similar term*] was taken as a proxy for schizophrenia)			

Topic Area	
1. Pharmacological	
Antidepressants and mood stabilisers	
Atypical antipsychotics	
Benzodiazepines	
Conventional antipsychotics	
Depot injections	
Other compounds (including those used in the management of side-effects)	
2. Psychological	
Cognitive–behavioural therapy	
Cognitive remediation	
Counselling and supportive therapy	
Family interventions	
Life skills training	
Multimodal interventions	
Psychoanalytic interventions	
Psychoeducation	
Social skills training	
3. Service system	
Assertive community treatment	
Case management (intensive, standard, user-led)	
Alternatives to admission	
Early intervention services	
Vocational rehabilitation	
Primary Outcomes	**Code options** Y N
● Adverse effects of treatment	
● Carer/family outcomes	
● Cognitive functioning	
● Compliance with:	
(a) Drug treatment	
(b) Other non-drug treatments	
● Death (any cause and sudden unexpected death or suicide)	
● Economic outcomes	
● Engagement	

● Hospital readmission	
● Involvement with criminal justice system	
● Mental state:	
(a) Criterion-based improvement (as defined in individual studies) with reference to the positive and negative symptoms of schizophrenia	
(b) Continuous measures of mental state	
● Occupational status	
● Other intervention specific outcomes	
● Participant satisfaction	
● Psychological well-being:	
(a) Criterion-based improvement (as defined in individual studies) with respect to general psychological well-being, such as self-esteem or distress	
(b) Continuous measures of psychological well-being	
● Quality of life	
● Relapse (as defined in the individual studies)	
● Social functioning	
● Any other unexpected or unwanted effect	

Note. Y = Yes; N = No; ? = Criterion not described adequately to classify as yes or no.

Appendix 11
Clinical study quality checklists

Table A11.1 Quality checklist for a systematic review (notes for reviewer are presented in italics)

Checklist completed by:	Report reference ID:
SECTION 1: VALIDITY	

Evaluation criteria		Comments
1.1	Does the review address an appropriate and clearly focused question?	*Unless a clear and well-defined question is specified, it will be difficult to assess how well the study has met its objectives or how relevant it is to the question you are trying to answer on the basis of its conclusions.*
1.2	Does the review include a description of the methodology used?	*A systematic review should include a detailed description of the methods used to identify and evaluate individual studies. If this description is not present, it is not possible to make a thorough evaluation of the quality of the review, and it should be rejected as a source of Level 1 evidence. (Though it may be useable as Level 4 evidence, if no better evidence can be found.)*
1.3	Was the literature search sufficiently rigorous to identify all relevant studies?	*Consider whether the review used an electronic search of at least one bibliographic database (searching for studies dating at least 10 years before publication of the review), and from the late 1990s onwards, the Cochrane Library. Any indication that hand searching of key journals, or follow-up of reference lists of included studies, was carried out in addition to electronic database searches can normally be taken as evidence of a well-conducted review.*
1.4	Was study quality assessed and taken into account?	*A well-conducted systematic review should have used clear criteria to assess whether individual studies had been well conducted before deciding whether to include or exclude them. At a minimum, the authors should have checked that there was adequate concealment of allocation, that the rate of drop out was minimised, and that the results were analysed on an "intention to treat" basis. If there is no indication of such an assessment, the review should be rejected*

		as a source of Level 1 evidence. If details of the assessment are poor, or the methods considered to be inadequate, the quality of the review should be downgraded.	
SECTION 2: OVERALL ASSESSMENT		Comments	Code
2.1	Low risk of bias	*All or most criteria met*	**A**
	Moderate risk of bias	*Most criteria partly met*	B
	High risk of bias	*Few or no criteria met*	C

Table A11.2 Quality checklist for a randomised controlled trial (notes for reviewer are presented in italics)

Checklist completed by:		Report reference ID:	
SECTION 1: INTERNAL VALIDITY			
Evaluation criteria		**Comments**	
1.1	Was the assignment of subjects to treatment groups randomised?	***If there is no indication of randomisation, the study should be rejected.*** *If the description of randomisation is poor, or the process used is not truly random (e.g., allocation by date, alternating between one group and another) or can otherwise be seen as flawed, the study should be given a lower quality rating.*	
1.2	Was an adequate concealment method used?	*Centralised allocation, computerised allocation systems, or the use of coded identical containers would all be regarded as adequate methods of concealment, and may be taken as indicators of a well-conducted study. If the method of concealment used is regarded as poor, or relatively easy to subvert, the study must be given a lower quality rating, and can be rejected if the concealment method is seen as inadequate.*	
SECTION 2: OVERALL ASSESSMENT		Comments	Code
2.1	Low risk of bias	*Both criteria met*	**A**
	Moderate risk of bias	*One or more criteria partly met*	**B**
	High risk of bias	*One or more criteria not met*	**C**

Appendix 12
Combined search filter for the identification of economic studies

MEDLINE, PreMEDLINE, EMBASE, PsycINFO, CINAHL, Cochrane Database of Systematic Reviews (CDSR), Database of Abstracts of Review of Effectiveness (DARE), Cochrane Controlled Trials Register (CCTR) were searched using the phrase combinations:

[(SCHIZO$ or HEBEPHRENI$ or OLIGOPHRENI$ or PSYCHOTIC$ or PSYCHOS#S) or ((CHRONIC$ or SEVER$) adj1 (MENTAL$ or PSYCHIATRIC) adj1 (ILL$ or DISEASE$ or PATIENT$ or DISORDER$ or DISABLED or DISABILIT$))]
and
[(COST$ adj2 (EFFECTIV$ or BENEFIT$ or UTILIT$ or MINIMI#ATION or CONSEQUENCE$ or OFFSET)) or ((ECONOMIC or COST$) adj2 (EVALUAT$ or ANALY$ or STUDY or STUDIES or ASSESS$))]

NHS Economic Evaluation Database (NHS EED), Health Technology Assessment Database (HTA) were searched using the phrase combination:

[(SCHIZO? or HEBEPHRENI? or OLIGOPHRENI? or PSYCHOTIC? or PSYCHOS?S) or ((CHRONIC? or SEVER?) and (MENTAL? or PSYCHIATRIC) and (ILL? or DISEASE? or PATIENT? or DISORDER? or DISABLED or DISABILIT?))]
and
[(COST? and (EFFECTIV? or BENEFIT? or UTILIT? or MINIMI?ATION or CONSEQUENCE? or OFFSET)) or ((ECONOMIC or COST?) and (EVALUAT? or ANALY? or STUDY or STUDIES or ASSESS?))]

Office of Health Economics Health Economic Evaluations Database (OHE HEED) was searched using the phrase combination:

[(SCHIZO* or HEBEPHRENI* or OLIGOPHRENI* or PSYCHOTIC* or PSYCHOSIS or PSYCHOSES) or ((CHRONIC* or SEVER*) and (MENTAL* or PSYCHIATRIC) and (ILL* or DISEASE* or PATIENT* or DISORDER* or DISABLED or DISABILIT*))]

[(COST* and (EFFECTIV* or BENEFIT* or UTILIT* or MINIMISATION or MINIMIZATION or CONSEQUENCE* or OFFSET)) or ((ECONOMIC or COST*) and (EVALUAT* or ANALY* or STUDY or STUDIES or ASSESS*))]

[CS= line1 AND line2]

Appendix 13
Databases searched for economic evidence

Database searched	Via interface	Search period
MEDLINE	OVID	1985 to Apr/1 2002
PreMEDLINE	OVID	17/04/2002
EMBASE (Excerpta Medica Database)	OVID	1985 to Week 15 2002
CINAHL (Cumultive Index to Nursing and Allied Health Literature)	OVID	1985 to Feb/4 2002
PsycINFO	OVID	1985 to Mar/3 2002
Cochrane Database of Systematic Reviews (CDSR)	OVID	1985 to Apr 2002
Database of Abstracts of Reviews of Effectiveness (DARE)	OVID	1985 to Apr 2002
Cochrane Controlled Trials Register (CCTR)	OVID	1985 to Apr 2002
HTA (Health Technology Assessment Database)	NHS Centre for Reviews and Dissemination website	1985 to Apr 2002
NHS EED (NHS Economic Evaluation Database)	NHS Centre for Reviews and Dissemination website	1985 to Apr 2002
OHE HEED (Office of Health Economics Health Economic Evaluations Database)	OHE HEED CD-ROM	1985 to Apr 2002

Appendix 14
Standard inclusion criteria
for economic studies

1   Evaluated interventions that the Guideline Development Group has primarily classified as recommended pharmacological, psychological and/or service interventions.

2   Was published between 1985 and 2002.

3   Used an analytical method of cost-effectiveness analysis (cost-minimisation analysis, cost–consequences analysis), cost–utility analysis, cost–benefit analysis, cost-analysis or cost–offset analysis.

4   Provided sufficient details regarding methods and results to enable judgement of the quality of the study, and use of the study's data and results (e.g., not only an abstract, poster, presentation, reply or commentary),

5   Was a primary economic study rather than a guideline or review.

6   The source of data for effect size measure(s) for the economic analysis was a meta-analysis, a single randomised controlled trial, a quasi-experimental study or a controlled study with concurrent controls. In the case of scarcity of economic evidence, high-quality mirror-image studies or controlled studies with historical controls were also considered.

7   Reported results for a study population with the age of illness onset between 18 and 60 years, which included a majority of participants with a diagnosis of schizophrenia spectrum disorder (schizotypal, schizoaffective, schizophreniform disorders) (note that the term 'severe mental illness' was used as a proxy for schizophrenia); or the costs of treatment could be estimated separately for these participants.

Was conducted in one or more OECD countries.

Appendix 15
Validity checklist for economic evaluations

Author: **Date:**

Title:

	Yes	No	NA
Study design			
1. The research question is stated	☐	☐	
2. The viewpoint(s) of the analysis are clearly stated	☐	☐	
3. The alternatives being compared are relevant	☐	☐	
4. The rationale for choosing the alternative programmes or interventions compared is stated	☐	☐	
5. The alternatives being compared are clearly described	☐	☐	
6. The form of economic evaluation used is justified in relation to the question addressed	☐	☐	
Data collection			
1. The source of effectiveness data used is stated	☐	☐	
2. Details of the design and results of effectiveness study are given	☐	☐	☐
3. The primary outcome measure(s) for the economic evaluation are clearly stated	☐	☐	
4. Methods to value health states and other benefits are stated	☐	☐	
5. Details of the subjects from whom valuations were obtained are given	☐	☐	
6. Indirect costs (if included) are reported separately			
7. Quantities of resources are reported separately from their unit costs	☐	☐	☐
8. Methods for the estimation of quantities and unit costs are described	☐	☐	
9. Currency and price data are recorded	☐	☐	
10. Details of currency of price adjustments for inflation or currency conversion are given	☐	☐	☐
11. Details of any model used are given	☐	☐	☐
12. The choice of model used and the key parameters on which it is based are justified	☐	☐	☐
Analysis and interpretation of results			
1. Time horizon of costs and benefits is stated	☐	☐	
2. The discount rate(s) is stated	☐	☐	☐
3. The choice of rate(s) is justified	☐	☐	☐
4. An explanation is given if costs or benefits are not discounted	☐	☐	☐

5.	Details of statistical tests and confidence intervals are given for stochastic data	☐	☐	☐
6.	The approach to sensitivity analysis is given	☐	☐	
7.	The choice of variables for sensitivity analysis is given	☐	☐	
8.	The ranges over which the variables are varied are stated	☐	☐	
9.	Relevant alternatives are compared	☐	☐	
10.	Incremental analysis is reported	☐	☐	☐
11.	Major outcomes are presented in a disaggregated as well as aggregated form	☐	☐	
12.	The answer to the study question is given	☐	☐	
13.	Conclusions follow from the data reported	☐	☐	
14.	Conclusions are accompanied by the appropriate caveats	☐	☐	

Appendix 16
Validity checklist for costing studies

Author: **Date:**

Title:

	Yes	No	NA
Study design			
1. The research question is stated	☐	☐	
2. The viewpoint(s) of the analysis are clearly stated and justified	☐	☐	
Data collection			
1. Details of the subjects from whom valuations were obtained are given	☐	☐	
2. Indirect costs (if included) are reported separately	☐	☐	☐
3. Quantities of resources are reported separately from their unit costs	☐	☐	
4. Methods for the estimation of quantities and unit costs are described	☐	☐	
5. Currency and price data are recorded	☐	☐	
6. Details of currency of price adjustments for inflation or currency conversion are given	☐	☐	☐
7. Details of any model used are given	☐	☐	☐
8. The choice of model used and the key parameters on which it is based are justified	☐	☐	☐
Analysis and interpretation of results			
1. Time horizon of costs is stated	☐	☐	
2. The discount rate(s) is stated	☐	☐	☐
3. Details of statistical tests and confidence intervals are given for stochastic data	☐	☐	☐
4. The choice of variables for sensitivity analysis is given	☐	☐	
5. Appropriate sensitivity analysis is performed	☐	☐	
6. The answer to the study question is given	☐	☐	
7. Conclusions follow from the data reported	☐	☐	
8. Conclusions are accompanied by the appropriate caveats	☐	☐	

Appendix 17
Economic data extraction form

Reviewer: Date of Review:

Authors:

Publication Date:

Title:

Country:

Language:

Economic study design:

☐ CEA   ☐ COA   ☐ CA
☐ CBA
☐ CUA
☐ CMA
☐ CCA

Modelling:

☐ No   ☐ Yes

Source of data for effect size measure(s):

                                     ☐ Meta-analysis
☐ RCT   ☐ RCT
☐ Quasi-experimental study   ☐ Quasi-experimental study
 Controlled study with concurrent controls   ☐ Controlled study with concurrent controls

☐ *Controlled study with historical controls*   ☐ *Controlled study with historical controls*

☐ *Mirror image (before–after) study*   ☐ *Mirror image (before–after) study*
                                     ☐ *Expert opinion*

Primary outcome measure(s) (please list):

_____

_____

Interventions compared (please describe):

Treatment: _____

Comparator: _____

Setting (please describe):

_____

_____

Patient population characteristics (please describe):

_____

_____

Perspective of analysis:

☐ Societal   ☐ Other:
☐ Patient and patient family
☐ Health care system
☐ Health care provider
☐ Individual clinician
☐ Insurer

Time frame of analysis: _____

Cost data:

☐ Primary   ☐ Secondary

                                   If secondary please specify: _____

Costs included:

Direct medical	*Direct non-medical*	*Productivity losses*
☐ direct treatment	☐ social care	☐ income forgone due to illness
☐ in-patient	☐ social benefits	☐ income forgone due to death
☐ out-patient	☐ travel costs	☐ income forgone by caregiver
☐ day care	☐ caregiver out-of-pocket	
☐ community health care	☐ criminal justice	
☐ medication	☐ training of staff	
☐ side-effect costs		

or

☐ staff
☐ medication
☐ labs/diagnostic
☐ overhead
☐ capital equipment
☐ real estate   Others: _____

Currency: _____

Year of costing: _____

Was discounting used? ☐ Yes, for benefits and costs   ☐ Yes, but only for costs   ☐ No

Rate: _____

Result(s): _____

_____

_____

Validity checklist score (Yes/NA/All):

……/……/…..

Risk of bias:

☐ High   ☐ Low

Comments, limitations of the study:

_____

_____

_____

Appendix 18 Evidence table template for clinical studies

Topic Area: **Sub-Topic Area:**

Author(s)		Interventions	Reported Outcomes (*including new RCTs*)
1. Review type 2. Funding 3. Period covered 4. Data analysis 5. No. of studies 6. No. randomised			
New RCTs			
Removed RCTs			

Additional notes for quality assessment
Author's objective
What methods were used to identify primary studies?
How were the inclusion criteria applied and what were they?
Criteria on which the validity (quality) of studies was assessed
How were the data extracted from the primary studies?

References to included studies

References to excluded studies

Characteristics of included studies

Study	Methods	Participants	Interventions	Outcomes	Notes

Appendix 19
Research recommendations

This section lists the research recommendations in this guideline.

Oral antipsychotics in the treatment of the acute episode

1. More long-term head-to-head RCTs of the atypical antipsychotic drugs are required, especially trials that include individuals in their first episode of schizophrenia, younger individuals and the elderly. (NICE 2002)

2. Direct comparisons between atypical antipsychotics are needed to establish their respective risk/long-term benefit, including effects upon relapse rates and persisting symptoms. Trials should pay particular attention to the long-term benefits and risks of the drugs, including diabetes, weight gain, EPS (including tardive dyskinesia), sexual dysfunction, lethargy and quality of life.

3. Further RCT-based cost-effectiveness studies comparing atypical antipsychotics to each other and to depot preparations are necessary.

4. Large-scale observational survey-based studies, including qualitative components, of the experience of drug treatments, for both conventional and atypical antipsychotics, should be undertaken. Studies should include data on service-user satisfaction, side-effects, preferences, provision of information and quality of life.

5. Further work is required on the nature and severity of antipsychotic drug discontinuation phenomena, including the re-emergence of psychotic symptoms, and their relationship to different antipsychotic withdrawal strategies.

Depot antipsychotic treatment

1. Further RCT-based cost-effectiveness studies are needed to establish the clinical and cost-effectiveness of depot and similar preparations of both conventional and atypical antipsychotics which should study their safety, efficacy, side-effect profile and impact upon quality of life.

Rapid tranquillisation

1. Quantitative and qualitative research is required investigating the utility, acceptability and safety of available drugs for urgent sedation (including atypical antipsychotics), employing larger samples, in settings that reflect current clinical practice, and systematically manipulating dosage and frequency of drug administration.

2. Quantitative and qualitative research is required to evaluate the role of non-pharmacological methods in behavioural control.

Treatment-resistant schizophrenia

1. Head-to-head comparative trials of clozapine against other atypicals and between other atypicals in treatment-resistant schizophrenia are required, including evaluation of their impact upon quality of life.

2. Further controlled studies are required to test the claims that clozapine is particularly effective in reducing hostility and violence, and the inconsistent evidence for a reduction in suicide rates in people with schizophrenia.

Combining antipsychotics

1. Adequately powered randomised controlled trials, reporting all relevant outcomes, including quality of life, are required to test the clinical efficacy and acceptability of combined antipsychotics (including clozapine) in those patients for whom monotherapy has proved unsatisfactory.

Cognitive–behavioural therapy

1. Adequately powered randomised controlled trials reporting all relevant clinical outcomes, including quality of life, are needed to further evaluate the use of cognitive–behavioural therapy in people at first episode of schizophrenia and people at risk of relapse.

2. Cognitive–behavioural therapy (CBT) is a relatively newly developed treatment option in the management of schizophrenia. Further research into the use and effects of CBT in the treatment of people with schizophrenia is needed to clarify the different roles and potential value of CBT in this context. Future studies should include reports on quality of life, and any adverse outcomes, including self-harm and death.

Family interventions

1. Adequately powered randomised controlled trials reporting all relevant clinical outcomes, including quality of life, are needed to evaluate the use of family interventions for the families of people with schizophrenia presenting for the first time.

2. Research into the methods for identifying which individuals would most benefit from family interventions and methods for promoting their effective implementation should be undertaken.

3. Further research is needed to evaluate the impact of family interventions upon the symptoms experienced by service users.

Community mental health health teams

1. High-quality research, including health economic outomes, should be conducted to establish the clinical and cost effectiveness, including the impact upon quality of life, of community mental health teams as compared to other ways of delivering care for people with schizophrenia.
2. Research studies to establish the relative effectiveness of specialist teams (e.g., crisis resolution and home treatment, and early intervention) as compared to community mental health teams, augmented or enhanced to deliver these functions.

Assertive outreach teams/assertive community treatment

1. Adequately powered randomised controlled trials reporting all relevant outcomes, including quality of life, are needed to establish the efficacy of assertive outreach teams (AOTs) for people with schizophrenia (and other serious mental disorders) in the UK. Studies should evaluate the suitability and efficacy of AOT for different service-user subgroups, and include economic analyses applicable for the UK setting.

Acute day hospitals

1. More high-quality, direct economic evaluations are necessary to establish the cost-effectiveness of acute day hospitals compared to other acute service provisions, such as crisis resolution and home treatment teams.

Vocational rehabilitation

1. Randomised controlled trials recording all relevant outcomes, including quality of life and self-esteem, should be conducted to establish the clinical, cost and occupational effectiveness of Supported Employment in the UK.
2. Research should be conducted recording all relevant outcomes, including quality of life and self-esteem, to identify the most beneficial types of work-related day-time activity for people with schizophrenia and other serious mental health problems.

Crisis resolution and home treatment teams

1. Adequately powered randomised controlled trials recording all relevant clinical, social and economic outcomes, including quality of life and the methods and effects of risk monitoring are needed, to compare acute day hospitals, inpatient units and crisis resolution and home treatment teams.

Early interventions

1. It is recommended that early intervention services are evaluated using adequately powered randomised controlled trials reporting all relevant clinical, social, occupational and economic outcomes, including quality of life and longer-term outcomes.

Primary–secondary care interface

1. An evaluation of a coordinated approach of primary and secondary care in the early diagnosis and management of people with schizophrenia is recommended.
2. It is recommended that the role of the general practice team in crisis management of people with schizophrenia be evaluated.
3. It is recommended that a randomised controlled trial on the role of case registers in the long-term management of people with schizophrenia in general practice be conducted.
4. It is recommended that more research be carried out on the development and evaluation of effective interventions for managing the physical health of people with schizophrenia in general practice.

References

Adams, C. E., Coutinho, E., Duggan, L., et al (2001) *Cochrane Schizophrenia Group*. In Cochrane Library, Issue 1. Oxford: Update Software.

Addington, J., el-Guebaly, N., Campbell, P., et al (1998) Smoking cessation treatment for patients with schizophrenia. *American Journal of Psychiatry*, **155**, 974–976.

Adesanya, A. & Pantelis, C. (2001) Adjunctive risperidone treatment in patients with 'clozapine-resistant schizophrenia' (letter). *Australian and New Zealand Journal of Psychiatry*, **34**, 533–534.

Allison, D. B., Mentore, J. L., Heo, M., et al (1999) Antipsychotic-induced weight gain: a comprehensive research synthesis. *American Journal of Psychiatry*, **156**, 1686–1696.

Altamura, A. C., Bobes, J., Cunningham Owens, D., et al (2000) Schizophrenia: diagnosis and treatment principles. Principles of Practice from the European Expert Panel on the Contemporary Treatment of Schizophrenia. *International Journal of Psychiatry in Clinical Practice*, **4**, 1–11.

American Hospital Association (1975) *A Patient's Bill of Rights*. Chicago: AHA.

American Psychiatric Association (1994) *Diagnostic and Statistical Manual of Mental Disorders*, 4th edn (DSM–IV). Washington, DC: APA.

Antai-Otong, D. (1989) Concerns of the hospitalized and community psychiatric client. *Nursing Clinics in North America*, **24**, 665–673.

Anthony, W. A. & Blanch, A. (1987) Supported employment for persons who are psychiatrically disabled: an historical and conceptual perspective. *Psychosocial Rehabilitation Journal*, **11**, 5–23.

Atakan, Z. & Davies, T. (1987) ABC of mental health. Mental health emergencies. *BMJ*, **314**, 1740–1742.

Atkins, G. L. & Bauer, J. L. (1992–93) Taming health care costs now. *Issues in Science and Technology*, **9**, 54–56, 58–60.

Atkinson, J. M., Coia, D. A., Gilmour, W. H., et al (1996) The impact of education groups for people with schizophrenia on social functioning and quality of life. *British Journal of Psychiatry*, **168**, 199–204.

Aubree, J. C. & Lader, M. H. (1980) High and very high dosage antipsychotics: a critical review. *Journal of Clinical Psychiatry*, **41**, 341–350.

Audini, B., Marks, I. M., Lawrence, R., et al (1994) Home-based versus out-patient/in-patient care for people with serious mental illness. Phase II of a controlled study. *British Journal of Psychiatry*, **164**, 204–210.

Audit Commission (1986) *Making a Reality of Community Care*. London: HMSO.

Ayllon, T. & Azrin, N. H. (1965) The measurement and reinforcement of behaviour of psychotics. *Journal of Experimental Analysis of Behavior*, **8**, 357–383.

Banerjee, S., Clany, C. & Crome, I. (2002) Coexisting problems of mental disorder and substance issue (dual diagnosis). An Information Manual – 2002. London: Royal College of Psychiatrists Research Unit.

Barbui, C., Saraceno, B., Liberati, A., et al (1996) Low dose neuroleptic therapy and relapse in schizophrenia: a meta-analysis of randomised controlled trials. *European Psychiatry*, **11**, 306–313.

Barnes, T. R. & Curson, D. A. (1994) Long-term depot antipsychotics. A risk-benefit assessment. *Drug Safety*, **10**, 464–479.

— & McPhillips, M. A. (1999) Critical analysis and comparison of the side-effect and safety profiles of the new antipsychotics. *British Journal of Psychiatry* (suppl. 38), 34–43.

—, McEvedy, C. J. & Nelson, H. E. (1996) Management of treatment resistant schizophrenia unresponsive to clozapine. *British Journal of Psychiatry* (suppl. 31), 31–40.

Barrowclough, C. & Parle, M. (1997) Appraisal, psychological adjustment and expressed emotion in relatives of patients suffering from schizophrenia. *British Journal of Psychiatry*, **171**, 26–30.

—, Tarrier, N., Lewis, S., et al (1999) Randomised controlled effectiveness trial of a needs-based psychosocial intervention service for carers of people with schizophrenia. *British Journal of Psychiatry*, **174**, 505–511.

Bateman, A. & Fonaghy, P. (1999) Effectiveness of partial hospitalization in the treatment of borderline personality disorder: a randomized controlled trial. *American Journal of Psychiatry*, **156**, 1563–1569.

Battaglia, J., Moss, S., Rush, J., et al (1997) Haloperidol, lorazepam, or both for psychotic agitation? A multicenter, prospective, double-blind, emergency department study. *American Journal of Emergency Medicine*, 15, 335–340.

Bäuml, J., Kissling, W. & Pitschel-Walz, G. (1996) Psychoedukative gruppen für schizophrene patienten: einfluss auf wissensstand und compliance. *Nervenheilkunde*, **15**, 145–150.

Bebbington, P. E. & Kuipers, E. (1994) The predictive utility of expressed emotion in schizophrenia. *Psychological Medicine,* **24**, 707–718.

Beck, A. T. (1976) *Cognitive Therapy and the Emotional Disorders.* New York: International Universities Press.

Belanger-Annable, M. C. (1985) Long-acting neuroleptics: technique for intramuscular injection. *Cancer Nurse*, **81**, 41–44.

Bell, M. & Lysaker, P. (1995) Paid work activity in schizophrenia: program costs offset by costs of rehospitalizations. *Psychosocial Rehabilitation Journal*, **18**, 25–34.

Bell, R., McLaren, A., Galanos, J., et al (1998) The clinical use of plasma clozapine levels. *Australian and New Zealand Journal of Psychiatry,* **32**, 567–574.

Bellack, A. S., Turner, S. M., Hersen, M., et al (1984) An examination of the efficacy of social skills training for chronic schizophrenic patients. *Hospital and Community Psychiatry*, **35**,1023–1028.

—, Sayers, M., Mueser, K. T., et al (1994) Evaluation of social problem solving in schizophrenia. *Journal of Abnormal Psychology*, **103**, 371–378.

—, Weinhardt, L. S., Gold, J. M., et al (2001) Generalization of training effects in schizophrenia. *Schizophrenia Research*, **48**, 255–262.

Benedict, R. H. B., Harris, A. E., Markow, T., et al (1994) Effects of attention training on information processing in schizophrenia. *Schizophrenia Bulletin,* **20**, 537–546.

Bennett, D. & Freeman, H. (1991) Principles and prospect. In *Community Psychiatry* (eds D. Bennett & H. Freeman), pp. 1–39. Edinburgh: Churchill Livingstone.

Berlin, J. A. (2001) Does blinding of readers affect the results of meta-analyses? *Lancet*, **350**, 185–186.

Bleuler, E. (1911) *Dementia Praecox or the Group of Schizophrenias* (translated by J. J. Zinkin, 1950). New York: International Universities Press.

Bleuler, M. (1978a) The long-term course of schizophrenic psychosis. In *The Nature of Schizophrenia* (eds L. C. Wynne, R. L. Cromwell & S. Matthysse). New York: Wiley.

— (1978b) *The Schizophrenia Disorders.* New Haven: Yale University Press.

Bloch, S., Szmukler, G. I., Herrman, H., et al (1995) Counseling caregivers of relatives with schizophrenia: themes, interventions, and caveats. *Family Process*, **34**, 413–425.

Bollini, P., Pampallona, S., Orza, M. J., et al (1994) Antipsychotic drugs: is more worse? A meta-analysis of the published randomized control trials. *Psychological Medicine*, **24**, 307–316.

Bond, G. R., Miller, L. D., Krumwied, R. D., et al (1988) Assertive case management in three CMHCs: a controlled study. *Hospital and Community Psychiatry*, **39**, 411–418.

—, Dietzen, L. L., Vogler, K., et al (1995) Toward a framework for evaluating cost and benefits of psychiatric rehabilitation: three case examples. *Journal of Vocational Rehabilitation*, **5**, 75–88.

Bondolfi, G., Dufour, H., Patris, M., et al (1998) Risperidone versus clozapine in treatment-resistant chronic schizophrenia: a randomized double-blind study. The Risperidone Study Group. *American Journal of Psychiatry*, **155**, 499–504.

Bouras, N., Tufnell, G., Brough, D. I., et al (1986) Model for the integration of community psychiatry and primary care. *Journal of the Royal College of General Practice*, **36**, 62–66.

Bradshaw, W. (2000) Integrating cognitive-behavioral psychotherapy for persons with schizophrenia into a psychiatric rehabilitation program: results of a three year trial. *Community Mental Health Journal*, **36**, 491–500.

Bramon, E., Kelly, J., van Os, J., et al (2001) The cascade of increasingly deviant development that culminates in the onset of schizophrenia. *NeuroScience News*, **4**, 5–19.

Breier, A., Meehan, K., Birkett, M., et al (2002) A double-blind, placebo-controlled dose-response comparison of intramuscular olanzapine and haloperidol in the treatment of acute agitation in schizophrenia. *Archives of General Psychiatry*, **59**, 441–448.

Brenner, H. D. (1986) On the importance of cognitive disorders in treatment and rehabilitation. In *Psychosocial Treatment of Schizophrenia* (eds J. S. Strauss, W. Boker & H. D. Brenner), pp. 136–151. Toronto: Hans Huber.

—, Dencker, S. J., Goldstein, M. J., et al (1990) Defining treatment refractoriness in schizophrenia. *Schizophrenia Bulletin*, **16**, 551–561.

Broadstock, M. (2001) The effectiveness and safety of drug treatment for urgent sedation in psychiatric emergencies. A critical appraisal of the literature. *NZHTA Report*, **4**.

Brody, D. S. (1980) The patient's role in clinical decision-making. *Annals of Internal Medicine*, **93**, 718–722.

Brown, G. W. & Rutter, M. (1966) The measurement of family activities and relationships: a methodological study. *Human Relations*, **19**, 241–263.

—, Monck, E. M., Carstairs, G. M., et al (1962) Influence of family life on the course of schizophrenic illness. *British Journal of Preventive and Social Medicine*, **16**, 55–68.

Brown, S. (1997) Excess mortality of schizophrenia. A meta-analysis. *British Journal of Psychiatry*, **171**, 502–508.

—, Birtwhistle, J., Row, L., et al (1999) The unhealthy lifestyle of people with schizophrenia. *Psychological Medicine*, **29**, 697–701.

—, Inskip, H. & Barraclough, B. (2000) Causes of the excess mortality of schizophrenia. *British Journal of Psychiatry*, **177**, 212–217.

Buchkremer, G., Schulze Monking, H., Holle, R., et al (1995) The impact of therapeutic relatives' groups on the course of illness of schizophrenic patients. *European Psychiatry*, **10**, 17–27.

Burns, T. & Cohen, A. (1998) Item-of-service payments for general practitioner care of severely mentally ill persons: does the money matter? *British Journal of General Practice*, **48**, 1415–1416.

— & Raftery, J. (1993) A controlled trial of home-based acute psychiatric services. II: Treatment patterns and costs. *British Journal of Psychiatry*, **163**, 55–61.

—, Beadsmoore, A., Ashok, V. B., et al (1993) A controlled trial of home-based acute psychiatric services. I: Clinical and social outcome. *British Journal of Psychiatry*, **163**, 49–54.

—, Millar, E., Garland, C., et al (1998) Randomized controlled trial of teaching practice nurses to carry out structured assessments of patients receiving depot antipsychotic injections. *British Journal of General Practice*, **48**, 1845–1848.

Burns, R., Creed, F., Fahy, T., et al (1999) Intensive versus standard case management for severe psychotic illness: a randomised trial. *Lancet*, **353**, 2185–2189.

Byford, S., Fiander, M., Barber, J. A., et al (2000) Cost-effectiveness of intensive v. standard case management for severe psychotic illness. UK700 case management trial. *British Journal of Psychiatry*, **176**, 537–543.

Cameron, E. (1947) The day hospital. An experimental form of hospitalization for psychiatric patients. *Modern Hospital*, **69**, 60–63.

Cannon, M. & Jones, P. (1996) Schizophrenia. *Journal of Neurology, Neurosurgery and Psychiatry*, **60**, 604–613.

Carande-Kulis, V. G., Maciosek, M. V., Briss, P. A, *et al* **(2000)** Methods for systematic reviews of economic evaluations for the Guide to Community Preventive Services. Task Force on Community Preventive Services. *American Journal of Preventive Medicine*, **18** (suppl. 1), 75–91.

Carpenter, W., Heinrichs, D. & Hanlon, T. (1987) A comparative trial of pharmacologic strategies in schizophrenia. *American Journal of Psychiatry*, **144**, 1466–1470.

Chakos, M., Lieberman, J., Hoffman, E., *et al* **(2001)** Effectiveness of second-generation antipsychotics in patients with treatment-resistant schizophrenia: a review and meta-analysis of randomized trials. *American Journal of Psychiatry*, **158**, 518–526.

Chandler, D., Spicer, G., Wagner, M., *et al* **(1999)** Cost-effectiveness of a capitated Assertive Community Treatment program. *Psychiatric Rehabilitation Journal*, **22**, 327–336.

Chong, S.-A., Tan, C. H. & Lee, H. S. (1996) Hoarding and clozapine-risperidone combination. *Canadian Journal of Psychiatry*, **41**, 315–316.

Chong, S. A. & Remington, G. (2000) Clozapine augmentation: safety and efficacy. *Schizophrenia Bulletin*, **26**, 421–440.

Citrome, L., Volavka, J., Czobor, P., *et al* **(2001)** Effects of clozapine, olanzapine, risperidone, and haloperidol on hostility among patients with schizophrenia. *Psychiatric Services*, **52**, 1510–1514.

Clarke, M. & Oxman, A. D. (eds) (2000) *Cochrane Reviewers' Handbook 4.1* (updated June 2000). In *Review Manager (RevMan)* (computer program), version 4.1. Oxford: Cochrane Collaboration.

Clark, R. E., Bush, P. W., Becker, D. R., *et al* **(1996)** A cost-effectiveness comparison of supported employment and rehabilitative day treatment. *Administration and Policy in Mental Health*, **24**, 63–77.

—, Xie, H., Becker, D. R., *et al* **(1998)** Benefits and costs of supported employment from three perspectives. *Journal of Behavioral Health Services and Research*, **25**, 22–34.

Coid, J. (1994) Failure in community care: psychiatry's dilemma. *BMJ*, **308**, 805–806.

Conley, R. R. & Buchanan, R. W. (1997) Evaluation of treatment-resistant schizophrenia. *Schizophrenia Bulletin*, **23**, 663–674.

Cookson, J., Taylor, D. & Katona, C. (2002) *Use of Drugs in Psychiatry* (5th edn). London: Gaskell.

Crammer, J. & Eccleston, D. A. (1989) Survey of the use of depot neuroleptics in a whole region. *Psychiatric Bulletin*, **13**, 517–520.

Creed, F., Black, D., Anthony, P., *et al* **(1990)** Randomised controlled trial of day patient versus in-patient psychiatric treatment. *BMJ*, **300**, 1033–1037.

—, Mbaya, P., Lancashire, S., *et al* **(1997)** Cost effectiveness of day and in-patient psychiatric treatment. *BMJ*, **314**, 1381–1385.

Crowther, R., Marshall, M., Bond, G., *et al* **(2001)** Vocational rehabilitation for people with severe mental illness (Cochrane Review). *Cochrane Library*, Issue 4. Oxford: Update Software.

Csernansky, J. & Okamoto, A. (2000) Risperidone vs haloperidol for prevention of relapse in schizophrenia and schizoaffective disorder: a long-term double-blind comparison. *Schizophrenia Research*, **41**, 198–199.

—, — & Brecher, M. (1999) Risperidone vs haloperidol: prevention of relapse in schizophrenia. *European Neuropsychopharmacology*, **9** (suppl. 5), S268.

Cunnane, J. G. (1994) Drug management of disturbed behaviour by psychiatrists. *Psychiatric Bulletin*, **18**, 138–139.

Cunningham Owens, D. G., Carroll, A., Fattah, S., *et al* **(2001)** A randomized, controlled trial of a brief interventional package for schizophrenic out-patients. *Acta Psychiatrica Scandinavica*, **103**, 362–369.

Curtis, J. L., Millman, E. J., Struening, E., *et al* (1992) Effect of case management on rehospitalisation and utilisation of ambulatory care services. *Hospital and Community Psychiatry*, **43**, 895–899.

Daniels, L. (1998) A group cognitive-behavioural and process-oriented approach to treating the social impairment and negative symptoms assocciated with chronic mental illness. *Journal of Psychotherapy Practice and Research*, **7**, 167–176.

David, A. S. & Adams, C. (2001) Depot antipsychotic medication in the treatment of patients with schizophrenia: (1) meta-review; (2) patient and nurse attitudes. *Health Technology Assessment*, **5**, 1–61.

Davies, L. M. & Drummond, M. F. (1994) Economics and schizophrenia: the real cost. *British Journal of Psychiatry* (suppl. 25), 18–21.

Davis, J. M. & Garver, D. L. (1978) Neuroleptics: clinical use in psychiatry. In *Handbook of Psychopharmacology* (eds L. Iversen, S. Iversen & S. Snyder). New York: Plenum Press.

—, Kane, J. M, Marder, S. R., *et al* (1993) Dose response of prophylactic antipsychotics. *Journal of Clinical Psychiatry*, **54** (suppl.), 24–30.

De Cangas, J. P. C. (1994) Le 'case management' affirmatif: une evaluation complete d'un programme du genre en milieu hospitalier. *Sante mentale au Quebec*, **19**, 75–92.

Department of Health (1998) *The New NHS, Modern and Dependable. A National Framework for Assessing Performance*. Wetherby: Department of Health.

— (2002) *National Service Framework for Mental Health: Modern Standards and Service Models*. http://www.doh.gov.uk/pub/docs/doh/mhmain.pdf

DerSimonian, R. & Laird, N. (1986) Meta-analysis in clinical trials. *Controlled Clinical Trials*, **7**, 177–188.

Dewan, M. J. & Koss, M. (1995) The clinical impact of reported variance in potency of antipsychotic agents. *Acta Psychiatrica Scandinavica*, **91**, 229–232.

Dick, P., Ince, A. & Barlow, M. (1985) Day treatment: suitability and referral procedure. *British Journal of Psychiatry*, **147**, 250–253.

—, Sweeney, M. L. & Crombie, I. K. (1991) Controlled comparison of day-patient and out-patient treatment for persistent anxiety and depression. *British Journal of Psychiatry*, **158**, 24–27.

Dixon, L. B., Lehman, A. F. & Levine, J. (1995) Conventional antipsychotic medications for schizophrenia. *Schizophrenia Bulletin*, **21**, 567–577.

Dobson, D. J. G., McDougall, G., Busheikin, J., *et al* (1995) Effects of social skills training and social milieu treatment on symptoms of schizophrenia. *Psychiatric Services*, **46**, 376–380.

Donlon, P. T., Swaback, D. O. & Osborne, M. L. (1977) Pimozide versus fluphenazine in ambulatory schizophrenics: a 12-month comparison study. *Diseases of the Nervous System*, **38**, 119–123.

Dorevitch, A., Katz, N., Zemishlany, Z., *et al* (1999) Intramuscular flunitrazepam versus intramuscular haloperidol in emergency treatement of aggressive psychotic behavior. *American Journal of Psychiatry*, **156**, 142–144.

Dowell, D. A. & Ciarlo, J. A. (1983) Overview of the community mental health centres program from an evaluation perspective. *American Journal of Psychiatry*, **19**, 95–125.

Drake, R. E., Becker, D. R. & Anthony, W. A. (1994) A research induction group for clients entering a mental health research project. *Hospital and Community Psychiatry*, **45**, 487–489.

—, McHugo, G. J., Bebout, R. R., *et al* (1999) A randomized controlled trial of supported employment for inner-city patients with severe mental illness. *Archives of General Psychiatry*, **56**, 627–633.

Drummond, M. F. & Jefferson, T. O. (1996) Guidelines for authors and peer reviewers of economic submissions to the BMJ. *BMJ*, **313**, 275–283.

Drury, V., Birchwood, M., Cochrane, R., *et al* (1996) Cognitive therapy and recovery from acute psychosis: a controlled trial. I. Impact on psychotic symptoms. *British Journal of Psychiatry*, **169**, 593–601.

Durson, S. M. & Deakin, J. F. (2001) Augmenting antipsychotic treatment with lamotrigine or topiramate in patients with treatment-resistant schizophrenia: a naturalistic case-series outcome study. *Journal of Psychopharmacology*, **15**, 297–301.

Dyck, D. G., Short, R. A., Hendry, M. S., et al (2000) Management of negative symptoms among patients with schizophrenia attending multiple-family groups. *Psychiatric Services*, **51**, 513–519.

Eccles, M. & Mason, J. (2001) How to develop cost-conscious guidelines. *Health Technology Assessment*, **5**, 1–69.

—, **Freemantle, N. & Mason, J. (1998)** North of England evidence based guideline development project: methods of developing guidelines for efficient drug use in primary care. *BMJ*, **316**, 1232–1235.

Eckman, T. A., Wirshing, W. C., Marder, S. R., et al (1992) Technique for training schizophrenic patients in illness self-management: a controlled trial. *American Journal of Psychiatry*, **149**, 1549–1555.

Ellison, M. L., Rogers, E. S., Sciarappa, K., et al (1995) Characteristics of mental health case management: results of a national survey. *Journal of Mental Health Administration*, **22**, 101–112.

Essock, S. M., Hargreaves, W. A., Covell, N. H., et al (1996) Clozapine's effectiveness for patients in state hospitals: results from a randomized trial. *Psychopharmacology Bulletin*, **32**, 683–697.

—, **Frisman, L. K. & Kontos, N. J. (1998)** Cost-effectiveness of assertive community treatment teams. *American Journal of Orthopsychiatry*, **68**, 179–190.

Falloon, I. R. H., Boyd, J. L., McGill, C. W., et al (1982) Family management in the prevention of exacerbations of schizophrenia: a controlled study. *New England Journal of Medicine*, **306**, 1437–1440.

Falvo, D. R. (1994) *Effective Patient Education. A Guide to Increased Compliance.* Gaithersburg, MD: Aspen.

Farde, L., Nordstrom, A. L., Wiesel, F. A., et al (1992) Positron emission tomographic analysis of central D1 and D2 dopamine receptor occupancy in patients treated with classical neuroleptics and clozapine. Relation to extrapyramidal side-effects. *Archives of General Psychiatry*, **49**, 538–544.

Faris, R. E. L. & Dunham, H. W. (1967) *Mental Disorders in Urban Areas: An Ecological Study of Schizophrenia and Other Psychoses.* Chicago, IL: University of Chicago Press.

Fekete, D. M., Bond, G. R., McDonel, E. C., et al (1998) Rural Assertive Community Treatment: a field experiment. *Psychiatric Rehabilitation Journal*, **21**, 371–379.

Fenton, F. R., Tessier, L. & Struening, E. L. (1979) A comparative trial of home and hospital psychiatric care: one-year follow-up. *Archives of General Psychiatry*, **36**, 1073–1079.

—, —, —, **et al (1984)** A two-year follow-up of a comparative trial of the cost-effectiveness of home and hospital psychiatric treatment. *Canadian Journal of Psychiatry*, **29**, 205–211.

Fenton, M., Coutinho, E. S. F. & Campbell, C. (2002a) Zuclopenthixol acetate in the treatment of acute schizophrenia and similar serious mental illnesses (Cochrane Review). *Cochrane Library*, Issue 2. Oxford: Update Software.

—, **Murphy, B., Wood, J., et al (2002b)** Loxapine for schizophrenia (Cochrane Review). *Cochrane Library*, Issue 2. Oxford: Update Software.

Fenton, W. S. & McGlashan, T. H. (1995) Schizophrenia: individual psychotherapy. In *Comprehensive Textbook of Psychiatry* (eds H. Kaplan & B. Sadock), pp. 1007–1018. Baltimore, MD: Williams & Wilkins.

—, **Mosher, L. R., Herrell, J. M., et al (1998)** Randomized trial of general hospital and residential alternative care for patients with severe and persistent mental illness. *American Journal of Psychiatry*, **155**, 516–522.

Fleischhacker, W. W. & Hummer, M. (1997) Drug treatment of schizophrenia in the 1990s. Achievements and future possibilities in optimising outcomes. *Drugs*, **53**, 915–929.

Ford, R., Beadsmoore, A., Ryan, P., *et al* **(1995)** Providing the safety net: case management for people with a serious mental illness. *Journal of Mental Health*, **4**, 91–97.

—, Raferty, J., Ryan, P., *et al* **(1997)** Intensive case management for people with serious mental illness – site 2: cost effectiveness. *Journal of Mental Health*, **6**, 191–199.

—, Minghella, E., Chalmers, C., *et al* **(2001)** Cost consequences of home-based and in-patient-based acute psychiatric treatment: results of an implementation study. *Journal of Mental Health*, **10**, 467–476.

Foster, K., Meltzer, H., Gill, B., *et al* **(1996)** Adults with a psychotic disorder living in the community. *OPCS Surveys of Psychiatric Morbidity in Great Britain*, Report 8. London: HMSO.

Francois, I., Gadreau, M., Gisselmann, A., *et al* **(1993)** Contribution to the economic evaluation in psychiatry – a comparison of two establishments for chronic schizophrenic patients in the CHRU of Dijon [in French]. *Journal d'Economie Médicale*, **11**, 185–199.

Franklin, J., Solovitz, B., Mason, M., *et al* **(1987)** An evaluation of case management. *American Journal of Public Health*, **77**, 674–678.

Freeman, D. J. & Oyewumi, L. K. (1997) Will routine therapeutic drug monitoring have a place in clozapine therapy? *Clinical Pharmacokinetics*, **32**, 93–100.

Freud, S. (1914) Reprinted (1953–1974) in the *Standard Edition of the Complete Psychological Works of Sigmund Freud* (trans. and ed. J. Strachey), vol. 14, p. 74. London: Hogarth Press.

— (1933) Reprinted (1953–1974) in the *Standard Edition of the Complete Psychological Works of Sigmund Freud* (trans. and ed. J. Strachey), vol. 22, p. 155. London: Hogarth Press.

Friedman, J., Ault, K. & Powchik, P. (1997) Pimozide augmentation for the treatment of schizophrenic patients who are trial responders to clozapine. *Biological Psychiatry*, **15**, 522–523.

Frith, C. D. (1992) *The Cognitive Neuropsychology of Schizophrenia.* Hillsdale, NJ: Lawrence Erlbaum.

Fromm-Reichmann, F. (1950) *Principles of Intensive Psychotherapy.* Chicago: University of Chicago Press.

Gaertner, I., Gaertner, H. J., Vonthein, R. I., *et al* **(2001)** Therapeutic drug monitoring of clozapine in relapse prevention: a five-year prospective study. *Journal of Clinical Psychopharmacology*, **21**, 305–310.

Galster, G. C., Champney, T. F. & Williams, Y. (1995) Costs of caring for persons with long-term mental illness in alternative residential settings. *Evaluation and Program Planning*, **17**, 3.

Garety, P. A. & Hemsley, D. R. (1994) *Delusions. Investigations into the Psychology of Delusional Reasoning.* UK: Psychology Press.

— & Jolley, S. (2000) Early intervention in psychosis. *Psychiatric Bulletin*, **24**, 321–323.

—, Fowler, D. & Kuipers, E. (2000) Cognitive-behavioral therapy for medication-resistant symptoms. *Schizophrenia Bulletin*, **26**, 73–86.

—, Kuipers, E., Fowler, D., *et al* **(2001)** A cognitive model of the positive symptoms of psychosis. *Psychological Medicine*, **31**, 189–195.

Garza-Trevino, E. S., Hollister, L. E., Overall, J. E., *et al* **(1989)** Efficacy of combinations of intramuscular antipsychotics and sedative-hypnotics for control of psychotic agitation. *American Journal of Psychiatry*, **146**, 1598–1601.

Gater, R., Goldberg, D., Jackson, G., *et al* **(1997)** The care of patients with chronic schizophrenia: a comparison between two services. *Psychological Medicine*, **27**, 1325–1336.

Geddes, J., Freemantle, N., Harrison, P., *et al* **(2000)** Atypical antipsychotics in the treatment of schizophrenia: systematic overview and meta-regression analysis. *BMJ*, **321**, 1371–1376.

Gelder, M., Mayou, R. & Geddes, J. (1997) *Oxford Textbook of Psychiatry.* Oxford: Oxford University Press.

Gervey, R. & Bedell, J. R. (1994) Psychological assessment and treatment of persons with severe mental disorders. In *Supported Employment in Vocational Rehabilitation* (ed. J. R. Bedell), pp. 170–175. Washington, DC: Taylor & Francis.

Gilbert, P. L., Harris, M. J., McAdams, L. A., *et al* (1995) Neuroleptic withdrawal in schizophrenic patients. A review of the literature. *Archives of General Psychiatry*, **52**, 173–188.

Gilbody, S. M., Bagnall, A. M., Duggan, L., *et al* (2002) Risperidone versus other atypical antipsychotic medication for schizophrenia (Cochrane Review). *Cochrane Library*, Issue 3. Oxford: Update Software.

Glazer, W. M. & Ereshefsky, L. (1996) A pharmacoeconomic model of outpatient antipsychotic therapy in 'revolving door' schizophrenic patients. *Journal of Clinical Psychiatry*, **57**, 337–345.

Glick, I. D., Fleming, L., DeChillo, N., *et al* (1986) A controlled study of transitional day care for non-chronically ill patients. *American Journal of Psychiatry*, **143**, 1551–1556.

Glynn, S. M., Randolph, E. T., Eth, S., *et al* (1992) Schizophrenic symptoms, work adjustment, and behavioral family therapy. *Rehabilitation Psychology*, **37**, 323–338.

Godlesky, L. S. & Sernyak, M. J. (1996) Agranulocytosis after addition of risperidone to clozapine treatment. *American Journal of Psychiatry*, **153**, 735–736.

Goldstein, M. J. (1996) Psychoeducational family programs in the United States. In *Handbook of Mental Health Economics and Health Policy,* vol. 1: *Schizophrenia.* (eds M. Moscarelli, A. Rupp & N. Sartorius). New York: John Wiley.

—, Rodnick, E. H., Evans, J. R., *et al* (1978) Drug and family therapy in the aftercare of acute schizophrenics. *Archives of General Psychiatry*, **35**, 1169–1177.

Green, M. F. (1992) Neuropsychological performance in the unaffected twin. *Archives of General Psychiatry*, **49**, 247.

Guest, J. F. & Cookson, R. F. (1999) Cost of schizophrenia to UK society. An incidence-based cost-of-illness model for the first 5 years following diagnosis. *Pharmacoeconomics*, **15**, 597–610.

Gulbinat, W., Dupont, A., Jablensky, A., *et al* (1992) Cancer incidence of schizophrenic patients: results of linkage studies in three countries. *British Journal of Psychiatry* (suppl. 161), 75–83.

Gunderson, J. G., Frank, A. F., Katz, H. M., *et al* (1984) Effects of psychotherapy in schizophrenia. II. Comparative outcome of two forms of treatment. *Schizophrenia Bulletin*, **10**, 564–598.

Gupta, S., Sonnenberg, S. J. & Frank, B. (1998) Olanzapine augmentation of clozapine. *Annals of Clinical Psychiatry*, **10**, 113–115.

Hadas-Lidor, N., Katz, N., Tyano, S., *et al* (2001) Effectiveness of dynamic cognitive intervention in rehabilitation of clients with schizophrenia. *Clinical Rehabilitation*, **15**, 349–359.

Haddock, G., Tarrier, N., Morrison, A.P., *et al* (1999) A pilot study evaluating the effectiveness of individual inpatient cognitive-behavioural therapy in early psychosis. *Social Psychiatry and Psychiatric Epidemiology*, **34**, 254–258.

Hale, A. S. & Wood, C. (1996) Comparison of direct treatment costs for schizophrenia using oral or depot neuroleptics: a pharmacoeconomic analysis. *British Journal of Medical Economics*, **10**, 37–45.

Hallam, A. & Schneider, J. (1999) Sheltered work schemes for people with severe mental health problems: service use and costs. *Journal of Mental Health*, **8**, 171–186.

Harding, C. M., Zubin, J. & Strauss, J. S. (1987) Chronicity in schizophrenia: fact, partial fact, or artifact? *Hospital and Community Psychiatry*, **38**, 477–486.

Harrington, M., Lelliot, P., Paton, C., *et al* (2002) Variation between services in polypharmacy and combined high dose of antipsychotic drugs prescribed for in-patients. *Psychiatric Bulletin*, **26**, 418–420.

Harris, A. E. (1988) Physical disease and schizophrenia. *Schizophrenia Bulletin*, **14**, 85–96.

Harris, E. C. & Barraclough, B. (1998) Excess mortality of mental disorder. *British Journal of Psychiatry*, **173**, 11–53.

Harrison, G., Owens, D., Holton, A., *et al* (1988) A prospective study of severe mental disorder in Afro-Caribbean patients. *Psychological Medicine*, **18**, 643–657.

Hasegawa, M., Gutierrez-Esteinou, R., Way, L., *et al* (1993) Relationship between clinical efficacy and clozapine concentrations in plasma in schizophrenia: effect of smoking. *Journal of Clinical Psychopharmacology*, **13**, 383–390.

Hatfield, B., Huxley, P. & Mohamad, H. (1992) Accommodation and employment: a survey into the circumstances and expressed needs of users of mental health services in a northern town. *British Journal of Social Work*, **22**, 60–73.

Hayashi, N., Yamashina, M., Igarashi, Y., *et al* (2001) Improvement of patient attitude toward treatment among inpatients with schizophrenia and its related factors: controlled study of psychological approach. *Comprehensive Psychiatry*, **42**, 240–246.

Hayes, R. L., Halford, W. & Varghese, F. T. (1995) Social skills training with chronic schizophrenic patients: effects on negative symptoms and community functioning. *Behavior Therapy*, **26**, 433–449.

Healey, A., Knapp, M., Astin, J., *et al* (1998) Cost-effectiveness evaluation of compliance therapy for people with psychosis [see comments]. *British Journal of Psychiatry*, **172**, 420–424.

Health Evidence Bulletins (1988) *Health Evidence Bulletins – Wales: Mental Health.* Cardiff: Welsh Office.

Heim, M., Wolf, S., Gothe, U., *et al* (1989) Cognitive training in schizophrenic diseases. *Psychiatrie, Neurologie und Medizinische Psychologie (Leipzig)*, **41**, 367–375.

Henderson, D. C. & Goff, D. C. (1996) Risperidone as an adjunct to clozapine therapy in chronic schizophrenics. *Journal of Clinical Psychiatry*, **57**, 395–397.

Hermanutz, M. & Gestrich, J. (1987) Cognitive training of schizophrenic patients. Description of the training and results of a controlled therapeutic study. *Nervenarzt*, **58**, 91–96.

Hersen, M. & Bellack, A. (1976) Social skills training for chronic psychiatric patients: rationale, research findings and future directions. *Comprehensive Psychiatry*, **17**, 559–580.

Herz, M. I., Endicott, J., Spitzer, R. L., *et al* (1971) Day versus in-patient hospitalization: a controlled study. *American Journal of Psychiatry*, **10**, 1371–1382.

—, Lamberti, J. S., Minz, J., *et al* (2000) A program for relapse prevention in schizophrenia: a controlled study. *Archives of General Psychiatry*, **57**, 277–283.

Hirsch, S. R. & Barnes, T. R. E. (1995) The clinical treatment of schizophrenia with antipsychotic medication. In *Schizophrenia* (eds S. R. Hirsch & D. R. Weinberger), pp. 443–468. Oxford: Blackwell.

Hogarty, G. E., Ulrich, R. F., Mussare, F., *et al* (1976) Drug discontinuation among long term, successfully maintained schizophrenic outpatients. *Diseases of the Nervous System*, **37**, 494–500.

—, Kornblith, S., Greenwald, D., *et al* (1997a) Three year trials of personal therapy among schizophrenic patients living with or independent of family. I: Description of study and effects on relapse rates. *American Journal of Psychiatry*, **154**, 1504–1515.

—, Greenwald, D., Ulrich, R., *et al* (1997b) Three year trials of personal therapy among schizophrenic patients living with or independent of family. II: Effects on adjustment of patients. *American Journal of Psychiatry*, **154**, 1514–1524.

Hoge, M. A., Davidson, L., Leonard, H. W., *et al* (1992) The promise of partial hospitalization: a reassessment. *Hospital and Community Psychiatry*, **43**, 345–354.

Hollister, L. E. (1974) Clinical differences among phenothiazines in schizophrenics. Introduction: specific indications for antipsychotics: elusive end of the rainbow. *Advanced Biochemical Psychopharmacology*, **9**, 667–673.

Holloway, F. & Carson, J. (1998) Intensive case management for the severely mentally ill. Controlled trial. *British Journal of Psychiatry*, **172**, 19–22.

Hornung, W. P., Holle, R., Schulze Monking, H., *et al* (1995) Psychoeducational-psychotherapeutic treatment of schizophrenic patients and their caregivers. Results of a one-year catamnestic study [in German]. *Nervenarzt*, **66**, 828–834.

Hoult, J., Reynolds, I., Charbonneau Powis, M., *et al* (1981) A controlled study of psychiatric hospital versus community treatment: the effect on relatives. *Australian and New Zealand Journal of Psychiatry*, **15**, 323–328.

Hu, T. W. & Jerrell, J. M. (1998) Estimating the cost impact of three case management programmes for treating people with severe mental illness. *British Journal of Psychiatry*, (suppl. 36), 26–32.

Hyde, C. E. & Harrower-Wilson, C. (1996) Psychiatric intensive care in acute psychosis. *International Clinical Psychopharmacology*, **11** (suppl. 2), 61–65.

—, — & Ash, P. E. (1998) Cost comparison of zuclopenthixol acetate and haloperidol. *Psychiatric Bulletin*, **22**, 140–143.

IRIS (2002) *Initiative to Reduce the Impact of Schizophrenia.* http://www.iris-initiative.org.uk

Isaac, M. N. (1996) Trends in the development of psychiatric services in India. *Psychiatric Bulletin*, **20**, 43–45.

Issakidis, C., Sanderson, K., Teesson, M., et al (1999) Intensive case management in Australia: a randomised controlled trial. *Acta Psychiatrica Scandinavica*, **99**, 360–367.

Jablensky, A., Sartorius, N., Ernberg, G., et al (1992) Schizophrenia: manifestations, incidence and course in different cultures. A World Health Organization ten-country study. *Psychological Medicine Monograph Supplement*, **20**, 1–97.

—, McGrath, J., Herrman, H., et al (2000) Psychotic disorders in urban areas. *Australian and New Zealand Journal of Psychiatry*, **34**, 221–236.

Jadad, A. R., Moore, R. A., Carroll, D., et al (1996) Assessing the quality of reports of randomized clinical trials: is blinding necessary? *Controlled Clinical Trials*, **17**, 1–12.

Janicak, P. G., Davis, J. M., Preskorn, S. H., et al (1993) *Principles and Practice of Psychopharmacotherapy.* Baltimore: Williams & Wilkins.

Jeffreys, S. E., Harvey, C. A., McNaught, A. S., et al (1997) The Hampstead Schizophrenia Survey 1991. I: Prevalence and service use comparisons in an inner London health authority, 1986-1991. *British Journal of Psychiatry*, **170**, 301–306.

Jerrell, J. M. (1995) Toward managed care for persons with severe mental illness: Implications from a cost-effectiveness study. *Health Affairs*, **14**, 197–207.

Jeste, D. V., Dgladsjo, J. A., Lindamer, L. A., et al (1996) Medical co-morbidity in schizophrenia. *Schizophrenia Bulletin*, **22**, 413–420.

Johannessen, J. O., McGlashan, T. H., Larsen, T. K., et al (2001) Early detection strategies for untreated first-episode psychosis. *Schizophrenia Research*, **51**, 39–46.

Johnson, S. (1997) *London's Mental Health: The Report for the King's Fund London Commission.* London: King's Fund.

—, Salkeld, G., Sanderson, K., et al (1998) Intensive case management: a cost effectiveness analysis. *Australian and New Zealand Journal of Psychiatry*, **32**, 551–559.

Johnstone, E. C. (1991) The nature and the management of schizophrenia. *Scottish Medical Journal*, **36**, 4–5.

—, Owen, D. G., Gold, A., et al (1984) Schizophrenic patients discharged from hospital – a follow up study. *British Journal of Psychiatry*, **145**, 586–590.

—, Connelly, J., Frith, C. D., et al (1996) The nature of 'transient' and 'partial' psychoses: findings from the Northwick Park 'Functional' Psychosis Study. *Psychological Medicine*, **26**, 361–369.

Jones, C., Cormac, I., Mota, J., et al (1999) Cognitive behaviour therapy for schizophrenia (Cochrane Review). *Cochrane Library*, Issue 1. Oxford: Update Software.

Jones, R. B., Atkinson, J. M., Coia, D. A., et al (2001) Randomised trial of personalised computer based information for patients with schizophrenia. *BMJ*, **322**, 835–840.

Joy, C. B., Adams, C. E. & Rice, K. (2002) Crisis intervention for people with severe mental illnesses (Cochrane Review). *Cochrane Library*, Issue 1. Oxford: Update Software.

Kane, J. M. (1987) Treatment of schizophrenia. *Schizophrenia Bulletin*, **13**, 133–156.

— (1990) Treatment programme and long-term outcome in chronic schizophrenia. *Acta Psychiatrica Scandinavica* (suppl. 358), 151–157.

— **(1992)** Clinical efficacy of clozapine in treatment-refractory schizophrenia: an overview. *British Journal of Psychiatry* (suppl. 17), 41–45.

— **& Marder, S. R. (1993)** Psychopharmacologic treatment of schizophrenia. *Schizophrenia Bulletin*, **9**, 287–302.

—, **Woerner, M. & Lieberman, J. (1985)** Tardive dyskinesia: prevalence, incidence, and risk factors. *Psychopharmacology Supplementum*, **2**, 72–78.

—, **Honigfeld, G., Singer, J., et al (1988)** Clozapine in treatment-resistant schizophrenics. *Psychopharmacology Bulletin*, **24**, 62–67.

—, **Schooler, N. R., Marder, S., et al (1996)** Efficacy of clozapine versus haloperidol in a long-term clinical trial. *Schizophrenia Research*, **18**, 127.

Kapur, S. & Remington, G. (2001) Dopamine D(2) receptors and their role in atypical antipsychotic action: still necessary and may even be sufficient. *Biological Psychiatry*, **50**, 873–883.

Kavanagh, S. & Opit, L. (1994) *Estimating the Prevalence of Schizophrenia: A Model for Service Development* (Discussion Paper 953). Canterbury: Personal Social Services Research Unit, University of Kent at Canterbury.

—, —, **Knapp, M., et al (1995)** Schizophrenia: shifting the balance of care. *Social Psychiatry and Psychiatric Epidemiology*, **30**, 206–212.

Kemp, N., Skinner, E. & Toms, J. (1984) Randomized clinical trials of cancer treatment – a public opinion survey. *Clinical Oncology*, **10**, 155–161.

Kemp, R., Hayward, P., Applewhaite, G., et al (1996) Compliance therapy in psychotic patients: a randomised controlled trial. *BMJ*, **312**, 345–349.

Kendrick, T. (1996) Cardiovascular and respiratory risk factors amongst general practice patients with long term mental illnesses. *British Journal of Psychiatry*, **169**, 733–739.

—, **Sibbald, B., Burns, T., et al (1991)** Role of general practitioners in care of long term mentally ill patients. *BMJ*, **302**, 508–510.

—, **Burns, T. & Freeling, P. (1995)** Randomised controlled trial of teaching general practitioners to carry out structured assessments of their long term mentally ill patients. *BMJ*, **31**, 93–98.

Kerr, I. B. & Taylor, D. (1997) Mental health emergencies. Caution is needed with rapid tranquillisation protocol. *BMJ*, **315**, 885.

Kinon, B. J., Kane, J. M., Johns, C., et al (1993) Treatment of neuroleptic-resistant schizophrenia relapse. *Psychopharmacology Bulletin*, **29**, 309–314.

Kissling, W. (1991) The current unsatisfactory state of relapse prevention in schizophrenic psychoses: suggestions for improvement. *Clinical Neuropharmacology*, **14** (suppl. 2), S33–S44.

Klein, D. F. & Davis, J. M. (1969) *Diagnosis and Drug Treatment of Psychiatric Disorders*. Baltimore: Williams & Wilkins.

Knapp, M. (1997) Costs of schizophrenia. *British Journal of Psychiatry*, **171**, 509–518.

—, **Marks, I. M., Wolstenholme, J., et al (1998)** Home-based versus hospital-based care for serious mental illness: controlled cost-effectiveness study over four years. *British Journal of Psychiatry*, **172**, 506–512.

—, **Chisholm, D., Leese, M., et al (2002)** European Psychiatric Services: Inputs Linked to Outcome Domains and Needs. Comparing patterns and costs of schizophrenia care in five European countries: the EPSILON study. *Acta Psychiatrica Scandinavica*, **105**, 42–54.

Koreen, A. R., Lieberman, J. A., Kronig, M., et al (1995) Cross-tapering clozapine and risperidone. *American Journal of Psychiatry*, **52**, 1690.

Koro, C. E., Fedder, D. O., L'Italien, G. J., et al (2002) Assessment of independent effect of olanzapine and risperidone on risk of diabetes among patients with schizophrenia: population based nested case-control study. *BMJ*, **325**, 243.

Kris, E. B. (1965) Day hospitals. *Current Therapeutic Research*, **7**, 320–323.

Kuipers, E. & Raune, D. (1999) The early development of EE and burden in the families of first onset psychosis. In *Early Intervention in Psychosis* (eds M. Birchwood & D. Fowler), pp. 128–140. Chichester: John Wiley.

—, **Fowler, D., Garety, P., et al (1998)** London–East Anglia randomised controlled trial of cognitive-behavioural therapy for psychosis. III: Follow-up and economic evaluation at 18 months. *British Journal of Psychiatry*, **173**, 61–68.

Laurier, C., Kennedy, W., Lachaine, J., et al (1997) Economic evaluation of zuclopenthixol acetate compared with injectable haloperidol in schizophrenic patients with acute psychosis. *Clinical Therapeutics*, **19**, 316–329.

Lecompte, D. & Pelc, I. (1996) A cognitive-behavioral program to improve compliance with medication in patients with schizophrenia. *International Journal of Mental Health*, **25**, 51–56.

Leff, J. P. (1978) Social and psychological causes of the acute attack. In *Schizophrenia: Toward a New Synthesis* (ed. J. K. Wing), pp. 139–166. New York. Grune & Stratton.

—, **Kuipers, L., Berkowitz, R., et al (1982)** A controlled trial of social interventions in the families of schizophrenic patients. *British Journal of Psychiatry*, **141**, 121–134.

—, **Berkowitz, R., Shavit, N., et al (1989)** A trial of family therapy v. a relatives group for schizophrenia. *British Journal of Psychiatry*, **154**, 58–66.

—, **Trieman, N. & Gooch, C. (1996)** Team for the assessment of psychiatric services (TAPS) project 33: Prospective follow-up study of long-stay patients discharged from two psychiatric hospitals. *American Journal of Psychiatry*, **153**, 1318–1324.

—, **Sharpley, M., Chisholm, D., et al (2001)** Training community psychiatric nurses in schizophrenia family work: a study of clinical and economic outcomes for patients and relatives. *Journal of Mental Health*, **10**, 189–197.

Lehman, A. F., Dixon, L. B., Kernan, E., et al (1995) Assertive treatment for the homeless mentally ill. In *Proceedings of the 148th Annual Meeting of the American Psychiatric Association*. Miami: American Psychiatric Association.

—, —, —, **et al (1997)** A randomized trial of assertive community treatment for homeless persons with severe mental illness. *Archives of General Psychiatry*, **54**, 1038–1043.

—, **Steinwachs, D. M. & PORT Co-investigators (1998)** Patterns of usual care for schizophrenia: initial survey results from the Schizophrenia Patient Outcomes Research Team (PORT) survey. *Schizophrenia Bulletin*, **24**, 11–20.

—, **Dixon, L., Hoch, J. S., et al (1999)** Cost-effectiveness of assertive community treatment for homeless persons with severe mental illness. *British Journal of Psychiatry*, **174**, 346–352.

—, **Goldberg, R., Dixon, L. B., et al (2002)** Improving employment outcomes for persons with severe mental illnesses. *Archives of General Psychiatry*, **59**, 165–172.

Leppig, M., Bosch, B., Naber, D., et al (1989) Clozapine in the treatment of 121 out-patients. *Psychopharmacology* (suppl. 99), S77–79.

Leucht, S. & Hartung, B. (2002) Benperidol for schizophrenia (Cochrane Review). *Cochrane Library*, Issue 2. Oxford: Update Software.

—, **Barnes, T. R. E., Kissling, W., et al (2003)** Relapse prevention in schizophrenia with new generation antipsychotics: a systematic review and explorative meta-analysis of randomized controlled trials. *American Journal of Psychiatry*, in press.

Levine, J., Barak, Y. & Granek, I. (1998) Cognitive group therapy for paranoid schizophrenics: applying cognitive dissonance. *Journal of Cognitive Psychotherapy*, **12**, 3–12.

Lewis, S., Tarrier, N., Haddock, G., et al (2002) Randomised, controlled trial of cognitive-behaviour therapy in early schizophrenia: acute phase outcomes. *British Journal of Psychiatry*, **181** (suppl. 43), 91–97.

Liberman, R. P., Cardin, V., McGill, C. W., et al (1987) Behavioral family management of schizophrenia: clinical outcome and costs. *Psychiatric Annals*, **17**, 610–619.

—, **Wallace, C. J., Blackwell, G., et al (1998)** Skills training versus psychosocial occupational therapy for persons with persistent schizophrenia. *American Journal of Psychiatry*, **155**, 1087–1091.

Liddel, J., Williamson, M. & Irwig, L. (1996) *Method for Evaluating Research and Guideline Evidence*. Sydney: New South Wales Health Department.

Lieberman, J. A., Jody, D., Geisler, S., et al (1989) Treatment outcome of first episode schizophrenia. *Psychopharmacology Bulletin*, **25**, 92–96.

—, **Alvir, J. M., Woerner, M., et al (1992)** Prospective study of psychobiology in first-episode schizophrenia at Hillside Hospital. *Schizophrenia Bulletin*, **18**, 351–371.

Lindsley, O. R. (1963) Direct measurement and functional definition of vocal hallucinatory symptoms. *Journal of Experimental Analysis of Behavior*, **2**, 269.

Linn, M. W., Caffey, E. M., Klett, C. J., et al (1979) Day treatment and psychotropic drugs in the aftercare of schizophrenic patients. *Archives of General Psychiatry*, **36**, 1055–1066.

Llorca, P. M., Lancon, C., Disdier, B., et al (2002) Effectiveness of clozapine in neuroleptic-resistant schizophrenia: clinical response and plasma concentrations. *Journal of Psychiatry and Neuroscience*, **27**, 30–37.

Loebel, A. D., Lieberman, J. A., Alvir, J. M., et al (1992) Duration of psychosis and outcome in first-episode schizophrenia. *American Journal of Psychiatry*, **149**, 1183–1188.

Lukoff, D., Wallace, C. J., Liberman, R., et al (1986) A holistic program for chronic schizophrenic patients. *Schizophrenia Bulletin*, **12**, 274–282.

Macias, C., Kinney, R., Farley, O. W., et al (1994) The role of case management within a community support system: partnership with psychosocial rehabilitation. *Community Mental Health Journal*, **30**, 323–339.

MacMillan, J. F., Crow, T. J., Johnson, A. L., et al (1986) Short-term outcome in trial entrants and trial eligible patients. *British Journal of Psychiatry*, **148**, 128–133.

Malmberg, L. & Fenton, M. (2001) Individual psychodynamic psychotherapy and psychoanalysis for schizophrenia and severe mental illness (Cochrane Review). *Cochrane Library*, Issue 4. Oxford: Update Software.

Mannion, L., Sloan, D. & Connolly, L. (1997) Rapid tranquillisation: are we getting it right? *Psychiatric Bulletin*, **20**, 411–413.

Marder, S. R., Wirshing, W. C., Mintz, J., et al (1996) Two year outcome of social skills training and group psychotherapy for outpatients with schizophrenia. *American Journal of Psychiatry*, **153**, 1585–1592.

Mari, J. & Streiner, D. (1999) Family intervention for schizophrenia (Cochrane Review). *Cochrane Library*, Issue 1. Oxford: Update Software.

Marland, G. R. & Sharkey, V. (1999) Depot neuroleptics, schizophrenia and the role of the nurse: is practice evidence based? A review of the literature. *Journal of Advanced Nursing*, **30**, 1255–1262.

Marshall, M. & Lockwood, A. (2002) Assertive community treatment for people with severe mental disorders (Cochrane Review). *Cochrane Library*, Issue 3. Oxford: Update Software.

—, — & **Gath, D. (1995)** Social services case-management for long-term mental disorders: a randomised controlled trial. *Lancet*, **345**, 409–412.

—, —, **Bradley, C., et al (2000)** Unpublished rating scales: a major source of bias in randomised controlled trials of treatments for schizophrenia. *British Journal of Psychiatry*, **176**, 249–252.

—, **Crowther, R., Almaraz-Serrano, A., et al (2001)** Systematic reviews of the effectiveness of day care for people with severe mental disorders: (1) Acute day hospital versus admission; (2) Vocational rehabilitation; (3) Day hospital versus outpatient care. *Health Technology Assessment*, **5**, 5. [Also available in Marshall, M., Crowther, R., Almaraz-Serrano, A. M., et al (2002) Day hospital versus out-patient care for psychiatric disorders (Cochrane Review). *Cochrane Library*, Issue 3. Oxford: Update Software.]

—, **Gray, A., Lockwood, A., et al (2002)** Case management for people with severe mental disorders (Cochrane Review). *Cochrane Library*, Issue 3. Oxford: Update Software.

Mason, J. (1999) Challenges to the economic evaluation of new biotechnological interventions in healthcare. *Pharmacoeconomics*, **16**, 119–125.

Mason, P., Harrison, G., Glazebrook, C., *et al* **(1996)** The course of schizophrenia over 13 years. A report from the International Study on Schizophrenia (ISoS) coordinated by the World Health Organization. *British Journal of Psychiatry*, **169**, 580–586.

May, P. R. A. (ed.) (1968) *Treatment of Schizophrenia.* New York: Science House.

—, Tuma, A. H. & Dixon, W. J. (1976a) Schizophrenia: a follow-up study of results of treatment. I. Design and other problems. *Archives of General Psychiatry*, **33**, 474–478.

—, —, —, *et al* **(1976b)** Schizophrenia: a follow-up study of results of treatment. II. Hospital stay over two to five years. *Archives of General Psychiatry*, **33**, 481–486.

McCarthy, R. H. & Terkelsen, K. G. (1995) Risperidone augmentation of clozapine. *Pharmacopsychiatry*, **28**, 61–63.

McCreadie, R. G. (1992) The Nithsdale schizophrenia surveys. An overview. *Social Psychiatry and Psychiatric Epidemiology*, **27**, 40–45.

— & Kelly, C. (2000) Patients with schizophrenia who smoke: private disaster, public resource. *British Journal of Psychiatry*, **176**, 109.

McCrone, P., Beecham, J. & Knapp, M. (1994) Community psychiatric nurse teams: cost-effectiveness of intensive support versus generic care. *British Journal of Psychiatry*, **165**, 218–221.

—, Thornicroft, G., Phelan, M., *et al* **(1998)** Utilisation and costs of community mental health services. PRiSM Psychosis Study 5. *British Journal of Psychiatry*, **173**, 391–398.

McEvoy, J. P., Schooler, N. R. & Wilson, W. H. (1991) Predictors of therapeutic response to haloperidol in acute schizophrenia. *Psychopharmacology Bulletin*, **27**, 97–101.

McFarlane, W. R., Lukens, E., Link, B., *et al* **(1995a)** Multiple-family groups and psychoeducation in the treatment of schizophrenia. *Archives of General Psychiatry*, **52**, 679–687.

—, Link, B., Dushay, R., *et al* **(1995b)** Psychoeducational multiple family groups: four-year relapse outcome in schizophrenia. *Family Processes*, **34**, 127–144.

McGorry, P. D., Edwards, J., Mihalopoulos, C., *et al* **(1996)** EPPIC: An evolving system of early detection and optimal management. *Schizophrenia Bulletin*, **22**, 305–326.

—, Yung, A. R., Phillips, L. J., *et al* **(2002)** A randomized controlled trial of interventions designed to reduce the risk of progression to first episode psychosis in a clinical sample with subthreshold symptoms. *Archives of General Psychiatry*, **59**, 921–928.

McGrew, J. H. & Bond, G. R. (1995) Critical ingredients of assertive community treatment: judgments of the experts. *Journal of Mental Health Administration*, **22**, 113–125.

—, —, Dietzen, L., *et al* **(1994)** Measuring the fidelity of implementation of a mental health program model. *Journal of Consulting and Clinical Psychology*, **62**, 670–678.

Macpherson, R., Jerrom, B. & Hughes, A. (1996) A controlled study of education about drug treatment in schizophrenia. *British Journal of Psychiatry*, **168**, 709–717.

Medalia, A., Aluma, M., Tryon, W., *et al* **(1998)** Effectiveness of attention training in schizophrenia. *Schizophrenia Bulletin*, **24**, 147–152.

—, Revheim, N. & Casey, M. (2000) Remediation of memory disorders in schizophrenia. *Psychological Medicine*, **30**, 1451–1459.

Meltzer, H. Y. & Okayli, G. (1995) Reduction of suicidality during clozapine treatment of neuroleptic-resistant schizophrenics: impact on risk benefit assessment. *American Journal of Psychiatry*, **152**, 183–190.

—, Gill, B., Petticrew, M., *et al* **(1995)** *Office of Population Censuses and Surveys: Surveys of Psychiatric Morbidity in Great Britain*, vol. 2. London: HMSO.

Meltzoff, J. & Blumenthal, R. L. (1966) *The Day Treatment Center: Principles, Application and Evaluation.* Springfield, IL: Charles C. Thomas.

Melzer, D., Hale, A. S., Malik, S. J., *et al* **(1991)** Community care for patients with schizophrenia one year after hospital discharge. *BMJ*, **303**, 1023–1026.

Mendelson, W. B. (1992) Clinical distinctions between long-acting and short-acting benzodiazepines. *Journal of Clinical Psychiatry*, **53** (suppl.), 4–7, discussion 8–9.

Merinder, L. B., Viuff, A. G., Laugesen, H., *et al* (1999) Patient and relative education in community psychiatry: a randomised controlled trial regarding its effectiveness. *Social Psychiatry and Psychiatric Epidemiology*, **34**, 287–294.

Merson, S., Tyrer, P., Onyett, S., *et al* (1992) Early intervention in psychiatric emergencies: a controlled clinical trial. *Lancet*, **339**, 1311–1314.

—, —, **Carlen, D., *et al* (1996)** The cost of treatment of psychiatric emergencies: a comparison of hospital and community services. *Psychological Medicine*, **26**, 727–734.

Mihalopoulos, C., McGorry, P. D. & Carter, R. C. (1999) Is phase-specific, community-oriented treatment of early psychosis an economically viable method of improving outcome? *Acta Psychiatrica Scandinavica*, **100**, 47–55.

Miller, D. D. (1996) The clinical use of clozapine plasma concentrations in the management of treatment-refractory schizophrenia. *Annals of Clinical Psychiatry*, **8**, 99–109.

—, **Fleming, F., Holman, T. L., *et al* (1994)** Plasma clozapine concentrations as a predictor of clinical response: a follow-up study. *Journal of Clinical Psychiatry*, **55** (suppl. B), 117–121.

Möller, H. J. & van Zerssen, D. (1995) Course and outcome of schizophrenia. In *Schizophrenia* (eds S. R. Hirsch & D. R. Weinberger), pp. 106–127. Oxford: Blackwell.

Moore, D. B., Kelly, D. L., Sherr, J. D., *et al* (1998) Rehospitalization rates for depot antipsychotics and pharmacoeconomic implications: comparison with risperidone. *American Journal of Health-System Pharmacy*, **55** (suppl. 4), S17–S19.

Morera, A. L., Barreiro, P. & Can-Munoz, J. L. (1999) Risperidone and clozapine combination for the treatment of refractory schizophrenia. *Acta Psychiatrica Scandinavica*, **99**, 305–307.

Mowerman, S. & Siris, S. G. (1996) Adjunctive loxapine in a clozapine-resistant cohort of schizophrenic patients. *Annals of Clinical Psychiatry*, **8**, 193–197.

Muijen, M., Cooney, M., Strathdee, G., *et al* (1994) Community psychiatric nurse teams: intensive support versus generic care. *British Journal of Psychiatry*, **165**, 211–217.

Mujica, R. & Weiden, P. (2001) Neuroleptic malignant syndrome after the addition of haloperidol to atypical antipsychotic. *American Journal of Psychiatry*, **158**, 650–651.

Murray, C. J. & Lopez, A. D. (1997) Global mortality, disability, and the contribution of risk factors: Global Burden of Disease Study. *Lancet*, **349**, 1436–1442.

Nazareth, I., King, M., Haines, A., *et al* (1993) Accuracy of diagnosis of psychosis on a general practice computer system. *BMJ*, **307**, 32–34.

NEPP (2002) *National Early Psychosis Project*. http://www.earlypsychosis.org/index.htm

NHS Executive (1996) *Clinical Guidelines: Using Clinical Guidelines to Improve Patient Care Within the NHS.* London: DoH.

NICE (2002) *Guidance on the Use of Newer (Atypical) Antipdychotic Drugs for the Treatment of Schizophrenia.* Technology Appraisal No. 43. London: National Institute for Clinical Excellence.

Nuechterlein, K. H. (1987) Vulnerability models for schizophrenia: state of the art. In *Search for the Causes of Schizophrenia* (eds H. Hafner, W. F. Gattaz & W. Janzarik), pp. 297–316. Heidelberg: Springer.

— **& Dawson, M. E. (1984)** A heuristic vulnerability/stress model of schizophrenic episodes. *Schizophrenia Bulletin*, **10**, 300–312.

— **& Subotnik, K. L. (1998)** The cognitive origins of schizophrenia and prospects for intervention. In *Outcomes and Innovation in Psychological Treatment of Schizophrenia* (eds T. Wykes, N. Tarrier & S. Lewis), pp. 17–41. Chichester: John Wiley & Sons.

O'Brien, C. P., Hamm, K. B., Ray, B. A., *et al* (1972) Group versus individual psychotherapy with schizophrenics. *Archives of General Psychiatry*, **27**, 474–478.

Office of National Statistics (1998) *Labour Force Survey (1997/8).* London: ONS.

Oh, P. I., Mittmann, N., Iskedjian, M., *et al* (2001) Cost-utility of risperidone compared with standard conventional antipsychotics in chronic schizophrenia. *Journal of Medical Economics*, **4**, 137–156.

Oltmanns, T. F. & Neale, J. M. (1975) Schizophrenic performance when distractors are present: attentional deficit or differential task difficulty? *Journal of Abnormal Psychology*, **84**, 205–209.

Oosthuizen, P., Emsley, R. A., Turner, J., et al (2001) Determining the optimal dose of haloperidol in first-episode psychosis. *Journal of Psychopharmacology*, **15**, 251–255.

Osborn, D. P. J. (2001) The poor physical health of people with mental illness. *Western Journal of Medicine*, **175**, 329–332.

Osser, D. N. & Sigadel, R. (2001) Short-term in-patient pharmacotherapy of schizophrenia. *Harvard Review of Psychiatry*, **9**, 89–104.

Pantelis, C., Taylor, J. & Campbell, P. (1988) The south Camden Schizophrenia survey. An experience of community based research. *Bulletin of the Royal College of Psychiatry*, **12**, 98–101.

Pasamanick, B., Scarpitti, F. R., Lefton, M., et al (1964) Home versus hospital care for schizophrenics. *JAMA*, **187**, 177–181.

—, — & Dinitz, S. (1967) *Schizophrenics in the Community: An Experimental Study in the Prevention of Hospitalization*. New York: Appleton-Century-Crofts.

Peacock, L. & Gerlach, J. (1994) Clozapine treatment in Denmark: concomitant psychotropic medication and hematologic monitoring in a system with liberal usage practices. *Journal of Clinical Psychiatry*, **55**, 44–49.

Peet, M. & Harvey, N. S. (1991) Lithium maintenance: 1. A standard education programme for patients. *British Journal of Psychiatry*, **158**, 197–200.

Pekkala, E. & Merinder, L. (2001) Psychoeducation for schizophrenia (Cochrane Review). *Cochrane Library*, Issue 4. Oxford: Update Software.

Peniston, E. & Kulkosky, P. (1988) Group assertion and contingent time-out procedures in the control of assaultive behaviors in schizophrenics. *Medical Psychotherapy*, **1**, 131–141.

Peralta, V., Cuesta, M. J., Caro, F., et al (1994) Neuroleptic dose and schizophrenic symptoms. A survey of prescribing practices. *Acta Psychiatrica Scandinavica*, **90**, 354–357.

Perry, P. J., Bever, K. A., Arndt, S., et al (1998) Relationship between patient variables and plasma clozapine concentrations: a dosing nomogram. *Biological Psychiatry*, **44**, 733–738.

Phelan, N., Stradins, L. & Morrison, S. (2001) Physical health of people with severe mental illness. *BMJ*, **322**, 442–444.

Pierides, M. (1994) Mental health services in Cyprus. *Psychiatric Bulletin*, **18**, 425–427.

Pilling, S., Bebbington, P., Kuipers, E., et al (2002a) Psychological treatments in schizophrenia: I. Meta-analysis of family intervention and cognitive behaviour therapy. *Psychological Medicine*, **32**, 763–782.

—, —, —, et al (2002b) Psychological treatments in schizophrenia: II. Meta-analyses of randomized controlled trials of social skills training and cognitive remediation. *Psychological Medicine*, **32**, 783–791.

Pilowsky, L. S., Ring, H., Shine, P. J., et al (1992) Rapid tranquillisation. A survey of emergency prescribing in a general psychiatric hospital. *British Journal of Psychiatry*, **160**, 831–835.

Piper, W. E., Rosie, J. S., Azim, H. F. A., et al (1993) A randomized trial of psychiatric day treatment for patients with affective and personality disorders. *Hospital and Community Psychiatry*, **44**, 757–763.

Posner, C. M., Wilson, K. G., Kral, M. J., et al (1992) Family psychoeducational support groups in schizophrenia. *American Journal of Orthopsychiatry*, **62**, 206–218.

Power, P., Elkins, K., Adlard, S., et al (1998) Analysis of the initial treatment phase in first-episode psychosis. *British Journal of Psychiatry* (suppl. 172), 71–76.

Preston, N. J. & Fazio, S. (2000) Establishing the efficacy and cost effectiveness of community intensive case management of long-term mentally ill: a matched control group study. *Australian and New Zealand Journal of Psychiatry*, **34**, 114–121.

Procopio, M. (1998) Sulpiride augmentation on schizophrenia. *British Journal of Psychiatry*, **172**, 449–450.

Procyshyn, R. M., Kennedy, N. B., Tse, G., *et al* (2001) Antipsychotic polypharmacy: a survey of discharge prescriptions from a tertiary care psychiatric institution. *Canadian Journal of Psychiatry*, **46**, 334–339.

Quatermaine, S. & Taylor, R. (1995) A comparative study of depot injection techniques. *Nursing Times*, **91**, 36–39.

Quinlivan, R., Hough, R., Crowell, A., *et al* (1995) Service utilisation and costs of care for severely mentally ill clients in an intensive case management program. *Psychiatric Services*, **46**, 365–371.

Rankin, S. H. & Stallings, K. D. (1996) *Patient Education: Issues, Principles, Practices.* Philadelphia: Lippincott-Raven.

Raskin, S., Katz, G., Zislin, Z., *et al* (2000) Clozapine and risperidone: combination/ augmentation treatment of refractory schizophrenia: a preliminary observation. *Acta Psychiatrica Scandinavica*, **101**, 334–336.

Reid, W. H., Mason, M. & Hogan, T. (1998) Suicide prevention effects associated with clozapine therapy in schizophrenia and schizoaffective disorder. *Psychiatric Services*, **49**, 1029–1033.

Reilly, J. G., Ayis, S. A., Ferrier, I. N., *et al* (2000) QTc-interval abnormalities and psychotropic drug therapy in psychiatric patients. *Lancet*, **355**, 1048–1052.

Rethink (2002) *Research.* http://www.rethink.org/information/research

Ricard, N., Sauriol, L., Belanger, M. C., *et al* (1999) Direct cost of care for patients with schizophrenia treated with haloperidol in an emergency unit. *Psychiatric Services*, **50**, 1287–1288.

Ridgeway, P. & Rapp, C. (1998) *Critical Ingredients Series.* Lawrence, KS: Kansas Department of Social and Rehabilitation Services, Commission on Mental Health and Developmental Disabilities.

Rogers, S. E., Sciarappa, K., MacDonald-Wilson, K., *et al* (1995) A benefit-cost analysis of a supported employment model for persons with psychiatric disabilities. *Evaluation and Program Planning*, **18**, 105–115.

Rosenheck, R. A. & Neale, M. S. (1998) Cost-effectiveness of intensive psychiatric community care for high users of inpatient services. *Archives of General Psychiatry*, **55**, 459–466.

—, Evans, D., Herz, L., *et al* (1999) How long to wait for a response to clozapine: a comparison of time course of response to clozapine and conventional antipsychotic medication in refractory schizophrenia. *Schizophrenia Bulletin*, **25**, 709–719.

—, Chang, S., Choe, Y., *et al* (2000) Medication continuation and compliance: a comparison of patients treated with clozapine and haloperidol. *Journal of Clinical Psychiatry*, **61**, 382–386.

Rossler, W., Loffler, W., Fatkenheuer, B., *et al* (1992) Does case management reduce rehospitalisation rates? *Acta Psychiatrica Scandinavica*, **86**, 445–449.

Roth, A., Fonagy, P., Parry, G., *et al* (1996) *What Works for Whom? A Critical Review of Psychotherapy Research.* New York: Guilford.

Royal College of Psychiatrists (1997) *The Association Between Antipsychotic Drugs and Sudden Death.* Council Report 57. London: RCP.

— (1998) *Management of Imminent Violence: Clinical Practice Guidelines to Support Mental Health Services.* Occasional Paper 41. London: RCP.

Salkever, D., Domino, M. E., Burns, B. J., *et al* (1999) Assertive community treatment for people with severe mental illness: the effect on hospital use and costs. *Health Services Research*, **34**, 577–601.

Sartorius, N. (2002) Iatrogenic stigma of mental illness. *BMJ*, **324**, 1470–1471.

Schizophrenia Patient Outcomes Research Team (1998) *Treatment Recommendations.* Rockville, MD: Agency for Healthcare Quality and Research. http://www.ahrq.gov/clinic/ schzrec.htm

Schooler, N. J., Keith, S. J., Severe, J. B., *et al* (1997) Relapse and rehospitalisation during maintenance treatment of schizophrenia. The effects of dose reduction and family treatment. *Archives of General Psychiatry*, **54**, 453–463.

Scottish Intercollegiate Guidelines Network (2001) *SIGN 50: A Guideline Developer's Handbook*. Edinburgh: SIGN.

Sedvall, G. & Farde, L. (1995) Chemical brain anatomy in schizophrenia. *Lancet*, **346**, 743–749.

Sensky, T., Turkington, D., Kingdon, D., et al (2000) A randomized controlled trial of cognitive-behavioral therapy for persistent symptoms in schizophrenia resistant to medication. *Archives of General Psychiatry*, **57**, 165–172.

Sernyak, M. J., Leslie, D. L., Alarcon, R. D., et al (2002) Association of diabetes mellitus with use of atypical neuroleptics in the treatment of schizophrenia. *American Journal of Psychiatry*, **159**, 561–566.

Shalev, A., Hermesh, H., Rothberg, J., et al (1993) Poor neuroleptic response in acutely exacerbated schizophrenic patients. *Acta Psychiatrica Scandinavica*, **87**, 86–91.

Shepherd, G. (1978) Social skills training: the generalisation problem – some further data. *Behavioural Research and Therapy*, **16**, 297–299.

—, Murray A. & Muijen, M. (1994) *Relative Values: The Different Views of Users, Family Carers and Professionals on Services for People with Schizophrenia*. London: Sainsbury Centre for Mental Health.

Shiloh, R., Zemishlany, Z., Aizenberg, D., et al (1997) Sulpiride augmentation in people with schizophrenia partially responsive to clozapine. A double-blind, placebo-controlled study. *British Journal of Psychiatry*, **171**, 569–573.

Simpson, D. & Anderson, I. (1996) Rapid tranquillisation: a questionnaire survey of practice. *Psychiatric Bulletin*, **20**, 149–152.

Singleton, N., Bumpstead, R., O'Brien, M., et al (2000) *Psychiatric Morbidity Among Adults Living in Private Households, 2000*. Report of a survey carried out by the Social Survey Division of the Office for National Statistics on behalf of the Department of Health, the Scottish Executive and the National Assembly for Wales. London: HMSO.

Slade, M., Rosen, A. & Shankar, R. (1995) Multidisciplinary mental health teams. *International Journal of Social Psychiatry*, **41**, 180–189.

Slade, P. D. & Bentall, R. P. (1988) *Sensory Deception: A Scientific Analysis of Hallucination*. London: Croom Helm.

Sledge, W. H., Tebes, J., Wolff N., et al (1996) Day hospital/crisis respite care versus inpatient care, part II: service utilization and costs. *American Journal of Psychiatry*, **153**, 1074–1083.

Smith, J. V. & Birchwood, M. J. (1987) Specific and non-specific effects of educational Intervention with families living with a schizophrenic relative. *British Journal of Psychiatry*, **150**, 645–652.

— & — (1993) The needs of high and low expressed emotion families: a normative approach. *Social Psychiatry and Psychiatric Medicine*, **28**, 11–16.

Snyder, S. H., Greenberg, D. & Yamumura, H. I. (1974) Antischizophrenic drugs: affinity for muscarinic cholinergic receptor sites in the brain predicts extrapyramidal effects. *Journal of Psychiatric Research*, **11**, 91–95.

Soares, B. G. O., Fenton, M. & Chue, P. (2002) Sulpiride for schizophrenia (Cochrane Review). *Cochrane Library*, Issue 2. Oxford: Update Software.

Solomon, P., Draine, J. & Meyerson, A. (1994) Jail recidivism and receipt of community mental health services. *Hospital and Community Psychiatry*, **45**, 793–797.

Speller, J. C., Barnes, T. R. E., Curson, D. A., et al (1997) One-year, low-dose neuroleptic study of in-patients with chronic schizophrenia characterised by persistent negative symptoms: amisulpride *v.* haloperidol. *British Journal of Psychiatry*, **171**, 564–568.

Spring, B. J. & Ravdin, L. (1992) Cognitive remediation in schizophrenia: should we attempt it? *Schizophrenia Bulletin*, **18**, 15–20.

Stack-Sullivan, H. (1947) *Conceptions of Modern Psychiatry*. Washington, DC: William Alanson White Psychiatric Foundation.

— (1974) *Schizophrenia as a Human Process*. London: Norton.

Stanton, A. H., Gunderson, J. G., Knapp, P. H., et al (1984) Effects of psychotherapy in schizophrenia. I. Design and implementation of a controlled study. *Schizophrenia Bulletin*, **10**, 520–563.

Steingard, S., Allen, M. & Schooler, N. R. (1994) A study of the pharmacologic treatment of medication-compliant schizophrenics who relapse. *Journal of Clinical Psychiatry*, **55**, 470–472.

Stubbs, J. H., Haw, C. M., Staley, C. J., et al (2000) Augmentation with sulpiride for a schizophrenic patients partially responsive to clozapine. *Acta Psychiatrica Scandinavica*, **102**, 390–394.

Sultana, A. & McMonagle, T. (2002) Pimozide for schizophrenia or related psychoses (Cochrane Review). *Cochrane Library*, Issue 2. Oxford: Update Software.

—, Reilly, J. & Fenton, M. (2002) Thioridazine for schizophrenia (Cochrane Review). *Cochrane Library*, Issue 2. Oxford: Update Software.

Takhar, J. (1999) Pimozide augmentation in a patient with drug-resistant psychosis previously treated with olanzapine. *Journal of Psychiatry and Neuroscience*, **24**, 248–249.

Tamminga, C. A., Thaker, G. K., Moran, M., et al (1994) Clozapine in tardive dyskinesia: observations from human and animal model studies. *Journal of Clinical Psychiatry*, **55** (suppl. 9), 102–106.

Tantam, D. & McGrath, G. (1989) Psychiatric day hospitals – another route to institutionalization? *Social Psychiatry and Psychiatric Epidemiology*, **24**, 96–101.

Tarrier, N., Barrowclough, C., Vaughn, C., et al (1988) The community management of schizophrenia: a controlled trial of a behavioural intervention with families to reduce relapse. *British Journal of Psychiatry*, **153**, 532–542.

—, Lownson, K. & Barrowclough, C. (1991) Some aspects of family interventions in schizophrenia. II. Financial considerations. *British Journal of Psychiatry*, **159**, 481–484.

—, Yusupoff, L., Kinney, C., et al (1998) Randomised controlled trial of intensive cognitive behavioural therapy for patients with chronic schizophrenia. *BMJ*, **317**, 303–307.

Task Force of the World Psychiatric Association (2002) The usefulness and use of second-generation antipsychotic medications. *Current Opinion in Psychiatry*, **15** (suppl. 1), S1–S51.

Tauscher, J. & Kapur, S. (2001) Choosing the right dose of antipsychotics in schizophrenia: lessons from neuroimaging studies. *CNS Drugs*, **15**, 671–678.

Taylor, D., Mace, S., Mir, S., et al (2000) A prescription survey of the use of atypical antipsychotics for hospital in-patients in the United Kingdom. *International Journal of Psychiatry in Clinical Practice*, **4**, 41–46.

—, Mir, S., Mace, S., et al (2002) Co-prescribing of atypical and typical antipsychotics prescribing sequence and documented outcome. *Psychiatric Bulletin*, **26**, 170–172.

Taylor, P. J. & Gunn, J. (1999) Homicides by people with mental illness: myth and reality. *British Journal of Psychiatry*, **174**, 9–14.

Test, M. A. & Stein, L. I. (1978) Training in community living: research design and results. In *Alternatives to Mental Hospital Treatment* (eds L. I. Stein & M. A. Test), pp. 57–74. New York: Plenum.

Thompson, K. S., Griffity, E. E. H. & Leaf, P. J. (1990) A historical review of the Madison Model of community care. *Hospital and Community Psychiatry*, **41**, 625–634.

Tompkins, L. M., Goldman, R. S. & Axelrod, B. N. (1995) Modifiability of neuropsychological dysfunction in schizophrenia. *Biological Psychiatry*, **38**, 105–111.

Tran, P. V., Hamilton, S. H., Kuntz, A. J., et al (1997) Double-blind comparison of olanzapine versus risperidone in the treatment of schizophrenia and other psychotic disorders. *Journal of Clinical Psychopharmacology*, **17**, 407–418.

—, Dellva, M. A., Tollefson, G. D., et al (1998) Oral olanzapine versus oral haloperidol in the maintenance treatment of schizophrenia and related psychoses. *British Journal of Psychiatry*, **172**, 499–505.

Tsaung, M. T., Perkins, K. & Simpson, J. C. (1983) Physical disease in schizophrenia and affective disorder. *Journal of Clinical Psychiatry*, **44**, 42–46.

Tuason, V. B. (1986) A comparison of parenteral loxapine and haloperidol in hostile and aggressive acutely schizophrenic patients. *Journal of Clinical Psychiatry*, **47**, 126–129.

Turkington, D. & Kingdon, D. (2000) Cognitive-behavioural techniques for general psychiatrists in the management of patients with psychoses. *British Journal of Psychiatry*, **177**, 101–106.

Tyrer, P. J. & Remington, M. (1979) Controlled comparison of day-hospital and out-patient treatment for neurotic disorders. *Lancet*, *i*, 1014–1016.

—, Morgan, J., Van Horn, E., *et al* (1995) A randomised controlled study of close monitoring of vulnerable psychiatric patients. *Lancet*, **345**, 756–759.

—, Evans, K., Gandhi, N., *et al* (1998) Randomised controlled trial of two models of care for discharged psychiatric patients. *BMJ*, **316**, 106–109.

—, Coid, J., Simmonds, S., *et al* (2002) Community mental health teams (CMHTs) for people with severe mental illnesses and disordered personality (Cochrane Review). *Cochrane Library*, Issue 1. Oxford: Update Software.

Tyson, S. C., Devane, C. L. & Risch, S. C. (1995) Pharmacokinetic interaction between risperidone and clozapine. *American Journal of Psychiatry*, **152**, 1401–1402.

US Department of Health and Human Services (1999) *Agency for Health Care Policy and Research. Treatment of Depression: Newer Pharmacotherapies (Electronic version)*. Evidence Report/Technology Assessment Number 7. AHCPR Publication No. 99-E014. Rockville, MD: US Department of Health and Human Services.

Van der Zwaag, C., McGee, M., McEvoy, J. P., *et al* (1996) Response of patients with treatment-refractory schizophrenia to clozapine within three serum ranges. *American Journal of Psychiatry*, **153**, 1579–1584.

Van Os, J., Takei, N., Castle, D. J., *et al* (1996) The incidence of mania: time trends in relation to gender and ethnicity. *Social Psychiatry and Psychiatric Epidemiology*, **31**, 129–136.

Vaughan, K., Doyle, M., McConaghy, N., *et al* (1992) The Sydney intervention trial: a controlled trial of relatives' counselling to reduce schizophrenic relapse. *Social Psychiatry and Psychiatric Epidemiology*, **27**, 16–21.

Vaughn, C. E. & Leff, J. P. (1976) The influence of family and social factors on the course of psychiatric illness. A comparison of schizophrenic and depressed neurotic patients. *British Journal of Psychiatry*, **129**, 125–137.

Walburn, J., Gray, R., Gournay, K., *et al* (2001) Systematic review of patient and nurse attitudes to depot antipsychotic medication. *British Journal of Psychiatry*, **179**, 300–307.

Wallace, C. J., Nelson, C. J., Liberman, R. P., *et al* (1980) A review and critique of social skills training with schizophrenic patients. *Schizophrenia Bulletin*, **6**, 42–63.

Waring, E. W., Devin, P. G. & Dewan, V. (1999) Treatment of schizophrenia with antipsychotics in combination (letter). *Canadian Journal of Psychiatry*, **44**, 189–190.

Warner, R. (1994) *Recovery from Schizophrenia* (2nd edn). New York: Routledge.

—, Huxley, P. & Berg, T. (2000) An evaluation of the impact of clubhouse membership on quality of life and treatment utilization. *International Journal of Social Psychiatry*, **45**, 4.

Weinberger, D. R., Berman, K. F. & Illowsky, B. P. (1988) Physiological dysfunction of dorsolateral prefrontal cortex in schizophrenia. III. A new cohort and evidence for a monoaminergic mechanism. *Archives of General Psychiatry*, **45**, 609–615.

Weisbrod, B. A., Test, M. A. & Stein, L. I. (1980) Alternative to mental hospital treatment. II. Economic benefit-cost analysis. *Archives of General Psychiatry*, **37**, 400–405.

Weldon, E., Clarkin, J., Hennessy, J. J., *et al* (1979) Day hospital versus outpatient treatment: a controlled study. *Psychiatric Quarterly*, **51**, 144–150.

Wierma, D., Kluiter, H., Nienhuis, F., *et al* (1989) *Day-treatment with Community Care as an Alternative to Standard Hospitalization: An Experiment in The Netherlands. A Preliminary Communication.* Groningen: Department of Social Psychiatry, University of Groningen.

Wolff, N., Helminiak, T. W., Morse, G. A., et al (1997) Cost-effectiveness evaluation of three approaches to case management for homeless mentally ill clients. *American Journal of Psychiatry*, **154**, 341–348.

World Health Organization (1992) *International Statistical Classification of Diseases and Related Health Problems* (ICD–10). Geneva: WHO.

Wright, P., Birkett, M., David, S. R., et al (2001) Double-blind, placebo-controlled comparison of intramuscular olanzapine and intramuscular haloperidol in the treatment of acute agitation in schizophrenia. *American Journal of Psychiatry*, **158**, 1149–1151.

Wykes, T. & van der Gaag, M. (2001) Is it time to develop a new cognitive therapy for psychosis – cognitive remediation therapy (CRT)? *Clinical Psychology Review*, **8** 1227–1256.

—, Reeder, C., Corner, J., et al (1999) The effects of neurocognitive remediation on executive processing in patients with schizophrenia. *Schizophrenia Bulletin*, **25**, 291–306.

Yuzda, M. S. K. (2000) Combination antipsychotics: what is the evidence? *Journal of Informed Pharmacotherapy*, **2**, 300–305.

Xiong, W., Phillips, M. R., Hu, X., et al (1994) Family-based intervention for schizophrenic patients in China: a randomised controlled trial. *British Journal of Psychiatry*, **165**, 239–247.

Zhang, M., Wang, M., Li, J., et al (1994) Randomised-control trial of family intervention for 78 first-episode male schizophrenic patients: an 18-month study in Suzhou, Jiangsu. *British Journal of Psychiatry* (suppl. 24), 96–102.

Zubin, J. & Spring, B. (1977) Vulnerability – a new view of schizophrenia. *Journal of Abnormal Psychology*, **86**, 103–126.